VULNERABLE
BUT
INVINCIBLE

Cover Design by Three Sisters Graphics

Cover Art
NIIHAU: When A Child Is Born
by
Guy Buffet

VULNERABLE BUT INVINCIBLE

A Longitudinal Study of Resilient Children and Youth

Emmy E. Werner
Ruth S. Smith

Foreword by Norman Garmezy

Adams • Bannister • Cox
New York

Adams • Bannister • Cox
460 Riverside Drive
New York 10027

Library of Congress Cataloging in Publication Data

Werner, Emmy E., 1929
Vulnerable, but invincible.

Reprint. Originally published: New York:
McGraw Hill, 1982.
Bibliography: P.
Includes index.
1. Children—Hawaii—Kauai—Longitudinal studies.
2. Socially handicapped children—Hawaii—Kauai—
Longitudinal studies. 3. Resilience (Personality trait)—
Longitudinal studies. I. Smith, Ruth S.
II. Title.
HQ792.U5W4   1989   305.2'3'0996951   89-313

ISBN 0-937431-03-6

In Memory of our mothers
and
with love to our mates

CONTENTS

LIST OF TABLES

TABLES IN APPENDIX

FOREWORD

A little more than a year ago while in residence as a Fellow at the Center for Advanced Study in the Behavioral Sciences I had the pleasure of meeting Dr. Emmy Werner for the first time. The circumstances surrounding that first meeting were these.

Michael Rutter and I had helped to organize a year-long seminar at the Center that included as co-participants Jerome Kagan, Herbert Leiderman, Lewis Lipsitt, Gerald Patterson, Julius Segal, and Judith Wallerstein.

Several years previously I had spent a year with Rutter as a Visiting Colleague in his Department of Child Psychiatry of the Institute of Psychiatry in London. During the year we discovered our community of interest in investigating an area of great neglect—the study of stress-resistant ("invulnerable") children. That common interest had energized the decision to organize a seminar at the Center in Stanford, California which came to fruition four years later.

The topical focus of the seminar was on Stress, Coping, and Development in Children and the task proved far more difficult than we had anticipated. The group oscillated between enthusiasm and discouragement as we discussed the vaguely defined concepts of *stress* and *coping*. One evident achievement of the group was the demonstration that we shared a common attribute—a tolerance for ambiguity.

One afternoon while sitting in my study I recognized the firm approaching footsteps of Michael Rutter. I am always delighted to see him and this day was no exception. He carried a manuscript in his hands, placed it on my desk, and said: "This comes closer to what we have been talking about than anything I have yet seen!"

The manuscript bore an intriguing title: *Vulnerable But Invincible: A Longitudinal Study of Resilient Children and Youth*. The authors were Emmy E. Werner in collaboration with Ruth Smith. Rutter had secured the final report of a large-scale research project that had received support from the Foundation for Child Development.

Once read there was no question but that Rutter was right, as usual. What we now had before us was the summary of an investigation that had begun in 1954 and now had been completed almost three decades later. Its original investigative team was an interdisciplinary one, composed of pediatricians, public health workers, and psychologists housed at the University of California and the University of Hawaii, who had joined with personnel of the Territory of Hawaii's Department of Health. Their mutual goals were two-fold. First, to follow the course of more than three thousand pregnancies on the island of Kauai; second, to pursue for a decade the growth and development of more than 1000 of the infants and their families. That goal was met with the publication of the first volume of what was to become a three-volume series. *The Children of Kauai* written by Werner and her colleagues appeared in 1971 and provided the initial data on the first decade of life for this cohort of children. In 1977 Volume II, *Kauai's Children Come of Age*, written by Werner and Smith, continued the follow-up of the original cohort to age 18. Attrition of the sample had been kept to a minimum. Through vigorous effort the investigators had managed to secure the continued cooperation of almost 90% of those who had participated in the study up to age ten. In the authors' words, extending the time span of the longitudinal study had enabled them "to take a look at the learning disabilities and behavior disorders diagnosed in childhood, at new problems and new promises in adolescence, at the predictive power of our diagnostic tools, and at the community's response to its 'youth at risk'."

Now we come to the final volume in the series published under the aegis of The Behavioral Sciences Program of McGraw-Hill's Professional and Reference Books Division. Here the emphasis of the previous two volumes has shifted somewhat. In *The Children of Kauai* the investigators had looked into the effects of cumulative stress on the children ranging from perinatal factors to poverty and inadequate caretaking. In this initial work one could read from a catalogue of distress: developmental disabilities, poor school achievement, physical handicap, intellectual retardation and the like. *Kauai's Children Come of Age* began an examination of the correlates of these antecedent stressors, focusing on the childrens' mental health problems and anti-social behaviors, emphasizing the roots of the cohort's vulnerability in biological and temperamental factors, socio-economic factors, inadequate caretaking, and socialization variations based upon cultural differences.

Volume III provides a shift in focus. The authors point out that one of every five children in the cohort developed "serious behavior or learning problems at *some time* during the first two decades of their lives." But now they have turned over the coin of vulnerability to examine the other side and there they find some unanticipated outcomes in their high-risk sample.

> Yet there were others, also *vulnerable*, exposed to poverty, perinatal stress and family instability, reared by parents with little education or serious mental health problems, who remained invincible, and developed into competent and autonomous young adults, who worked well, played well, loved well, and expected well. This report is an account of our search for the roots of their resilience, for the sources of their strength.

No wonder then at the excitement this report engendered in our Seminar group. Studies of stress and coping in children are beginning to appear in the literature with a frequency never before seen. Whereas previously the ascriptor terms *stress* and *coping* revealed relatively small numbers of references in the annual indices of our various scientific abstracts, today there is clear evidence that we are on the threshold of a *Zeitgeist*. Studies of stress in children are beginning to proliferate. Its roots are many: from psychiatry we perceive a growing concern for the study of developmental antecedents to the severe mental disorders; from developmental biology comes an awareness of biological factors that conduce to growth and adaptation; from developmental psychologists we see an increase of interest in the study of prosocial behaviors; from developmental psychopathologists we are witness to a growing involvement in studying children who are "at risk" for later maladaptation; from sociology there is the continuation of a research literature that emphasizes the significance of role and of culture in accentuating or mitigating stress factors in society.

Today one can peruse any recent index of the *Psychological Abstracts* with satisfaction, finding pages of citations of a literature focused on stress and coping in children. Resilience, ego strength, stress-resistance are becoming part of our scientific language.

Manfred Bleuler, the great Swiss psychiatrist, who spent a considerable part of his career studying, from a longitudinal perspective, the natural history of schizophrenic individuals and their offspring, recently noted that on the basis of repeated observations of the sons and daughters of mental patients—observations made possible by his role over many years as virtually the family physician for their sick parents—that he had observed an adaptive facet in the offspring that could have been missed by investigators who became acquainted with them for "purely scientific purposes."

In his volume *The Schizophrenic Disorders: Long-Term Patient and Family Studies* (Yale University Press, 1978) Bleuler provides a deeply compassionate portrait of these so-called high-risk children and their *positive* attributes. His observations deserve quotation:

> Many of these probands' children I had to counsel professionally, principally because of the distress that the psychosis of their parents had caused them. I shared with these children their concern for the sick parents when things went bad for them—and their joy and pleasure when their parents improved. I have often seen these probands' children weep, I have met them on the stairs and in the halls of the clinic, bearing flowers and gifts as they went to visit their parents. And I saw them again repeatedly, sometimes years apart, or heard of them and their fate for years, while visiting other patients. From this different way of meeting them, I was bound to come up with a different evaluation of their personalities. Personality phenomena that appeared to me as the physician (and perhaps, sometimes, a personal friend as well) of the probands' children, much more as perfectly natural behavior patterns for a healthy individual undergoing difficult circumstances in connection with his family. . . . I saw how children worried about their parents, how they struggled against it when their parents were to be transferred to other clinics because, perhaps, visiting them would be more difficult then. I found out how many of these children of my patients made economic sacrifices or interrupted their professional training in order to help their parents, or how a son might undertake to manage the household to take the place of his hospitalized mother. A school-age girl cleverly evaded the truant officer in order to be able to care devotedly for her smaller siblings, necessarily neglected by the sick mother. And I saw frequently, too, how these children were confused in their relations to the opposite sex, because of the schizophrenia of their father or mother. Invariably they felt guilty toward a love partner; they worried whether, faced with the probability of becoming ill or of their future offspring becoming ill, marriage would be a responsible step to take. What appeared to be a form of schizoid autism in an erotic situation, without knowing their internal sufferings, was actually the understandable, rather dramatic reaction of a warm-hearted, sensitive human being. In short, it was inevitable that I should find considerably more mentally sound and fewer psychopaths than I would have, if I had seen my probands' children in but a single interview and only for the purpose of scientific inquiry (pp. 380–381).

Bleuler has reported in these high-risk offspring a greater occupational proficiency than the parents had maintained, a higher occupa-

tional level achieved, a heightened social mobility, a higher proportion
who were demonstrably capable of sustaining a happy and successful
marital relationship.

Bleuler emphasizes that

. . . only a minority of the children of schizophrenics are in any way
abnormal or socially incompetent. The majority of them are healthy
and socially competent, even though many of them have lived
through miserable childhoods, and even though there are reasons to
suspect adverse hereditary taints in many of them. Keeping an eye
on the favorable development of the majority of these children is just
as important as observing the sick minority. It is surprising to note
that their spirit is not broken, even of children who have suffered
severe adversities for many years. In studying a number of the family histories, one is even left with the impression that pain and suffering has a steeling—a hardening—effect on the personalities of some
children, making them capable of mastering their lives with all its
obstacles, in defiance of all their disadvantages. (p. 409).

Here is the "paradox" to which that pioneer in the study of vulnerability and coping in children, Lois Murphy, alluded two decades
ago in *The Widening World of Childhood.* How, she asked, was it possible for an achievement-oriented nation like the United States to
present such a vast "problem" literature in its scientific study of children—"a literature often expressing adjustment difficulties, social fail-
ures, blocked potentialities, and defeat."

It is possible only if our mental health practitioners and researchers are predisposed by interest, investment, and training in see-
ing deviance, psychopathology, and weakness wherever they look.

That imbalance is being righted today. Murphy widened the world
of childhood to embrace more than vulnerability; she added coping and
growth (Murphy and Moriarty, 1976). Numerous recent volumes have
traversed a similar path. This long-term follow-up of Kauai's children
is part of that new emergence, adding to our knowledge by demonstration, as Bleuler has, that even among high-risk children there are the
resilient and the invincible ones.

At the beginning of this brief essay I noted that I first became
acquainted with Dr. Werner through her research report. That ac-
quaintanceship grew when our Center seminar group invited her to
meet with us at Stanford.

When I read Dr. Bleuler's writings I sense the compassion and the
humanity of this wise psychiatrist who has devoted his life to the study
of schizophrenia and to helping his patients to recover in mind and

spirit. I believe these aspects of Bleuler's personality play a significant role in the manner in which he perceives patients. Dr. Emmy Werner forms a comparable image for me. When she appeared at the Center we observed a modest, charming, witty, invigorating person whose dedication both to her project and to her cohort of children now grown to adulthood marked her as humanist and scientist.

Her writing reveals her humanistic as well as her scientific credentials. Her background further confirms the scientist side. After receiving a doctorate in psychology at the University of Nebraska she began her academic career as an Assistant Professor in the highly regarded Institute of Child Development of the University of Minnesota. Subsequently she served as Visiting Scientist and Chief, Behavioral Sciences Unit, Perinatal Research Branch, National Institute of Neurological Diseases and Blindness. Currently she is Professor of Human Development at the University of California, Davis. She has also served as a consultant to The Children's Bureau of the Department of Health, Education and Welfare, The Ford Foundation, UNESCO and UNICEF. She is the author of *Cross-Cultural Child Development: A View from the Planet Earth,* a volume that reflects her deep attachment to the many children of different cultures that she has studied. She has had long-term interests in the consequences of reproductive and environmental casualties and this interest has led her to the identification and study of various groups of children who may be at risk: those born to teenage parents; the learning disabled; the minimally brain-damaged; children of poverty; multi-racial children, and nutritionally deficient children among others.

This volume is an achievement. Longitudinal research is difficult to conduct and even more difficult to sustain. Dr. Werner and Ms. Smith have accomplished both and have done so with a high-risk, multi-racial cohort of children, predominantly of Oriental and Polynesian descent, following the sample, with minimal attrition, from pre-birth (the study began in the mother's fourth week of pregnancy) to their mid-twenties.

The fact that their data enable them to compare, over this age span, differences between resilient children and those who have had difficulty coping should be of interest not only to researchers in developmental biology, developmental psychology, child clinical psychology, child psychiatry, obstetrics, and pediatrics, but also to those who are engaged in the practice of social work, public welfare, child clinical psychology, and public health nursing.

Finally, I would note that there is an inadvertent political aspect to this research program. The United States has been built on successive waves of immigrants who knew depreviation and stress and whose own resilience was, in some manner, passed on to successive generations that transformed our nation. The politicization of research has inherent dangers and I have no desire to advance that unwholesome course. But I do firmly believe in a viewpoint that I expressed in the closing paragraphs of an article I wrote when I first became interested in studying vulnerable and stress-resistant children.

> 'Vulnerables' have long been the province of our mental health disciplines; but prolonged neglect of the 'invulnerable' child—the healthy child in an unhealthy setting—has provided us with a false sense of security in erecting prevention models that are founded more on values than on facts.
> . . . these 'invulnerable' children remain the 'keepers of the dream.' Were we to study the forces that move such children to survival and to adaptation, the long-range benefits to our society might be far more significant than are the many efforts to construct models of primary prevention to curtail the incidence of vulnerability.

Dr. Werner and Ms. Smith have permitted us to see the two sides of a coin, one marked "resilience" and the other "maladaptation." Their work serves the cause of scientific investigation and its potential application to society's betterment.

NORMAN GARMEZY
Minneapolis, Minnesota

ACKNOWLEDGMENTS

Our thanks and appreciation go to Dr. Orville Brim, president, Ms. Jane Dustan, vice-president, and to the board of directors of the Foundation for Child Development in New York for their financial support and their faith in our venture into the lives of the resilient children.

The Foundation for Child Development is a private foundation that makes grants to educational and charitable institutions. Its main interests are in research, social and economic indicators of children's lives, advocacy and public information projects, and service experiments that help translate theoretical knowledge about children into policies and practices that affect their daily lives.

The Foundation was incorporated as a voluntary agency in New York in 1900 and established as the Association for the Aid of Crippled Children in 1908. The Association was publicly supported by voluntary contributions until 1944, when substantial funds were received from the estate of Milo M. Belding in memory of his wife, Annie K. Belding, who had given many years of service to the Association. In 1972, in recognition of its evolving program and of its status as a grant-giving organization, the Association changed its name to the Foundation for Child Development.

Additional financial support for this research was given by the University of California at Davis Faculty Research Committee and the Experiment Station of the College of Agricultural and Environmental Sciences.

Kim Johnston, our research assistant and reliable yeo-"woman" throughout this project, calmly and assuredly kept our files in order and the stressful life events of the investigators "under control." Leanne Friedman Everett, our computer programmer, provided her technical skills, her songs, and never-ending patience; and Drs. Keith Barton, Louise Bachtold, and Brenda Bryant gave helpful statistical and editorial advice. Janis Castile typed several versions of this manuscript with her usual speed, precision, and flair. Thomas H. Quinn, Michael Hennelly, Karen Seriguchi, Christine Aulicino, and Paul Malchow transformed it into a book. We salute them all with deep appreciation.

Our sincere thanks go also to a number of other colleagues who read versions of this manuscript and gave us inestimable advice, comments, and constructive criticism. Among them are Dr. Nicholas Anastasiow, Hunter College in New York; Dr. Norm Garmezy, University of Minnesota; Dr. Michael Rutter, Institute of Psychiatry, London; and Dr. Marian Sigman, University of California at Los Angeles.

Our respect and admiration go to the resilient children and their families on Kauai, who gave us hope, and to the members of the Department of Mental Health of the State of Hawaii, who cared about them.

Department of Applied Behavioral Sciences   Emmy E. Werner
University of California, Davis

Haena, Kauai, Hawaii   Ruth S. Smith

VULNERABLE
BUT
INVINCIBLE

CHAPTER 1

INTRODUCTION

*And so I went on a journey to answer for myself a few
questions: What are our most human qualities? What sets
us apart from animal and machine? From the masses and
the monster? How can we believe in our infinite
possibilities when our limitations are so conspicuous? And
hope? What is this stubborn thing in man that keeps him
forever picking the lock of time? . . . The odds are
against him, the odds have always been against him, and
he knows it, but he has never believed it. . . .*

LILLIAN SMITH
The Journey (1954)

In the year in which Lillian Smith posed these questions, a team of
pediatricians, psychologists, and public health workers began a search
of their own that lasted for more than two decades. As it happened to
the poet, a few of our questions were never answered, and others
changed into new questions along the way.

The children whose lives we followed from their prenatal period to
young adulthood live on the island of Kauai, the "Garden Island," at
the northwest end of the main islands in the Hawaiian chain. They
were born in 1955, when Hawaii was still a territory, and came of age
when the islands had become the 50th state of the Union.

The population of this island is a kaleidoscope of ethnic groups:
Japanese, Pilipino, part- and full-Hawaiians, Portuguese, Puerto Ricans, Chinese, Koreans, and a small group of Anglo-Caucasians. They
are, for the most part, descendants of immigrants from Southeast Asia
and Europe who came to Hawaii to work for the sugar and pineapple
plantations. More than half of the children in this cohort grew up in
families whose fathers were semi- or unskilled laborers, and whose
mothers did not graduate from high school.

Our study began with an assessment of the reproductive histories
and the physical and emotional condition of the mothers in each trimester of pregnancy from the fourth week of gestation to delivery. It con-

1

tinued with an evaluation of the cumulative effects of perinatal stress and the quality of the caretaking environment on the physical, cognitive, and social development of their offspring in infancy, childhood, and adolescence.

In our first book about *The Children of Kauai* (Werner, Bierman & French, 1971) we presented a perspective on the magnitude of fetal and perinatal casualties in this community and documented the cumulative effects of perinatal stress, poverty, and a disordered caretaking environment on the development of children from birth to age 10.

Our main focus then was on youngsters who suffered from developmental disabilities—that is, physical handicaps, mental retardation, and serious school achievement problems—and our major concern was with prevention and early intervention.

In our second book, *Kauai's Children Come of Age* (Werner & Smith, 1977), we examined mental health problems and antisocial behavior in childhood and adolescence, and the likelihood of their persistence into young adulthood. We documented the biological and temperamental underpinnings of these problems, the relationship between social class and vulnerability, the pervasive effects of caretaker-child interaction, and cultural differences in socialization.

Throughout our follow-up studies we focused on a *combination* of biological, social, and psychological factors that were predictive of serious coping problems and examined the responses of health, mental health, and social service agencies to high-risk children and youth.

The results of our study, based on a whole population of children in a community over two decades of their lives, provide us with a perspective that cannot be obtained from short-term studies of problem children. While this report focuses on the vulnerability of young people, we could not help but be deeply impressed by the resiliency of most children and their potential for positive growth. Most young people in this cohort were competent in coping with their problems, chose their parents as their models, found their family and friends to be supportive and understanding, and expressed a strong sense of continuity in family-held values attached to education, occupational preferences, and social expectations.

In this cohort of 698, however, 204 children developed serious behavior or learning problems at *some time* during the first two decades of their lives. Some were exposed to major biological insults that prevented adequate development; many more lived in chronic poverty, or in a persistently disorganized family environment that prevented normal integration. Frequently, several of these factors interacted and exposed these children and youth to cumulative stresses too difficult to cope with unaided.

Yet there were others, also *vulnerable*—exposed to poverty, biological risks, and family instability, and reared by parents with little education or serious mental health problems—who remained *invincible* and developed into competent and autonomous young adults who "worked well, played well, loved well and expected well" (Garmezy, 1976). This report is an account of our search for the roots of their resilience, for the sources of their strength.

HISTORICAL CONTEXT OF THE STUDY

After decades of concern with pathology, child-development research began to focus in the mid- to late-1970s on self-righting tendencies in the human organism that appear to move children toward normal development under all but the most adverse circumstances (Sameroff & Chandler, 1975).

Major forces in this swing of the pendulum have been renewed interests in evolution and the new field of sociobiology (Freedman, 1979; Wilson, 1978), an outpouring of research on the competencies of infants (Osofsky, 1979), and a few longitudinal studies, begun shortly after birth, some of which are still in progress. They have provided us with an increased awareness of children's *coping skills*, that is, their *adaptation under relatively difficult circumstances in the face of challenges, frustrations, and threats* (White, 1974).

Only a handful of the prospective studies of the development of children's coping patterns have come of age, but they offer a perspective to the clinical profession that is more balanced, and that appears more hopeful, than the view glimpsed from retrospective investigations of children and youth with problems. Such "follow-back" studies have often created an unjustified impression of an inevitability of outcome.

Two types of investigations are especially relevant to our concern and will be discussed within the context of the findings of our own study. First, there is a handful of longitudinal studies that have extended over a decade or more, of normal children of above-average intelligence, living in predominantly middle-class and stable homes. Foremost among them are the Ego Resiliency and Growth and Guidance Studies of the Institute of Human Development at the University of California at Berkeley (Block & Block, 1980; Haan, 1977); the Coping Project of the Menninger Foundation in Topeka, Kansas (Murphy & Moriarty, 1976); the New York Temperament Studies (Thomas & Chess, 1977); and the Harvard Preschool Project (White, Kaban & Attanucci, 1979). Second, there are prospective studies of high-risk children exposed to reproductive risk, poverty, or parental mental illness (Anthony, 1978; Broman, Nichols & Kennedy, 1975; Garmezy, 1976; Rutter, 1979).

All have made us aware of the *resilience* of children, that is, their *capacity to cope effectively with the internal stresses of their vulnerabilities* (such as labile patterns of autonomic reactivity, developmental imbalances, unusual sensitivities) *and external stresses* (such as illness, major losses, and dissolution of the family). Even through the most stressful experiences in the most terrible homes, some individuals appear to emerge unscathed and to develop a stable, healthy personality.

Explanations for this emergence have been slow in forthcoming (Escalona, 1968). This state of affairs is, in part, due to a paucity of long-term studies of whole populations of children and, in part, to the models of human development that have influenced the collection and analysis of empirical data.

MODELS OF HUMAN DEVELOPMENT

In a state-of-the-art review, Garmezy (1974) noted that the determination of a child as vulnerable or at high risk is derived from several basic models that have characterized speculations about the etiology of behavior disorders: (1) genetic predisposition, (2) pathological disorganization within the near environment (the family), or (3) within the molar (sociocultural) environment of the child, and (4) deprivation within the prenatal or neonatal periods.

When our study began in the mid-fifties, many developmental psychologists, child psychiatrists, and allied mental health professionals adhered to a *main-effect* model of child development. Its central premise was that constitution and environment exert influences on development that are *independent* of each other. Thus, most prospective studies of high-risk infants, for example, focused attention selectively on either biological risk (such as reproductive or perinatal complications) or environmental deprivation (such as chronic poverty). As time went by, long-range predictions based on such unilateral assessments proved to be disappointing.

In our longitudinal study on Kauai, it soon became clear that to venture a guess at (or predict) the probabilities of developmental outcomes we had to consider *both* the child's constitutional make-up and the quality of his or her caretaking environment. Other investigators, especially those affiliated with the largest of the prospective studies of risk factors on the U.S. mainland—the Collaborative Perinatal Project (NCPP), sponsored by the National Institutes of Health—came to similar conclusions (Broman et al., 1975; Smith et al., 1972). Thus, since the mid-sixties, more developmental researchers and mental health practitioners have turned to an *interactional* model of human development.

An added perspective has emerged since the mid-seventies, a shift from a static, linear model of interaction to a more dynamic *transactional model* (Sameroff & Chandler, 1975; Wertheim, 1978). This model of psychosocial development has roots in the Piagetian tradition and in general systems theory (Bertalanffy, 1968; Piaget, 1971).

From this vantage point the child's development is perceived to be more than a simple reaction to the caregiving environment: It is an active, ongoing attempt to organize his or her world. The transactions between the constitutional characteristics of the child and the quality of the caregiving environment *across time* determine the quality of the outcome. Breakdown from this point of view is seen as a consequence of some *continuous* malfunction in the organism-environment transactions that prevents the child from organizing his world adaptively.

Given the apparently genetically programmed self-organizing and self-righting tendencies of the human organism (Waddington, 1966), two possible explanations have been suggested for deviant development. The first is that a severe enough insult to the organism's integrative ability prevents the functioning of its self-righting ability; the second possibility is that adverse environmental forces present *throughout development* prevent the normal integration that would occur in a more favorable setting (Sameroff & Chandler, 1975). As we shall see, rather than being separate, these two sources of stress appear to be closely interrelated throughout the child's development.

It is the balance between risk, stressful life events, and protective characteristics in the child and his caregiving environment that appears to account for the range of outcomes encountered in our study. The relative impact of these factors may differ, however, with the stages of the life cycle, the sex of the child, and the cultural context in which s/he grows up.

SOME DIRECTIONS FOR FUTURE RESEARCH

We do not as yet fully understand how children's coping patterns are shaped by their situation and personality and how these patterns change during the course of development (Monat & Lazarus, 1977). We especially need to examine sex differences in the antecedents and correlates of resilience. There is fairly consistent evidence of sex differences in children's responses to family stress (Rutter, 1970). Nationwide, reported rates of disordered behavior differ significantly for boys and girls, and the sex ratio of problem behavior changes from childhood to adolescence (Gore, 1979). Hence, we might also expect to find some sex differences in behavior characteristics and competencies that allow boys and girls to cope *positively* with life's difficulties.

We have as yet only a few clues, mostly from case studies and autobiographies of the gifted (e.g., Angelou, 1970; Darrel, 1973; Goertzel et al., 1978; Wiesel, 1969), about the early sources of security that enable resilient men and women to cope successfully with poverty, prejudice, and family disintegration in their childhood and youth. The long-term effects of these informal sources of support within the extended family, among peers, and in school, as well as the prevailing values system(s) that provide such security, need to be studied more systematically in longitudinal research.

The few longitudinal studies that have followed children's coping patterns into adolescence have dealt with a select and privileged sample of the human race: bright, urban, middle-class whites. Prospective studies of high-risk children include black children from poverty-stricken homes as well, but have, as yet, not come of age.

There is need, then, for a broader perspective, one which places children's sources of competence and support in a wider sociocultural context. The Kauai Longitudinal Study provides such a unique opportunity:

It is based on a large, multiracial cohort of children.
It represents *all* births in an entire community.
It has followed the children, with little sample attrition, from the perinatal period to the threshold of adulthood.

The objectives of this report are:

1. To provide a longitudinal perspective on children's capacity to cope with perinatal stress, poverty, and parental psychopathology;
2. To examine sex differences in vulnerability and resiliency in the first and second decades of life;
3. To identify protective factors within the child and the caregiving environment that differentiate high-risk children who are resilient from those who develop serious learning and behavior problems.

THE PLAN OF THIS BOOK

We introduce the reader to the setting of the study and to the methods we used to assess the physical and psychological status of the children and the quality of their caregiving environment in Chapters 2 and 3. We next give a brief overview of what it was like to grow up vulnerable and examine sex differences in vulnerability and resiliency in the first and second decades of life (Chapters 4 and 5).

We then identify characteristics of the person and of the caregiving environment that distinguished high-risk resilient children from peers of the same age and sex who developed serious learning and behavior problems. We present these data for each of four segments of the life cycle (infancy, toddlerhood, middle childhood, and late adolescence) for children growing up in chronic poverty (Chapters 6–10) and for offspring of psychotic parents (Chapter 11).

We subsequently take a look at the interrelationships, across time, between significant child and caregiver variables that contributed to the making of resiliency in high-risk children. Finally, we introduce a model that shows the interrelationship between risk factors and stressful life events that increased vulnerability on the one hand, and protective factors within the child and the caregiving environment that increased stress resistance, on the other.

The resilient children and youth tell their own stories in a series of selected case studies (Chapter 13). We close the report with a discussion of the implications of our findings for research and social action (Chapter 14).

Throughout this book we present relevant vignettes from our files and interviews to illustrate the interplay between risk, stressful life events, and protective factors on the development of resilient boys and girls. We hope thus to present an effective balance between the statistical findings of our study that depict group trends and individual life histories that illustrate stability and change in human development. The interested reader is referred to the Appendix for a detailed account of the statistical analyses of our data that includes the results of parametric and nonparametric tests of significance, correlations, multiple regression, and discriminant function analyses.

CHAPTER 2

THE SETTING

KAUAI AND ITS PEOPLE

The island of Kauai lies in the northwest end of the Hawaiian chain, some 100 miles and half an hour's flight from Honolulu. Roughly circular in shape and about 30 miles in diameter, it ranks fourth among the islands in geographical size and population. Kauai's people, numbering close to 32,000, live in small towns scattered around the shoreline and connected by a highway that reaches three-quarters of the way around the island, ending in the north, where cliffs rise steeply from the ocean's edge. The rainy central part of the island is mostly uninhabited.

Kauai has great natural beauty, encompassing mountains, cliffs and canyons, rain forests, sandy beaches, and pounding surf. As the oldest of the Hawaiian islands, and the last of its independent kingdoms, its history and legends reflect a certain maverick spirit that has come to characterize its people and their lifestyles.

Settled in the 8th century A.D. or earlier by canoe voyages from the Marquesas and Society Islands and populated in the 12th and 13th centuries by migrations from Tahiti, the Hawaiian Islands were rediscovered by Captain James Cook, England's great seagoing explorer, whose first landing occurred on Kauai in 1778. In the years that followed, an increasing number of vessels stopped at the island's Waimea port to trade and replenish their supplies. The first Christian mission was established on Kauai in 1820, and New Englanders set about teaching first royalty and then the common people to read and write in their native tongue and in English. The island's first sugar plantation was founded in Koloa in 1835 and is still in operation today. The development of the plantations was the initial stimulus to the influx of what today constitutes Kauai's multiracial population. Chinese, Portuguese from the Azores and Madeira Islands, and Japanese were imported for plantation labor prior to the 1900s, with Puerto Ricans and Koreans coming to the islands during the early 20th century, and large numbers of Pilipino immigrants arriving until shortly after the end of World War II.

The rate at which different immigrant groups advanced up the socioeconomic ladder has varied. The *haole* (stranger) Caucasians of North European and North American ancestry differed from the other immigrants, since they came to Hawaii not as plantation laborers but in upper- and middle-class positions, first as missionaries, then as businessmen and plantation managers and supervisors. The *haoles,* the Chinese, and the Koreans have been the most mobile socially, followed closely by the Japanese, who are predominant in the middle class of the island. The Portuguese, Puerto Ricans, and Pilipinos have been the least mobile; together with the Hawaiians and part-Hawaiians they are found predominantly in the lower and lower-middle classes. Relative to their length of stay on the island, the Pilipino and Portuguese show a slower rate of upward mobility than the other ethnic groups. The Japanese, in contrast, have moved quickly from plantation labor to supervisory, professional, and business positions.

Two Decades of Change

When our study began in 1954, Hawaii was still a territory; 5 years later, in 1959, the islands became the 50th state of the Union. Statehood brought rapid economic changes and population shifts. Whereas Kauai's economy had once been based almost entirely on sugar and pineapple production, the 1960s saw a rapid expansion of the tourist industry. Today the island is visited by more than half a million tourists each year.

Sugar continues to be Kauai's major agricultural enterprise and will doubtless retain its primary position in the foreseeable future, but increasing consideration is being given to diversified agriculture. With increased mechanization, urbanization, and new local and export markets, job opportunities for Kauai's youth are shifting. Other economic changes have been brought about by an increase in the government work force and in retail trade and construction. The space age has also reached Kauai. Major scientific-military installations were developed on the west side of the island, which have provided important contributions to space explorations and general strategic defense. They opened up new possibilities to Kauai's people as well as introducing a new population to the island.

These economic and population shifts have had a significant effect on Kauai's young people. No longer willing to settle for the predictable futures of their fathers, but not necessarily prepared for other alternatives, some have left the island for Honolulu and the mainland. Others are experimenting with alternative lifestyles or are involving themselves actively in the controversies surrounding these changes. Ecology groups have sprung up to resist the influx of developers and their efforts to build more hotels and condominiums and to introduce a pace of life that some youth feel may destroy their heritage.

The arrival of so-called hippies, primarily from the West Coast of the mainland, when our cohort was entering their teen years added to the turbulence of this period. This group's search for serenity and inner awareness through drugs, their desire for a simple life, and their rejection of established values brought social changes and conflicts totally outside the experience of the islanders. The harassment of one group by the other became a not-uncommon occurrence. Although much misinformation exists on the prevalence of drug abuse, all concerned agree that it has become a significant problem on the island. There has also been a significant increase in serious offenses, such as murder, manslaughter, burglary, and theft, recorded in the annual police reports, and in the number of motor vehicle accidents on the island.

In an effort to cope with the many changes of the past few decades, the educational and social agencies of the community have added new programs, and private groups have increased their services.

Health, Education, and Social Services on Kauai

From the beginning of our study excellent provisions were available on the island for health and medical care. Virtually all plantation employees and their families were enrolled in medical care and hospitalization plans. All pregnant women had ready access to prenatal care in a physician's office or dispensary, delivery in one of the two general hospitals on the island, and medical and hospital care for their infants.

Medical services have greatly expanded in the past two decades. Thirteen physicians practiced on Kauai when the study began, seven associated with the plantations, four in private practice, and two serving as government physicians. There were thirty-six practicing physicians 20 years later. Probably the greatest contribution has been the recruitment of medical specialists—from one board-certified practitioner to the coverage of 22 basic specialties. Three hospitals now serve the population and a greater level of care is noted in them, including family-planning services and the implementation of Hawaii's liberalized abortion laws.

When our study children entered school, there were fifteen elementary schools (eleven public, four parochial) and three high schools on the island. In addition to existing classes for the mentally retarded and learning disabled, new programs were added in the late 1960s for potential drop-outs—work motivation classes, special classes for pregnant teenagers, services of outreach counselors, and off-campus classrooms. The Special Services office of the Department of Education maintains a staff consisting of a coordinator, psychological examiners, speech and hearing specialists, social workers, and visiting teachers, as well as diagnostic-prescriptive teachers to assist children with special educational needs. The growth of our cohort also saw the expansion of the Kauai Community College. Starting with a student enrollment of about 250 in 1965, this branch of the University of Hawaii serves now more than 1000 students.

The State Health Department administers Kauai Children's Services, a coordinated multidisciplinary and one-door entry approach with services related to child development, developmental disabilities, learning disabilities, mental health, mental retardation, pediatrics, orthopedics, cardiology, and other special fields. Specialists from Honolulu together with local public health nurses, physicians, social workers, and psychologists are available for diagnosis and treatment. The Kauai Community Mental Health Service has a staff of two psychiatrists, a clinical psychologist, two social workers, and two paramedical assistants, including a special children's mental health team funded by the State of Hawaii.

Other social agencies have expanded staff and services as well. The Family Court and the Divisions of Public Welfare and Vocational Rehabilitation in the Department of Social Services and Housing all maintain extensive case loads. The Police Department has increased its services to provide a special female counselor in its Juvenile Crime Prevention Unit and a school relations officer at one of the high schools.

The Big Brothers and Big Sisters Association of Kauai, a nongovernmental organization, was formed and flourished during the cohort's teen years. Other voluntary organizations, such as the YWCA, YMCA, Civil Air Patrol, Catholic Youth Organization, Boy and Girl Scouts, and athletic groups, provide recreational and learning experiences for all who care to participate. The Kauai Community Services

Council, through its sponsorship of such programs as the Committee on Substance Abuse, the Kauai Immigration Services Committee, and the Serenity House, a halfway house for recovering alcoholics, and through its role as a coordinating and educational body for community services, has broadened its base of service operations. Rehabilitation Unlimited Kauai, with its vocational evaluation and training programs and sheltered workshop, provides one of the island's major resources for both youth and adults. Kauai Economic Opportunity, Inc., and Headstart have developed programs to assist residents of all age groups in poverty-stricken areas.

In retrospect one wonders if any other generation among Kauai's children have been exposed to so many and such rapid changes in such short a time as the children and youth who participated in this study.

THE STUDY POPULATION

Table 1 presents some relevant demographic data on the 1955 birth cohort.

Socioeconomic status ratings are based on the father's occupation, income level, steadiness of employment, and condition of housing. The rating is based primarily on father's occupation, categorized by one of five groups: (1) professional; (2) semiprofessional, proprietorial, and managerial; (3) skilled trade and technical; (4) semiskilled; and (5) day laborer and unskilled.

"Ethnicity" is based on a cultural definition and refers to the country of origin of the child's immigrant ancestors—i.e., whether they were Chinese, Japanese, Pilipino, Puerto Rican, or Portuguese

Table 1: Distribution of 1955 Birth Cohort by Ethnicity and Socioeconomic Status (Kauai Longitudinal Study)

| | | % in Each SES Category | | |
| | | Upper | Middle | Lower |
Ethnic Group	N	(1,2)	(3)	(4,5)
Japanese	217	14.3	54.4	31.3
Part- and Full-Hawaiian	147	2.0	31.3	66.7
Pilipino	115	2.6	15.7	81.7
Other Ethnic Mixtures	105	5.7	26.7	67.6
Portuguese	42	7.1	33.3	59.5
Anglo-Caucasians (haoles)	17	76.5	23.5	0

(Lind, 1967). It has remained a custom in Hawaii to designate whites of North European or North American ancestry as *haoles* (strangers). A person of any Hawaiian ancestry, no matter how slight the admixture of native blood, if it is recognized and known, is designated as part-Hawaiian. Since 1950, part-Hawaiians have been combined with pure Hawaiians in most census tables. Other ethnic mixtures include children of two different non-white and non-Hawaiian parents; on Kauai they are mostly children of younger Japanese mothers and older Pilipino fathers. All ethnic groups, of course, share a common local island culture. The majority of the children are of Asian and Polynesian descent (Japanese, Hawaiian, part-Hawaiian, and Pilipino) and more than half come from poor families.

METHODOLOGY

We give now a brief account of the ways in which we assessed the children and their family environment in infancy, childhood, and adolescence. These issues are discussed at length in our previous publications, especially Chapters 3 and 4 of *The Children of Kauai* (Werner, Bierman & French, 1971) and Chapter 3 of *Kauai's Children Come of Age* (Werner & Smith, 1977). These works also contain the instruments we used in data collection. A summary of the data base for the present report can be found in the Appendix.

CENSUS AND CAMPAIGN FOR EARLY PREGNANCY REPORTS

In the first phase of the study, beginning in 1954, five public health nurses and one social worker, all residents of Kauai, set about obtaining a household census. They listed the occupants of each dwelling and recorded demographic information and brief personal data, including a reproductive history of all women 12 years of age and older. Those of childbearing age were asked if they were pregnant. A report card with a postage-free envelope was left with each woman, with a request that she mail it to the Department of Health as soon as she believed herself to be pregnant.

The campaign to get women to report as soon as they believed themselves to be pregnant was conducted once each trimester, simultaneously with the periodic interviews of all pregnant women. The interviewers were local residents who knew the community and had the trust and cooperation of the mothers. They were trained by the resident research director (a sociologist) in the use of specially prepared interview forms. The local physicians were asked to submit monthly a list of women who had come to them for prenatal care. The physicians were supplied with special forms, serving as a source of pregnancy reports to the study. The Kauai District Health Department laboratory, from which prenatal serology was ordered by the physicians, became an additional source of reports.

The prenatal interviews, and prenatal, hospital, labor, delivery, and newborn records from the local physicians, as well as live-birth and death certificates, were also included in the records of the study.

ASSESSMENT OF PRE/PERINATAL COMPLICATIONS

A clinical perinatal rating, based on the presence of conditions thought to have had a possible deleterious effect on the fetus or newborn infant, was made for each child in the 1955 birth cohort. After reviewing extensive records, a pediatrician scored the severity of some 60 selected complications or events that could occur during the prenatal, labor, delivery, and neonatal periods, as follows: 0–not present, 1–mild, 2–moderate, and 3–severe. (A summary of the scoring system for prenatal-perinatal complications is presented in the Appendix.) After all conditions were scored, the pediatrician assigned to each infant an overall score from 0 to 3. This was based on a clinical judgment taking into consideration the number, type, and severity of unfavorable conditions present. In general, this overall score is the same as the value assigned to the most severe condition present. Cases with overall scores of 2 and 3 were reviewed by a second pediatrician on the research staff, and all scoring was checked by a statistician for consistency.

HOME VISITS IN YEAR 1

In the postpartum period and when the babies were 1 year old, public health and social workers interviewed the mothers at home. The mothers rated their infants on a number of temperamental characteristics, such as activity level, social responsiveness, and ease of handling, and reported any distressing habits, such as frequent head-banging, temper tantrums, or irregular sleeping or feeding habits. During the home visits the interviewers also checked a series of adjectives that described the mother's interaction with the infant and asked about any stressful life events that had occurred between birth and the baby's first birthday.

PEDIATRIC AND PSYCHOLOGIC EXAMINATIONS IN YEAR 2

Two practicing pediatricians from Honolulu, both diplomates of the American Board of Pediatrics, periodically came to Kauai to conduct the medical examinations. The median age at examination was 20 months, with 95 percent of the children examined before age 2. The examinations, based on a systematic appraisal of all organ systems, were conducted principally to assess physical status and to search for congenital and acquired defects. Nutrition, sleeping and feeding habits, toilet training, speech, and social and motor development were also appraised. In addition to recording specific findings, the pediatricians were asked to indicate their impressions of each child's overall physical and intellectual status by rating him or her as superior, normal, low-normal, or retarded, in each area. The pediatricians' judgments were based on their examinations, observations of the children's behavior, and questioning of the mothers. They also recorded their recommendations for further study by the children's physicians or by a specialist provided by the Crippled Children's Branch of the Children's Health Services Division.

Independently, two psychologists from the University of Hawaii assessed the children's cognitive development with the Cattell Infant Intelligence Scale and self-help skills with the Vineland Social Maturity Scale. The examiners also completed a series of adjective checklists describing the behavior of the toddler and the parent-child interaction during the testing session, and asked the mother about any stressful life events that had occurred in the family between year 1 and year 2.

ASSESSMENT OF THE EARLY FAMILY ENVIRONMENT: BIRTH THROUGH YEAR 2

The quality of the early caretaking environment was evaluated on the basis of information obtained from the periodic home interviews conducted by public health and social workers in the prenatal and postpartum periods and when the infants were 1 year old. Additional data were obtained from interviews with the mothers during the developmental examinations of their toddlers.

The following dimensions were used to reflect intellectual stimulation, material opportunities, and emotional support available to the young child:

1. *Mother's educational level*, based on number of years of schooling (from school records that also included parental IQ scores for 485 parents).
2. *Socioeconomic Status (SES)*, at birth and age 2, based on father's occupation, standard of living, condition of housing, and crowding (observed during home visits).
3. *Family Stability* (birth to age 2), based on information from the interviews on the legitimacy or illegitimacy of the child, presence or absence of the father, marital discord, alcoholism, parental mental health problems, and long-term separation of the child from the mother without an adequate substitute caretaker.

This information was rated on a 5-point scale from very favorable (1) to very unfavorable (5) by two graduate students, one in psychology, the other in social work. The ratings were made without any knowledge of the children's perinatal scores or of the results of the 2-year follow-up. The two raters scored 15 percent of the total sample twice, independently of each other, until they had reached a percentage agreement in the high eighties and nineties. The correlations between the three environmental ratings were (r): SES/family stability .21; SES/mother's education .33; mother's education/family stability .03.

10-YEAR FOLLOW-UP

The design we followed in the 10-year follow-up utilized the experience we had gained in a pretest in which all procedures were tested with 75 children slightly older than the study group. As a result of this experience, we eliminated the routine pediatric examination we had originally planned for each child because we discovered no findings pertinent to the study beyond those recorded in the extensive medical and school health records already available.

The field staff collected existing information about each of the children from the following sources:

Records of the Crippled Children's Branch, the Mental Health Services Division, the Department of Social Services, and the schools' Department of Special Services.
School records, including grades, results of previous intelligence and achievement tests, and of speech, hearing, and vision examinations conducted at the school.

Records of physicians and hospitals for children who had physical handicaps, illnesses, or accidents.

The staff obtained *new* information about each child from:

A questionnaire filled out by his current teacher, including grades in reading, arithmetic, and writing (grammar and spelling), and a checklist of physical, intellectual, and emotional problems observed in the classroom.

A home interview with the mother, covering illnesses, accidents, and hospitalizations in the interval between 2 years and 10 years of age; changes in the home environment; the mother's impressions of the child's school performance; and behavior problems observed at home.

Results of two group tests—the Bender Gestalt and the Primary Mental Abilities (PMA) test—sampling reasoning, verbal, numerical, spatial, and perceptual-motor skills.

A panel of the resident staff, consisting of a pediatrician, a psychologist, and a public health nurse, reviewed each child's record to determine if the information was complete and if there was evidence of any physical defect or handicap, or evidence of any intellectual or emotional problem. They determined whether further diagnostic procedures were needed to complete their appraisal of the child's status at age 10. The panel judged that some 30% of the children needed additional diagnostic examinations. Each examination was then conducted by an appropriate specialist. The combined screening and diagnostic information was again reviewed by the panel. They prepared a final need-assessment of each child, estimating the effect of any existing handicap on his or her school progress and the need for various types of future care.

ASSESSMENT OF THE FAMILY ENVIRONMENT: YEARS 2 THROUGH 10

The assessment of the caretaking environment at age 10 was based on standardized interviews with the mother or mother substitute, conducted by public health nurses and social workers who visited the home. The main purpose of the interviews was to obtain information about the quality of the family environment in which the child had grown up from age 2 to age 10.

The rating of the family's *socioeconomic status at age 10* combined information on father's occupation, income level in terms of plantation pay scales, steadiness of employment, and condition of housing. It was based primarily on father's occupation, which was categorized into one of five levels: (1) professional; (2) semiprofessional, proprietorial, and managerial; (3) skilled trade and technical; (4) semiskilled; (5) day laborer and unskilled.

The rating of *emotional support* took into account the information given in the interview on interpersonal relations between the parents and the child, opportunities for satisfactory identification, methods of discipline and ways of expressing approval, and the presence or absence of stressful life events encountered by the child and his or her family between the ages of 2 and 10.

The rating of *educational stimulation* took into account the opportunities provided for enlarging the child's vocabulary, the intellectual interests and activities of the family, the values placed by the family on education, the work habits emphasized in the home, the facilities and help provided by the parents, the availability of learning supplies, books, and periodicals, and the opportunities for exploration of the community at large (recreational facilities, library).

All ratings were made by a clinical psychologist on a 5-point scale from very favorable (1) to very unfavorable (5). An item was included in the environmental ratings only when two independent scorers reached an agreement at least 90% of the time.

All environmental ratings were made independently of any knowledge of the perinatal scores of the children or the results of the follow-up studies. The intercorrelations between the ratings ranged from .57 (socioeconomic status/educational stimulation) to .37 (socioeconomic status/emotional support).

The environmental ratings made of the study group at age 10 were somewhat lower than those made at age 2. Whereas 30% of the 2-year-olds were rated as living in homes of low socioeconomic status, 55% of the 10-year-old group were rated as such; those in the middle group had decreased from 59% to 34% and the proportion with the highest ratings remained the same, about 11%. The shift in ratings of socioeconomic status can be explained by the closing of several pineapple canneries and plantations, which had provided seasonal work for many mothers. In addition, more children had been born, especially among the poor.

Although the ratings of "emotional support" when the children were age 10 and of "family stability" when they were age 2 are not strictly comparable, we noted a slight downward shift from preschool to school age. Three out of four Kauai families were given a favorable rating in "family stability" when the children were 2; only two out of three families received "average" or "above average" ratings in "emotional support" when the children were 10.

The rating of "educational stimulation" at age 10 showed that the study families were about evenly divided between those with "adequate" to "high" ratings and those with "low" to "very low" ratings. The proportion of families at the lower end of the scale is not surprising, considering the rather low educational level of the Kauai population, its rural character, and the large percentage of workers in the semiskilled and unskilled classes. In 1950, the median year of schooling completed by Kauai women, aged 25 and over, was eighth grade, and for Kauai males, 25 years and over, only sixth grade. The lower educational level of the men reflects the presence of the older immigrant sector of the population, especially the Pilipinos.

18-YEAR FOLLOW-UP

The follow-up at age 18 consisted of a survey of the entire cohort via a search of educational, health, mental health, and social service agency records, and tests of ability and achievement (SCAT and STEP) routinely administered in the schools. It also included an in-depth study via clinical interviews and personality tests (California Personality Inventory and Nowicki Locus of Control Scale) of youth with serious mental health and/or learning disabilities and of a control group without problems, matched for age, sex, ethnicity, and socioeconomic status.

Stage 1: The Record Search

During our previous follow-up studies at years 2 and 10, we had been impressed by the amount of useful information available in the educational, health, and social service records of the community agencies on the island. We obtained permission to examine the records of the following agencies for data on referral (date, source, and reason), diagnosis, type of services rendered, and outcome:

1. Department of Education, Office of Guidance and Special Services: records of periodic evaluations of all children placed in special classes for the mentally retarded, in learning disability classes, in special motivation classes for potential drop-outs; records of special services for behavior, health, and learning problems.

2. Department of Health, Divisions of Mental Health, Mental Retardation, and Public Health Nursing: records of all youth referred to community mental health services as outpatients or admitted to psychiatric hospitals; records of all youth with significant health problems, including the mentally retarded, and boys and girls served through Crippled Children's Services and the Public Health Nursing Branch.
3. Department of Social Services and Housing, Division of Vocational Rehabilitation: records of youth who were physically disabled or slow learners and who were placed in work-study or Job Corps programs.
4. Department of Social Services and Housing, Division of Public Welfare: records of all youth eligible for welfare benefits and families eligible for Aid to Dependent Children (ADC); foster home placements; home visits of social workers to families "in trouble."
5. Family Court and Kauai Police Department: records of all contacts with law enforcement agencies, delinquent acts (including possession and sale of drugs); placement on probation or in Hawaii youth correctional facilities, and suicide attempts.
6. Rehabilitation Unlimited Kauai: records of severely retarded and multiply handicapped youth who worked in sheltered workshops and were participating in prevocational evaluation and training programs.
7. G. N. Wilcox Memorial Hospital and Health Center and Kauai Veterans Memorial Hospital: Records of teenage deliveries and abortions among the women in the 1955 birth cohort.

A similar search was made of the Department of Education (Special Services), Department of Social Services, and Family Court records in Honolulu and on the other islands to which some youth from the 1955 cohort had moved. We also obtained permission to check the Mental Health Register of the State of Hawaii, which contained information on in- and outpatient treatment and referrals for mental health problems for members of the 1955 birth cohort and their families.

Stage 2: Group Tests and Questionnaires

TESTS OF ABILITY AND ACHIEVEMENT. The district superintendent, Department of Education, Kauai, gave us permission to copy from the records of the Special Services Division the following scores from group ability and achievement tests that had been routinely administered in grades 8, 10, and 12 in the high schools on the island: Mid-percentile scores on the verbal, quantitative, and total scales of the Cooperative School and College Ability Tests (SCAT 1966) and mid-percentile scores on the reading, writing, and mathematics scales of the Sequential Tests of Educational Progress (STEP 1966).

PERSONALITY TESTS. The California Psychological Inventory (CPI) (Gough, 1969) and the Nowicki Strickland Locus of Control Scale (Duke and Nowicki, 1973; Nowicki and Strickland, 1973) were administered in group sessions to members of the 1955 cohort still attending high schools on the island. Follow-up sessions were scheduled for youth who could not be reached in the first round of testing. "Problem" youth were given the tests at the time of the interview if they had not participated previously in a group testing session.

BIOGRAPHICAL QUESTIONNAIRE. A brief biographical questionnaire asking for information on educational status and plans, vocational status and plans, marriage and health status, and stressful life events experienced in adolescence, was mailed to members of the 1955 cohort in a self-addressed and stamped return envelope. For "problem" youth and controls this information was obtained during the course of the interview.

Stage 3: The Interviews

Semistructured interviews explored the youths' attitude toward school, their current interests and activities, their occupational plans, the extent of their participation in work and social life. The youths were asked about their preference in friends, their perspectives on their own strenghs and weaknesses, the values they held, the things they worried about, and their opinions on drugs, sex, and race relationships. The interviews lasted, on the average, about 2 hours.

ASSESSMENT OF THE ENVIRONMENT: YEARS 10 THROUGH 18

Among the 18-year interviews were a number of questions that dealt with the nature of the caregiving environment the youth had grown up in during adolescence. It explored their attitudes toward kin and neighbors, stressful life events experienced in adolescence, their feelings of security or conflict about their family and the degree of their identification with their father and mother. We also asked for an evaluation of the help received from formal and informal sources of support—such as community agencies, teachers, ministers, older friends, peers, and siblings. These contacts were verified in the records of social service agencies and also provided an independent check on major stressful life events reported by the youth themselves.

Every effort was made to trace all youth who had been at risk and those in the control group, including those who had moved to other islands in the State of Hawaii (mostly Honolulu, Oahu) and the mainland (mostly California). Ninety percent of the interviews were conducted by the resident psychologist on Kauai, the others by the project director in California and two graduate students in Honolulu. Reliability of interview ratings made independently from knowledge of the other follow-up data ranged from the high eighties to the nineties.

Attrition Rates

The promise of a relatively stable sample on the island of Kauai remained justified, even during a period of rapid social change. Throughout the two decades of the study attrition was low: 96% of the 1955 birth cohort participated in the 2-year follow-up, 90% in the 10-year follow-up, and 88% in the 18-year follow-up. By comparison, the two largest follow-up studies on the U. S. mainland, the Berkeley Growth Study and the Berkeley Guidance Study (Block, 1971) and the St. Louis study of former child guidance clinic cases by Robins (1966), were able to reach 70% and 82% of their original target groups, respectively.

This relatively low rate of attrition for a longitudinal study involving many persons over a long time-span is a tribute to the cooperation of an immensely helpful island community—to the education, health, and social agencies, to the parents, and especially to the youth themselves.

CHAPTER 4

GROWING UP VULNERABLE

The Kauai Longitudinal Study is unique in that it covered all pregnancies and births that occurred in an entire community—across a wide socioeconomic and ethnic spectrum—and followed the study group for nearly two decades. The study was conducted on an island with educational, medical, and public health facilities that compared favorably with most communities of similar size on the United States mainland. Yet the magnitude of the casualties among the children and youth in this cohort was impressive.

THE CASUALTIES OF PREGNANCY AND THE FIRST DECADE OF LIFE

Deleterious biological effects resulting in reproductive casualties exerted their peak influence in the very early weeks of pregnancy, when 90% of the fetal losses occurred. Of pregnancies reaching 4 weeks gestation, an estimated 237 per 1000 ended in loss of the conceptus. The rate of loss formed a decreasing curve from a high of 108 per 1000 women in the 4–7 week period to a low of 3 in 32–35 weeks of gestation.

In contrast, neonatal and infant mortality rates were very low, reflecting a minimum number of unfavorable influences in the first weeks of postnatal life: There were only 13.8 deaths under 28 days per 1000 liveborn and all were attributed to pre- and perinatal causes. The liveborn were classified as to presence and severity of handicapping conditions and estimates were made of the type of care required.

24

At birth, 9% of the cohort had some congenital defects, of which 3.7% were serious enough to require long-term, specialized care for either severe physical handicaps and/or severe mental retardation. Eight percent of the liveborn weighed below 2500 gm. About half of these low-birthweight babies remained in the hospital for special medical and nursing care after the mother was discharged.

By age 2, pediatricians found 14% of the children to be below the norm in physical development. This included children with congenital defects of the central nervous, musculo-skeletal, and cardiovascular systems, and children born prematurely or "under par" in physical development. Of the infants weighing 2500 gm or less at birth, 34% were judged to be below normal in physical status compared to 13% of the heavier infants.

Sixteen percent of the children in the cohort were considered to be below normal in intellectual development, and 12% were rated below normal in social development by the psychologists. Judgments were based on results of the Cattell and Vineland tests and behavior observations during the developmental examinations. Of the children rated below normal, most were low in only one area of development. The greater the perinatal stress, however, the higher was the chance that a child would be rated low in more than one area.

Had the 2-year follow-up been restricted to pediatric examinations, only 46% of all below normal children would have been detected. Had the follow-up study been limited to psychological examinations, a little over two-thirds (70%) would have been pinpointed. This finding highlights the need for the use of multiple criteria and interdisciplinary cooperation in the assessment of young children.

At age 10, an interdisciplinary panel consisting of a pediatrician, a psychologist, and a public health nurse reviewed each child's record to isolate any evidence of significant physical, learning, or behavior problems and to identify any need for medical treatment, remedial education, or mental health care. The following groups of children were identified:[1]

7% in need of continuous medical care for moderate to marked physical handicaps (congenital and acquired defects of the central nervous system, vision, or hearing, heart anomalies, and orthopedic problems).

[1]On the basis of combined screening and diagnostic examinations (psychological and medical), school records, and behavior checklists filled out independently by teachers and parents.

14% in need of long-term (more than 6 months) remedial education in such basic skills as reading, spelling, grammar, arithmetic.

3% in need of placement in special classes for the mentally retarded.

3% in need of placement in classes for the learning disabled. These were children of normal intelligence with serious reading and perceptual-motor or attention problems.

4% in need of long-term (more than 6 months) mental health services. Four out of five in this group of children were "acting out"; the others were diagnosed as having childhood neuroses or as schizoid or sociopathic personalities.

10% in need of short-term (less than 6 months) mental health services. The overwhelming majority in this group were shy or anxious children who lacked self-confidence and had developed chronic nervous habits to deal with their insecurities.

In sum: During the months of pregnancy and the first decade of life, the casualties in this cohort amounted to about one-half of those conceived and to about one-third of the liveborn. The greatest need for services at age 10, required by almost one-third of the children, was for long-term educational or mental health services, or both.

THE CASUALTIES OF THE SECOND DECADE OF LIFE

By age 18, 15% of the cohort had a record of serious delinquencies documented in the files of the Police Department and the Family Court. Among the delinquents were youth who were or had been involved in larceny, burglary, malicious injury, assault and battery, sexual misconduct, including rape; possession, sale, and abuse of hard drugs; and in repeated acts of truancy, running away from home, curfew violations, and unlawful hunting. (Excluded were traffic citations and occasional trespassing of property.)

Mental health problems by age 18 were found among 70 youth, approximately 10% of the cohort. These were documented in the Mental Health Register, the records of the Department of Health's Division of Mental Health, and other Social Service records. They included youth who had made one or more suicide attempts; youth who had been sent to the Hawaii State Mental Hospital or local hospitals for mental health reasons; youth treated as outpatients of the Kauai Community Health Center; and youth who, on the basis of our 18-year interviews, were judged to have serious conflicts and high anxiety that led to maladaptive behavior.

The majority of the troubled youth had a record of multiple problems, e.g., a combination of delinquency and mental health problems, for boys, or mental health problems and teenage pregnancies, for the girls. Significant mental health problems were noted in most teenage mothers.

In sum: Approximately one out of every five youth in this cohort developed *serious* coping problems at *some time* during the second decade of their lives—some because of major biological insults that prevented adequate development, many more because of the poverty of their homes or because a persistently disorganized family environment prevented normal integration.

THE JOINT INFLUENCE OF REPRODUCTIVE RISK AND THE QUALITY OF THE CAREGIVING ENVIRONMENT

The interplay between the caretakers' attitudes toward the baby's arrival and perinatal risk factors depends on the social context in which the family lives and is already discernible in prenatal interviews with pregnant women.

Attitudes Toward Pregnancy

Our analysis of the prenatal interviews indicated that emotional factors predictive of reproductive risk for women from middle-class families differed from the factors predictive for women with little economic or emotional support. Among middle-class women, negative feelings about the pregnancy, psychological trauma experienced during the pregnancy, and the woman's anxiety and inability to express herself freely during the prenatal interviews were significant predictors of such perinatal risk factors as prematurity (birthweight below 2500 gm); difficult delivery (prolonged first stage of labor); poor condition of newborn (respiratory distress, jaundice, convulsions, gastro-intestinal problems); congenital defects; and central nervous system dysfunctions noted in the neonatal period. First-trimester interviews yielded more items predictive of perinatal risk factors than later prenatal interviews for middle-class women.

Fewer prenatal interview items were significant predictors of perinatal risk factors among poor women or women living in unstable, disorganized homes. In all three trimesters, the father's unhappiness about the coming baby (as perceived by the woman) and, in the second and third trimester, the woman's lack of physical preparedness for the baby were significant predictors of such perinatal risk factors as difficult labor, low birthweight, and poor condition of the newborn. The anxiety expressed by the poor mothers in the prenatal interviews tended to reflect *long-term chronic life stresses;* the anxiety expressed by the middle-class mothers tended to focus more specifically on the *pregnancy experience.*

Pre/perinatal Risk: Short versus long-term effects

For 56% of the children in this cohort, the prenatal and perinatal periods were free from complications as we defined them (see scoring system in Appendix Table A-O). Thirty-one percent suffered complications of only a mild nature (score of 1); for 10%, complications of moderate severity were present (score of 2); and for 3% they were considered severe (score of 3). Of the infants who died before the 2-year follow-up, more than three-fourths were from the very small group with severe perinatal complications. Among the surviving children, only 2% had severe complications.

During the developmental examinations at 20 months, we found a *direct* relationship between severity of perinatal stress and the proportion of children considered to be below normal in physical, intellectual, or social development. This trend was especially pronounced among children who had experienced moderate or severe perinatal stress. In the latter group were children with major congenital defects, who required long-term medical care (see Table 2).

By age 10, differences between children exposed to various degrees of perinatal complications and those born without perinatal stress were less pronounced than at 20 months and centered on a small group of survivors of moderate and severe perinatal stress. The greatest effect of perinatal complications was found in the proportion of children with physical handicaps related to central nervous system (CNS) impairment, children requiring placement in special institutions or classes for the mentally retarded (MR) or learning disabled (LD) and children in need of long-term mental health (LMH) services of more than six months duration.

By age 18, four of five survivors of the small group who had suffered severe perinatal stress had persistent and serious physical, learning, or mental health problems. The rate of mental retardation in this group was ten times, the rate of serious mental health problems was five times, and the rate of serious physical handicaps was more than twice that found in the total cohort. Among the survivors of moderate perinatal stress, the rate of serious mental health problems was three times, and the rate of mental retardation and of teenage pregnancies was twice that of their peers in the 1955 cohort.

Table 2: 2-, 10- and 18-Year Outcomes by Severity of Perinatal Stress: 1955 birth cohort, Kauai Longitudinal Study

	Total Cohort (N:698) %	Moderate Perinatal Stress (N:69) %	Severe Perinatal Stress (N:14) %
CRITERIA AT AGE 2			
Pediatrician's rating of physical health status below normal	14.2	23.1	35.7
Psychologist's rating of intellectual development below normal	13.5	21.5	28.6
Cattell IQ > one SD below mean	9.6	15.4	21.4
CRITERIA AT AGE 10			
Physical handicap	6.0	7.0	22.2
PMA IQ > one SD below mean	10.7	9.9	30.6
In MR class or institution	2.3	3.5	16.7
CRITERIA AT AGE 18			
Physical handicap	6.0	6.0	14.5
Mental retardation	3.0	6.0	29.0
Serious mental health problem	3.0	9.0	14.5
Delinquency record	15.0	17.0	21.5
Teenage pregnancy	6.0 (F)	14.0 (F)	——
Proportion of children and youth with some problem at 2, 10, or 18 years	33.0	36.0	79.0

At each of the follow-up stages, however, we found significant interaction effects between characteristics of the caretaking environment and degrees of perinatal stress that produced the largest deficits for the most disadvantaged children (see Table 3).

As early as 20 months, these effects were seen in several ways. First, children growing up in middle-class homes who had experienced the *most severe* perinatal complications had mean scores on the Cattell Infant Scale almost comparable to children with *no* perinatal stress who were living in poor homes. Second, the most developmentally retarded children (in physical as well as intellectual status) were those who had experienced *both* the most severe perinatal complications *and* who were also living in the poorest homes. Third, SES differences pro-

Table 3: Proportion of Children with Physical Health Problems, Mean Cattell IQ at Age 2, and Mean PMA IQ at Age 10 by Socioeconomic Status and Degree of Perinatal Stress: 1955 birth cohort, Kauai Longitudinal Study

Variable	Severity of Perinatal Complications			
Physical Health Status at Age 2 (below normal)	None (N:388) %	Mild (N:222) %	Moderate (N:69) %	Severe (N:14) %
(very) high SES	7.5	16.7	16.7	50.0
middle SES	10.9	15.9	22.0	22.2
(very) low SES	12.2	13.8	21.4	66.7
Cattell IQ at Age 2	Mean Score (and Standard Deviation)			
(very) high SES	102 (12)	100 (11)	104 (20)	95 (13)
middle SES	100 (12)	100 (11)	98 (14)	91 (8)
(very) low SES	98 (11)	96 (12)	93 (12)	61 (37)
PMA IQ at Age 10	Mean Score (and Standard Deviation)			
(very) high SES	112 (11)	113 (12)	114 (11)	110 (11)
middle SES	108 (12)	106 (13)	105 (12)	101 (13)
(very) low SES	99 (11)	100 (11)	99 (12)	94 (14)

vided for a *greater* difference in mean Cattell scores (34 points) for children who had experienced severe perinatal stress than did perinatal complications for children living in a favorable environment (4 points).

Although the correlation between SES and family stability ratings was low (r. 21), the difference in mean Cattell scores at 20 months between children who had experienced *severe* perinatal stress, but who were growing up in a *stable* family environment (94), and those with *serious* perinatal stress who were living in an *unstable* caretaking environment (77) was nearly as dramatic as that found for differences between children from middle-class and poor homes. Unstable caretaking environments also produced a significant increase in the proportion of children in poor health at 20 months, especially among those who had undergone severe perinatal stress, in spite of the availability of prepaid and easily accessible health care services provided by the plantations.

The effects of the caretaking environment appeared even more powerful at age 10: First, children *with* and *without* severe perinatal stress who had grown up in middle-class homes *both* achieved mean PMA IQ scores well above the average. Second, PMA IQ scores were seriously depressed in children from *low* SES homes, particularly if they had experienced *severe* perinatal stress. Third, the family's socioeconomic status showed significant associations with the rate of serious learning and behavior problems. By age 18, ten times as many youth with serious coping problems were living in poverty as had survived serious perinatal stress.

In sum: Perinatal complications were consistently related to later impaired physical and psychological development *only* when combined with persistently poor environmental circumstances (e.g., chronic poverty, family instability, or maternal mental health problems). Children who were raised in more affluent homes, with an intact family and a well-educated mother, showed few, if any, negative effects from reproductive stress, unless there was severe central nervous system impairment.

THE BIDIRECTIONALITY OF CHILD-CARETAKER EFFECTS

Although most of the children and youth with serious and persistent learning and behavior problems in this community were poor, it needs to be kept in perspective that *poverty alone* was not a sufficient condition for the development of maladaptation (see Table 4 and Appendix A-1).

Table 4: Social Class Distribution of Males and Females in the 1955 Birth Cohort (Kauai) by Presence and Persistence of Coping Problems at 10 and 18

MALES

SES at 10	Total (N:318)		M without Problems at 10 and 18 (N:158)		M with Problems at 10 only (N:105)		M with Problems at 10 and 18 (N:55)	
	%	N	%	N	%	N	%	N
Upper (1,2)	10.1	32	14.6	23	7.7	8	1.8	1
Middle (3)	37.4	119	44.9	71	33.3	35	23.6	13
Lower (4,5)	52.5	167	40.3	64	59.0	62	74.5	41

FEMALES

SES at 10	Total (N:325)		F without Problems at 10 and 18 (N:212)		F with Problems at 10 only (N:59)		F with Problems at 10 and 18 (N:54)	
	%	N	%	N	%	N	%	N
Upper (1,2)	8.4	27	9.4	21	10.2	6	—	0
Middle (3)	33.5	109	38.2	81	35.6	21	13.0	7
Lower (4,5)	58.5	189	51.8	110	54.3	32	87.0	47

In *both* poor and middle-class homes, infants with "difficult" temperaments who interacted with distressed caretakers in a disorganized, unstable family, had a greater chance of developing serious and persistent learning and behavior problems than infants perceived as rewarding by their caretakers and who grew up in stable, supportive homes. Let us briefly illustrate this bidirectionality of child-caretaker effects by a comparison of the records of children with learning disabilities and long-term mental health problems.[2]

Children with learning disabilities (3% of the 1955 cohort) had been diagnosed by a panel consisting of a pediatrician, a psychologist, and a public health nurse, on the basis of the combined results of psychological and medical examinations, grades, and behavior checklists filled out independently by parents and teachers. Placement in an LD class was recommended when a child displayed serious reading problems (more than 1 year below Chronological age (CA), in spite of normal intelligence; a great deal of scatter on the Wechsler Intelligence Scale for Children (WISC) subtests [more than 1 standard deviation (SD) difference between verbal and performance IQ]; large numbers of errors on the Bender-Gestalt (B-G) test; difficulties in attention and information processing; and persistent hyperkinetic behavior, both in the home and the classroom.

The children in need of long-term mental health services (4% of the cohort) had been identified on the basis of behavior checked independently by parents and teachers and confirmed by individual diagnostic examinations. The majority of children in this group were considered to be "acting out"; the others had been diagnosed as having childhood neuroses or as schizoid or sociopathic personalities by child psychiatrists or clinical child psychologists.

Sixty percent of the LMH children and 30% of the LD children had records of moderate perinatal stress, low birthweight, congenital defects, or CNS dysfunctions. Controls of the same age and sex, from the same SES and ethnic background, did not display these factors to a significant extent.

More frequently noted among the LMH and LD children than among the controls were infant temperamental traits that appeared distressing and nonrewarding to the caretakers and that may have contrib-

---

[2]The interested reader is referred to Chapters 5–7 of *Kauai's Children Come of Age* (Werner & Smith, 1977) for a detailed report on the children with learning disabilities and childhood mental health problems.

uted to initial difficulties in attachment and bonding. These disturbed child-caretaker transaction patterns were observed in the postpartum period and during home visits at year 1 by public health nurses and were noted independently by psychologists and pediatricians during the developmental examinations at 20 months.

Often a mother with a low level of education attempted unsuccessfully to cope with the needs of an infant who was perceived by her as not responsive (not cuddly, not affectionate) or too active and fretful, and who had sleeping and/or feeding habits that were distressing to her. The disturbed nature of this interaction was accentuated in an atmosphere of family instability, e.g., where there was mental illness, parental discord, or desertion, divorce, or death.

By the second year, caregiver and child appeared caught in a vicious cycle of increasing frustration, characterized by parental behavior that was perceived as "careless," "erratic," "indifferent," "ambivalent," or "overprotective" by psychologists during the 20-month examination.

By the tenth year, public health nurses, social workers, and teachers who were unaware of the earlier child-caregiver transactions noted a pronounced lack of emotional support in the homes of most of the children in need of long-term mental health services whose problems persisted throughout adolescence.

THE PROGNOSIS FOR CHILDREN WITH LEARNING DISABILITIES. For the overwhelming majority in this group serious problems persisted throughout adolescence: Agency records for *four out of five* indicated continued academic underachievement, confounded by absenteeism, truancy, a high incidence of repetitive, impulsive acting-out behavior that led to problems with the police for the boys and sexual misconduct for the girls, and other mental health problems less often recognized and attended to. Rates of contact with community agencies were nine times as high as that for control-group youth matched by age, sex, socioeconomic status, and ethnicity.

Group tests at age 18 showed continued perceptual-motor problems for most, as well as deficiencies in verbal skills and serious underachievement in reading and writing. Self-reports revealed a pervasive lack of self-assurance and interpersonal competency, and a general inadequacy in utilizing their intellectual resources. High "external" scores on the Locus of Control Scale were indicative of the youths' feeling that their actions were not under their control. Professional assistance in adolescence was considered of "little" help by them. Only *one out of four* in this group was rated improved by age 18, the lowest proportion among all the groups of youth at risk.

THE PROGNOSIS FOR CHILDREN CONSIDERED IN NEED OF LONG-TERM MEN-TAL HEALTH SERVICES AT AGE 10. During adolescence more than *three out of four* in this group had contacts with community agencies, the majority as consequences of persistent, serious behavior problems. Rates of contact (many with multiple agencies), were six times as high as that for controls matched by age, sex, socioeconomic status, and ethnicity.

Psychosomatic and psychotic symptoms, sexual misconduct or problems with sexual identity, assault and battery, theft and burglary, drinking and drug abuse, and continued poor academic performance, coupled with absenteeism and truancy, left these youth few construc-tive options for the future as they reached young adulthood.

The majority had recognized a need for help, but turned to their peers for the assistance they did not seek or obtain from their families. Only *one out of three* was judged to have improved by age 18; the improvement rate rose to *one out of two* among the minority (one out of three) for whom there was some community intervention in adoles-cence.

THE PROGNOSIS FOR CHILDREN CONSIDERED IN NEED OF SHORT-TERM MENTAL HEALTH SERVICES AT AGE 10. The prognosis was much more favor-able for the children who, at age 10, had been considered in need of mental health services of less than 6 months duration. In the absence of early biological stress and early family instability, the majority of child-hood behavior problems in this group appeared to be temporary, though at the time painful reactions to stressful life events.

Only *one out of ten* had been the beneficiary of intervention by community agencies, but *six out of ten* were rated improved by age 18. With few exceptions the improved cases had been troubled by a lack of self-confidence, anxiety and/or chronic nervous habits in childhood. Among the *four out of ten* who remained unimproved by age 18 were most of the children characterized by high anxiety *and* acting-out be-havior at age 10.

In sum: The majority of problems identified in middle childhood had improved spontaneously by the time the cohort reached age 18, although positive changes in behavior were noted more often for mid-dle-class than lower-class children. Children with learning and/or be-havior problems that *persisted* into late adolescence had higher rates of moderate to severe perinatal stress, low birthweight, and "chronic conditions leading to minimal brain dysfunctions" noted by pediatricians in infancy *and* tended to live more often in chronic poverty or amidst parental psychopathology than children whose problems were transient. They also tended to elicit more negative responses from their caretakers.

CHAPTER 5

SEX DIFFERENCES IN VULNERABILITY AND RESILIENCY

Resilience, *n. 1. The capability of a strained body to recover its size and shape after deformation caused especially by compressive stress. 2.* An ability to recover from or adjust easily to misfortune or change.

Resiliency, *n: RESILIENCE*

Across the first two decades of life, we noted some significant sex differences in the proportion of males and females with serious physical, learning, and behavior problems, and in the stressful life events associated with deviant outcomes among boys and girls. Sex differences in susceptibility to biological and psychosocial stress changed *with time,* and with the different cognitive and social demands of childhood and adolescence. Overall, more females than males in this birth cohort appeared to be able to cope successfully, in spite of reproductive risks, chronic poverty, or family distress.

Let us first take a closer look at significant sex differences in the occurrence of physical, learning, and behavior problems in the first two decades of life and at major life stresses reported by each sex in childhood and adolescence. We will then consider some of the factors that may make one sex more vulnerable than the other at different points in their lifetimes.

SEX DIFFERENCES IN VULNERABILITY IN THE FIRST DECADE

At birth, more boys than girls in our study had been exposed to moderate or marked perinatal stress (M: 3.6%; F: 2.7%). More than half (8 of 15) of the boy babies, but less than one-fifth (2 of 11) of the girl babies with the most serious perinatal complications died in infancy, most in the neonatal period. Four-fifths (80%) of *all* the deaths among the boys in this cohort up to age 2, and two-thirds (67%) of all the deaths among the girls were due to severe pre-perinatal complications.

Among the survivors, the incidence of perinatal complications, by degree of severity, was approximately the same for boys and girls (2%), but more of the most seriously stressed girls stayed alive. A slightly higher proportion of boy babies had recognizable congenital defects at birth (M: 10.2%; F: 7.9%), but a higher proportion of girl babies weighed less than 2500 gm when they were born (M: 6.5%; F: 9.5%).

Between birth and age 2, more boys than girls had been exposed to serious and/or repeated illnesses or accidents. The proportion of children judged to be below normal in physical status by the pediatricians at age 2 was approximately the same for both sexes (M: 13%; F: 15%).

By age 2, a higher proportion of boys than girls (M: 7%; F: 4%) obtained Cattell IQ's below 80 on a psychological examination that measured adaptive, sensorimotor, and emerging language skills; and more boys than girls were rated below normal or retarded in intellectual development in independent assessments by the pediatricians.

Boys, as a group, also had lower mean scores than the girls on the Vineland Social Maturity Scale (M: Mean SQ: 114, SD: 15; F: Mean SQ: 118, SD: 14) and appeared to lag somewhat behind the girls in self-help skills and social competence.

Between the ages of 2 and 10, more boys than girls in this cohort had records of serious or repeated illnesses or accidents. At age 10, boys had nearly twice the proportion of minor physical handicaps than did girls (M: 20.7%; F: 11.8%); but there were no sex differences in the proportion of moderate to marked physical handicaps requiring continuous medical care.

By age 10, boys had a considerably higher proportion (51.0%) of minor and major school achievement problems than did girls (37.0%). Significantly more boys (46.9%) than girls (33.6%) received poor grades (D or F) in basic skill subjects, such as reading, writing, and arithmetic. Nearly twice as many boys (9.2%) than girls (4.7%) were diagnosed as having serious language disabilities on the basis of psychological tests.

Significantly more boys (30.9%) than girls (22.0%) had behavior problems that interfered with their school achievement in the elementary grades. Among the various symptoms checked by teachers during observations of classroom behavior, "hyperkinetic" symptoms, i.e., restless, distractible behavior, were checked for more than twice as many boys (8.7%) as girls (3.2%). A higher proportion of boys (8.4%) than girls (5.0%) had chronic nervous habits as well.

Among the children considered in need of special educational services by the interdisciplinary panel (consisting of a pediatrician, a psychologist, and a public health nurse), more boys than girls were judged to be either in need of long-term (more than 6 months) remedial education, or in need of placement in a learning disability class. More boys than girls were placed in classes or institutions for the mentally retarded (M: 15; F: 10), as well. More boys than girls were considered to be in need of long-term mental health care by age 10, on the basis of psychological and medical examinations and behavior checklists filled out independently by teachers and parents (M: 14; F: 11).

Boys who were at high risk because of constitutional factors (moderate to severe perinatal stress; congenital defects) were more vulnerable amidst a disordered caretaking environment than girls with the same predisposing conditions. There were significant sex differences in the effects of poverty, family instability, and lack of educational stimulation in the home, which led to a higher rate of childhood problems (i.e., need for long-term remedial education, need for long-term mental health services, repeated serious delinquencies) for high-risk boys than for high-risk girls.

Stressful Life Events Associated with Serious Learning and/or Behavior Problems in Childhood

Among stressful life events that discriminated significantly for *both* sexes between children who had developed serious learning and/or behavior problems by age 10 and peers who were free of such problems were: birth of a younger sibling before the index child was 2 years old; maternal mental health problems between ages 2 and 10; change of schools between ages 6 and 10; and the presence of a handicapped brother in the household who had serious learning and/or behavior problems himself. Among both sexes significantly more such stressful life events were reported for lower-class than middle- and upper-class children.

By age 10, more stressful childhood events discriminated between *boys* with and without serious coping problems than between girls. Among significant life stresses associated with serious learning and/or behavior problems for the boys in childhood were: the departure of an older sibling from home; sporadic employment of the mother (of less than 3 months duration); serious marital discord among the parents; prolonged absence of the father (of more than 1 year's duration); or

Table 5: Stresses Associated with Serious Coping Problems in
Childhood: Males, 1955 birth cohort, Kauai

Stressful Life Events or Chronic Difficulties	M without Problems (N:206) %	M with serious Learning and/or Behavior Problems (N:88) %
IN INFANCY		
Mother pregnant or birth of younger sib before M was 2 years old	15.0	35.2
IN CHILDHOOD		
Sibling left household	6.8	29.5
Mother worked short-term outside of household	9.2	20.5
Serious marital discord	4.4	13.6
Maternal mental health problems	1.0	10.2
Father permanently absent	3.4	10.2
Mother remarries, stepfather moves into house	.5	6.8
Child changed schools	1.0	6.8
Father lost job	0	5.7
Brother handicapped or with serious learning or behavior problems	1.0	5.7
Sister handicapped or with serious learning or behavior problems	.5	2.3
Close friend dies or moves away	0	2.3

replacement of the natural father by a stepfather after a divorce (see
Table 5).

Among significant life events associated with childhood learning
and/or behavior problems in *girls* were: serious illness of the father, the
death of a brother, and having a handicapped sister with serious learning and/or behavior problems (see Table 6).

SEX DIFFERENCES IN VULNERABILITY IN ADOLESCENCE

With the exception of two deaths from accident and drowning (both
boys) in the time period between 10 and 18 years, there were no significant sex differences in rates of recorded serious illnesses among the
adolescents in the Kauai Longitudinal Study.

Table 6: Stresses Associated with Serious Coping Problems in Childhood: Females, 1955 birth cohort, Kauai

Stressful Life Events or Chronic Difficulties	F without Problems (N:233) %	F with Serious Learning and/or Behavior Problems (N:54) %
IN INFANCY		
Mother pregnant or birth of younger sib before F was 2 years old	18.5	59.3
Serious marital discord	.4	9.3
Maternal mental health problems	0	3.7
IN CHILDHOOD		
Serious illness of father	11.2	25.9
Loss of brother by death	.9	9.3
F changed schools	1.3	9.3
Sister handicapped or with serious learning or behavior problems	1.7	11.1
Brother handicapped or with serious learning or behavior problems	.9	7.4
Maternal mental health problems	.9	7.4

Nearly three times as many boys than girls had records of serious delinquencies (M: 77; F: 26) by age 18, but the sex ratio of other disordered behavior shifted from a majority of boys in childhood to a majority of girls in late adolescence. By age 18 more than twice as many girls as boys (M: 23; F: 47) had developed serious mental health problems. These included youth who had been sent to the Hawaii State Mental Hospital or local hospitals for mental health care, youth who were or had recently been under treatment as outpatients of the Kauai Community Mental Health Center, and teenage girls in the cohort who had mental health problems associated with their pregnancies.

More boys than girls with serious learning and/or behavior problems in childhood had *improved* by age 18, and *new* problems in the second decade appeared more frequently among the girls than the boys.

The total number of *boys* with serious problems in our cohort dropped from 88 (out of 342) in the first decade to 66 in the second decade, while the total number of *girls* with serious behavior problems rose from 54 (out of 356) in the first decade to 69 in the second decade.

This shift was due mainly to a decrease in need for long-term remedial educational services among the boys and an increase in serious mental health problems among the girls in late adolescence.[1]

Stressful Life Events Associated with Serious Coping Problems in Adolescence

Among stressful life events that discriminated significantly for *both* sexes between youth who were delinquent and/or had developed serious mental health problems by age 18, and peers without such

Table 7: Factors Associated with Serious Coping Problems in Adolescence: Males, 1955 birth cohort, Kauai

Stressful Life Events or Chronic Difficulties	M without Problems (N:206) %	M with Serious Mental Health Problems and/or Delinquencies (N:66) %
IN INFANCY		
Mother pregnant or birth of younger sib before M was 2 years old	15.0	40.9
IN CHILDHOOD		
Older sib left household	6.8	31.8
Serious marital discord	4.4	19.7
Maternal mental health problems	1.0	12.1
Father lost job	.5	10.6
Father permanently absent	3.4	9.1
M changed schools in lower grades	1.0	7.6
Brother handicapped, with serious learning or behavior problems or in trouble with law	1.0	6.1
Mother remarried, stepfather moves in house	.5	4.5
IN ADOLESCENCE		
Problems in relationship with father	6.8	22.7
Financial problems	4.9	16.7
Maternal mental health problems	1.0	16.7
Problems in relationship with mother	2.9	12.1

[1]For a more detailed discussion of the teenage pregnancies on Kauai, see Chapter 8 in *Kauai's Children Come of Age* (Werner & Smith, 1977) and a report on High Risk Families in Rural Hawaii, by Smith (1980).

problems were: difficulties in the relationship with the father during adolescence; problems in the relationship with the mother, including maternal mental health problems, and financial problems reported by the teenagers. In *both* sexes, lower-class youth reported more stressful life events during their teens than did adolescents who grew up in middle- and upper-class homes. (See Tables 7 and 8.)

A number of additional stressful life events were associated with serious coping problems among adolescent girls. Among them were: teenage pregnancy; teenage marital stress; serious marital discord between the parents; divorce or permanent separation of one parent from the family; temporary absence of one or the other parent; and departure of a favorite sibling from the household.

Discussion

Our data, from a predominantly Asian and Polynesian population, corroborate findings reported from longitudinal studies on the mainland that include white, black, and Hispanic children.

A report from the largest of these studies, the Collaborative Perinatal Project (NCPP), sponsored by the National Institute of Neurological and Communicative Disorders and Stroke, is based on a sample of some 37,945 infants in the first year of life, and on smaller samples from the thirteen participating institutions across the United States who provided data on the physical, neurological, and psychological development of the children from birth to age 4. Some 55% of the NCPP population is black; 95% are ward patients (Broman, Nichols & Kennedy, 1975; Singer, Westphal & Niswander, 1968).

Significant sex differences, showing males to be at a disadvantage, were found on all examinations, the neonatal exam, the 8-months performance on the Bayley Scales of Infant Development (both Mental and Motor), the 12-months neurological examinations, the speech and hearing examinations at 3 years, and the psychological examinations at 4 years, which included the Stanford-Binet Intelligence Test.

Details of the mechanisms behind these early sex differences are still debated by biological and behavioral scientists.

A number of factors seem to combine to make life generally more difficult for young boys than for young girls:

1. *Genetic factors.* The X chromosome contains at least 100 important genes other than those specifically related to reproduction. The female has two of these genes (and 4–5% more chromosomal material), compared with the hemizygous male, and hence may be able to marshall more resistance to external haz-

Table 8: Factors Associated with Serious Coping Problems in Adolescence: Females, 1955 birth cohort, Kauai

Stressful Life Events or Chronic Difficulties	F without Problems (N:233) %	F with Serious Mental Health Problems and/or Delinquencies (N:69) %
IN INFANCY		
Mother pregnant or birth of younger sib before F was 2 years old	18.5	55.1
Serious marital discord	.5	5.8
Maternal mental health problems	0	2.9
F was adopted	0	2.9
IN CHILDHOOD		
Maternal mental health problems	.9	13.2
Sister handicapped or with serious learning or behavior problems	1.7	10.3
Brother handicapped or with serious learning or behavior problems	.9	7.4
F changed schools	1.3	4.4
F was placed in foster home	0	2.9
Death of brother	.9	2.9
IN ADOLESCENCE	(N:102)	(N:69)
Problems in family relationship	9.8	55.1
Teenage pregnancy	2.0	43.5
Financial problems	7.8	40.6
Problems in relationship with mother	3.9	37.7
Problems in relationship with father	2.0	36.2
Teenage marriage	1.0	15.9
Father permanently absent (deserted, divorced)	3.9	15.9
Mother permanently absent (divorced)	2.0	14.5
Maternal mental health problems	1.0	14.5
Severe marital discord	2.0	13.0
Problem with peers	3.9	13.0
Mother temporarily absent	2.9	13.0
Father temporarily absent	1.0	11.6
Sibling left home	0	7.2
Teenage marital stress	0	7.2

ards of development. These differences are presumably more likely to reveal themselves when the young organism is stressed.

The other possibility involves the tendency for a mother, without Y chromosomal genes, to become sensitized to foreign products produced by Y chromosomes and to try to reject them, thus creating a relatively unhealthy prenatal environment for the male embryo. This might produce minimal neurological damage prenatally and contribute to the greater incidence of behavioral disorders and mental retardation observed in males in childhood (Robinson, 1969).

2. *Rate of development.* Girls mature faster than boys at all ages up to late adolescence. The difference in physical growth rate is as much as several weeks at birth, approximates 1 year at the time of starting school and reaches almost 2 years at puberty (Rutter, 1970). Boys' rate of intellectual development is slower as well: Virtually all evidence indicates that girls not only say their first word sooner and are able to articulate at an earlier age than boys, but, once having reached this stage, they tend to progress verbally at a more rapid rate than boys (Maccoby & Jacklin, 1974). These developmental differences suggest that boys may experience more difficulties than girls in the elementary grades. The evidence uniformly indicates that this was the case among the children on Kauai.

3. *Aggressiveness.* Another factor that probably creates problems for boys is their aggressiveness. Young boys appear to have, on the whole, a lower frustration threshold than girls, and are more impulsive and given to physical quarrels. Thus, boys may more often get into trouble with parents and teachers, and this, in turn, may increase the number of disturbances they experience at home and in the classroom (Gove, 1979).

4. Finally, *sex-role expectations* are more stringent for young boys than young girls. At an early age, boys learn that they are expected to be masculine, and that they must earn their masculine identity. In contrast, young girls are allowed more leeway in childhood, and it is only in adolescence that behaving in a "feminine" manner becomes a serious issue.

The evidence suggests that children learn appropriate sex-role behavior primarily as a consequence of contact with an adult model of the same sex, yet young boys have a more limited amount of such contact in our culture, since they live in a predominantly feminine world, at home and in school (Lynn, 1974).

In sum, the physical immaturity of boys, the expectations for male sex-role behavior, and the feminine environment in which they live may work both separately and in concert to increase the amount of stress experienced by them in *childhood*.

There are reasons to believe that, at least in our culture, the relative stress (i.e., undesirable or threatening life events) experienced by the sexes changes as they move from childhood into adolescence. This is quite apparent when we examine the number and types of stressful life events reported for males and females in our birth cohort in their first and second decades of life.

Our findings have support from other sources. Gove (1979) has examined the reported rates of persons 19 years old and younger who received psychiatric treatment in public and private mental hospitals, general hospitals, and outpatient clinics on the U.S. mainland. These data, collected by the National Institute of Mental Health, show that, while young boys have higher rates of treated mental illness than do young girls, by late adolescence, girls have as high, if not higher, rates as their male counterparts.

Boys perform better academically in adolescence, when they start to catch up with girls in verbal skills. Academic work also now mainly requires analytic problem-solving skills and an increased focus on mathematics and the sciences. In these fields, boys, as a whole, tend to outperform girls (Maccoby & Jacklin, 1974).

On the other hand, adolescent girls undergo marked pressure to adopt a traditional feminine role and *not* to compete in the masculine world. Thus, in adolescence, girls tend to go through a process many boys went through earlier, that is, of trying to cope with a set of social sex-role expectations that may *limit* their behavior and the expression of their competence (Gove, 1979).

Unlike males, females now tend to perceive their fate as depending more on the actions of others and may feel this lack of control to be frustrating (most excruciating in the case of unmarried pregnant teenagers). Just as *aggressiveness* tended to get boys into trouble in childhood, *dependency* may become a major problem for girls in adolescence.

EARLY PREDICTORS OF SERIOUS COPING PROBLEMS IN CHILDHOOD AND ADOLESCENCE

How well did each set of variables assessed in this study (the biological, the behavioral, and the environmental data) identify males and females who developed serious coping problems in childhood and/or adolescence?[2]

---

[2]For a detailed discussion of early predictors of problems, see Chapter 13 in *Kauai's Children Come of Age* (Werner & Smith, 1977).

In general, predictions from earlier data, i.e., from birth and infancy to age 2, and from age 2 to age 10, ran more accurately for the girls than the boys, reflecting sex differences in the rate of physical, cognitive, and social development.

Predictors of 2-year Outcomes

Exposure to moderate or marked perinatal stress, a congenital defect, and a poor standard of living at birth were predictive of poor developmental outcomes at age 2 for *both* sexes. Maternal behavior ratings of low activity level and low social responsiveness added to the predictive power for the boy infants; a low level of maternal education added to the predictive power for the girl infants.

Predictors of 10-year Outcomes

A Cattell IQ score below 80 at age 2 was the best single predictor of a diagnosis of *mental retardation* at age 10 for both males and females. The predictive power of the results of the infant test increased with the addition of information on biological factors (presence of congenital defects) in the girls, and with the addition of data reflecting early emotional instability in the home (low family stability, psychological trauma during mother's pregnancy) for the boys.

Predictive of a *learning disability* for *both* sexes was a combination of biological insult to the central nervous system around birth and an early home environment low in stability. Infant temperamental traits nonrewarding for the mother, such as very high or very low activity levels, appeared more frequently in boys who were later diagnosed as having learning disabilities than in girls.

In both sexes an interaction between biological impairment around birth, a low standard of living, and infant temperamental characteristics perceived as distressing or nonrewarding by the mother were moderately predictive of *mental health problems* that required long-term care.

Predictors of 18-year Outcomes

A combination of a need for long-term mental health services (more than 6 months), remedial education, and a moderate to marked physical handicap by age 10 was the most powerful predictor of serious *mental health problems* in late adolescence for the males. A combination of a learning disability, with need for mental health services, and a moderate to marked physical handicap by age 10 was a fairly powerful predictor of serious mental health problems in late adolescence for the females. The predictability of later mental health problems improved considerably from the early to the middle childhood years.

The single most powerful predictor of *delinquency* among girls in adolescence was a recognized need for long-term mental health services by age 10. Most delinquent boys had learning problems and were in need of long-term remedial education at age 10. Predictions increased if we took into account the family's socioeconomic status (low), maternal education (low), and the presence of physical handicaps at birth or age 10.

Key Predictors

About a dozen variables were among the key predictors of serious coping problems in our study. Among the variables that characterized the caregiving environment were a low level of maternal education; a low standard of living, especially at birth, but also at ages 2 and 10; and a low rating of family stability between birth and age 2. Among the *biological* variables were moderate to severe perinatal stress, the presence of a congenital defect at birth, and of a moderate to marked physical handicap at age 10. Among the *behavioral* variables were maternal ratings of very low or very high infant activity level at year 1, a Cattell IQ score below 80 at age 2, a PMA IQ score below 90 at age 10, and a recognized need for placement in a class for the learning disabled or for six months or more of mental health services by age 10. (App. A-2)

Singly or in combination these variables appeared in our multiple regression equations as key predictors of serious learning and behavior problems in childhood and adolescence, with the predictive power increasing steadily from birth to age 2, from ages 2 to 10, and from ages 10 to 18. Predictions for children from poor homes could be made with greater certainty than for children from middle-class homes, reflecting a greater likelihood of some *continuous* malfunction of the child-care-taker/environment interaction across time for the children of poverty than for the children of affluence.

The presence of *four or more* of these predictors in the records of the children by age 2 appeared to be a realistic dividing line between most children in this cohort who developed serious learning and/or behavior problems by age 10 or age 18, and most of the boys and girls who were able to cope successfully with the developmental tasks of childhood and adolescence. We chose this cut-off point to select the resilient children and their control-group peers for the present study (see Table 9).

Table 9: Cumulating Predictors of Serious Coping Problems in Children and Youth (Kauai Longitudinal Study, 1955 Cohort)

			Criteria			
Number of Predictors Present	MR by 10	LD by 10	LMH by 10	Delinquents by 18	Mental Health Problems by 18	No Problem at 10 or 18
1 or more	100.0	100.0	100.0	100.0	100.0	97.6
2 or more	100.0	100.0	100.0	100.0	100.0	70.6
3 or more	100.0	100.0	92.0	90.0	88.0	49.2
4 or more	100.0	81.0	75.0	72.0	70.0	26.9
5 or more	88.0	54.0	54.0	54.0	50.0	9.1
6 or more	60.0	27.0	37.0	30.0	27.0	2.2
7 or more	44.0	18.0	16.5	16.0	18.0	.6
8 or more	20.0	4.5	4.0	9.0	7.5	0
9 or more	16.0	4.5	4.0	3.0	3.0	0
10 or more	12.0	0	4.0	3.0	3.0	0

THE CHILDREN OF THE RESILIENCY STUDY

The 42 girls and 30 boys who are the target group of our resiliency study had *each* encountered at least *four or more* cumulative risk factors by age 2, but all managed to cope successfully with chronic poverty and, in addition, with constitutional vulnerabilities or family distress. None, as far as we can tell, developed any serious learning or behavior problems in childhood or adolescence. The "resilient" youth have since crossed the threshold of young adulthood, the age (late teens and early twenties) at which admission to mental hospitals and need for mental health care reaches a peak.[3]

As far as we can tell from interviews and from their record in the community, they manage to do well in their work, family, and social life, and they are realistic in their goals and expectations. They have learned "to work well and love well," in accord with Freud's definition of mental health.

From a comparison of their coping patterns and informal sources of support with those of others of the same age, sex, and socioeconomic status who developed serious problems, we hope to find some clues about the self-righting tendencies of the human organism.

[3]We are aware that the maximum period of risk for mental breakdown is still ahead of them. This dilemma we share with others who have ventured into prospective studies of the "invincible" offspring of psychotic parents (Anthony, 1974; Garmezy, 1974c; Pines, 1979).

The two comparison groups also lived in chronic poverty, and their records contained four or more of the risk factors that had identified the majority of the children with serious learning and/or behavior problems in this birth cohort.[4]

Comparison Group I consisted of 39 females and 51 males who had developed serious learning and behavior problems by age 10. Included were children in need of long-term (more than 6 months) remedial education or placement in special classes (LD, EMR) and children in need of long-term mental health care by age 10. *All* children with mental health problems had serious learning problems as well.

Comparison Group II consisted of 43 females and 49 males with a record of serious delinquencies and/or mental health problems at age 18 (verified by the police, the Family Court, the schools, the Kauai Community Mental Health Center, and the Mental Health Register of the State of Hawaii). There was considerable overlap among these problems. The majority of the high-risk youth had multiple problems.

[4]There were no significant ethnic differences between the resilient children and the two comparison groups, but there were no Anglo-Caucasians amongst them. None of the *haoles* on Kauai lived in chronic poverty.

CHAPTER 6

RESILIENT INFANTS: CONSTITUTIONAL ENDOWMENT AND CARETAKING ENVIRONMENT

The resilient children in our study were all born and reared in families that were poor, judging by the breadwinner's occupation, level of income, and condition of housing. Most fathers were semi- or unskilled laborers on the sugar plantations of the island. Most mothers had not graduated from high school and about half had eight grades or less of formal schooling.

These children had also higher than average rates of constitutional vulnerabilities, including more than twice the proportion of low-birthweight (LBW) babies than was found in the total cohort (16.7% vs. 7.4%). Most of the LBW infants needed special care and stayed in the hospital for a few days after their mothers went home (F: 11.9%; M: 6.7%) (see Tables 10 and 11).

The resilient boys and girls shared these characteristics with the high-risk boys and girls who later developed serious coping problems. However, a smaller proportion of the resilient infants had congenital defects. At the birth of their child, the mothers of the resilient boys were significantly younger (average age: below 30) than the mothers of the boys in the two control groups. The fathers of the resilient girls

50

Table 10: Characteristics of the Females in the Resiliency
Study: Birth to Year 1 (1955 cohort, Kauai, low SES homes)

Characteristics of the Infant: Birth to Year 1	High-Risk F Resilient % (N:42)	High-Risk F Problems at 10 % (N:39)	High-Risk F Problems at 18 % (N:43)
BIRTH ORDER:			
First born	28.6	18.0	25.6
Second born	21.4	25.6	25.6
Third born	11.9	17.9	16.3
Fourth born	11.9	15.4	14.0
Fifth born and later born	26.2	15.7	16.3
PERINATAL STRESS:			
Moderate-Marked	12.0	28.2	20.9
Congenital Defects at Birth	0	23.1	25.6
Low Birthweight (LBW) (below 2500 gm)	16.7	15.4	4.7
Required care for LBW condition in hospital after mother discharged	11.9	7.7	4.7
MOTHER'S PERCEPTION OF INFANT AT YEAR			
is "very active"	75.0	57.9	62.8
is "cuddly, affectionate"	80.0	63.2	75.6
is "good-natured, easy to deal with"	52.4	56.4	54.8
has distressing habits	33.3	40.5	42.9

were significantly older (average age: above 30) than the fathers of the
girls who later developed serious problems. (For a distribution of parental ages and the results of tests of significance, see Appendix Tables
A-3 to A-7.)

STRESSFUL LIFE EVENTS IN INFANCY

Among stressful life events, recorded for each child on the basis of
information obtained during home visits and interviews in the postpartum period and at year 1, were temporary or prolonged disruptions in
the family, and temporary or prolonged separations from the mother.

Categorized as *temporary disruption in the family* were temporary

Table 11: Characteristics of the Males in the Resiliency Study:
Birth to Year 1 (1955 cohort, Kauai, low SES homes)

Characteristics of the Infant: Birth to Year 1	High-Risk M Resilient % (N:30)	High-Risk M Problems at 10 % (N:51)	High-Risk M Problems at 18 % (N:49)
BIRTH ORDER:			
First born	43.3	17.7	12.2
Second born	20.0	7.8	10.2
Third born	3.3	29.4	28.6
Fourth born	10.0	15.7	14.3
Fifth born and later born	23.4	29.4	34.7
PERINATAL STRESS:			
Moderate-Marked	20.0	15.7	12.2
Congenital Defects at Birth	13.3	25.5	20.4
Low Birthweight (LBW) (below 2500 gm)	16.7	9.8	10.2
Required care for LBW condition in hospital after mother discharged	6.7	4.0	6.1
MOTHER'S PERCEPTION OF INFANT AT YEAR 1			
is "very active"	70.0	40.8	56.3
is "cuddly, affectionate"	66.7	50.0	62.5
is "good-natured, easy to deal with"	63.3	42.9	46.6
has distressing habits	46.7	41.7	33.3

unemployment of the father; parents busy with new business; moves to a new home or with another family; addition of another child; another pregnancy; baby's short-term illness; other children cared for in the home.

   Prolonged disruption in the family included parental mental health problems; parental alcoholism; chronic illness of parent; long periods of unemployment; family on relief; serious family conflict; separation; desertion; divorce; parent in jail; sudden death of parent.

   Categorized as *temporary separation from the mother* were occasions when the mother had worked during the baby's first year of life, but when the infant was adequately cared for at home; or when the mother was separated from the child while she was in the hospital giving birth to a new baby; and other separations of more than 1 day, but less than 1 week.

Prolonged separations from the mother included maternal employment since the baby was born, without adequate child care; or where the infant was staying or sleeping overnight at another house while the mother went to work; and other separations of 1 week or more, including hospitalization.

Neither the resilient boys nor the resilient girls differed from same-sex comparison groups in proportions exposed to temporary family disruptions and temporary separations from their mothers. But resilient infants, especially resilient girls, encountered fewer prolonged separations from their mothers in the first year of life than high-risk children who later developed serious coping problems (see Tables 12 and 13).

Table 12: Characteristics of the Females' Caretaking Environment: Birth to Year 1 (1955 cohort, Kauai, low SES homes)

Characteristics of Caretaking Environment	High-Risk F Resilient % (N:42)		High-Risk F Problems at 10 % (N:39)		High-Risk F Problems at 18 % (N:43)	
Mother's educational level (grade 8 or less)	45.2		56.4		51.2	
Temporary disruption in family	38.1		43.6		34.9	
Prolonged disruption in family	14.3		15.4		14.0	
Temporary separation from mother	35.0		34.2		32.6	
Prolonged separation from mother	2.5		15.8		11.6	
Attention given to infant by primary caretaker: A great deal	66.7		47.2		53.7	
Mother's Way of Coping	*Mean*	*S.D.*	*Mean*	*S.D.*	*Mean*	*S.D.*
Ratio: $\frac{\text{Positive adjectives}}{\text{Total}}$	.75	.29	.64	.38	.63	.36
Ratio: $\frac{\text{Negative adjectives}}{\text{Total}}$	.24	.27	.32	.34	.34	.33

Table 13: Characteristics of the Males' Caretaking
Environment: Birth to Year 1 (1955 cohort, Kauai, low SES
homes)

Characteristics of Caretaking Environment	High-Risk M Resilient % (N:30)		High-Risk M Problems at 10 % (N:51)		High-Risk M Problems at 18 % (N:49)	
Mother's educational level (grade 8 or less)	43.3		51.0		49.0	
Temporary disruption in family	40.0		27.5		35.4	
Prolonged disruption in family	6.7		18.0		16.7	
Temporary separation from mother	33.3		32.0		27.1	
Prolonged separation from mother	10.0		14.0		12.5	
Attention given to infant by primary caretaker: A great deal	63.3		46.8		47.8	
Mother's Way of Coping	Mean	S.D.	Mean	S.D.	Mean	S.D.
Ratio: Positive adjectives / Total	.75	.29	.66	.39	.71	.32
Ratio: Negative adjectives / Total	.23	.26	.30	.37	.25	.31

CHARACTERISTICS OF CAREGIVERS AND INFANTS

The resilient infants differed significantly from their age-mates who later developed serious learning and/or behavior problems in the amount of attention given to them by their primary caretaker during the first year of life. The majority of resilient boys and girls had been given a great deal of attention.

Adjectives checked significantly more often for the mothers of resilient infants were "self-confident" (for mothers of both resilient boys *and* girls); "intelligent" and "self-controlled" (for mothers of resilient girls); "indulgent" and "unemotional" (for mothers of resilient boys).

Resilient boy babies had an additional advantage: A significantly higher proportion amongst them than among boys who later developed problems were first-born sons. There were more first-born infants than infants born in other ordinal positions among the resilient girls as well, but differences between them and the same-sex comparison groups were not statistically significant.

Resilient infants not only received, but *elicited* a great deal of attention. Temperamental characteristics that significantly differentiated resilient infants from future problem children were activity level and social responsiveness.

At age 1, mothers of resilient boys characterized a significantly higher proportion of their sons as "very active" and as "good natured and easy to deal with" than mothers of boys in the two comparison groups. Mothers of resilient girls characterized a higher proportion of their daughters as "very active" and as "cuddly and affectionate" than mothers of girls in the two comparison groups.

A number of these characteristics may be seen in the early records of Edward and Theresa, two of our resilient children.

Edward, the first child of Pilipino parents, was a low-birthweight infant, prone to minor illnesses in infancy. His father was a plantation laborer, and his mother, while remaining at home, did ironing for some of the single men in the camp. The family lived in an old plantation house, described as clean and adequately furnished, but lacking in most of the amenities helpful to the physical care of an infant. Although the socioeconomic rating was low, family stability was considered high. The mother attended school through the ninth grade in the Philippines and was considered by the visiting public health nurse to be "stable, responsible, energetic, reasonably relaxed, and self-controlled"— a woman who "takes things in stride, is self-confident, patient, and warm-hearted." Edward, at 1 year, was "alert, looked happy." The mother considered him to be a very active infant, relatively easy to deal with. She indicated that she was practically always with him, that he received "plenty" of attention, and that his father spoiled him and "satisfied all his whims." This pattern apparently continued through his first 2 years. During a period of the mother's hospitalization for tuberculosis, Edward, still an only child, was cared for by a neighbor, and his activity level and social responsiveness was noted to be above average. At an age when many babies retreat from strangers, Edward had good rapport with them and reached out to others. The parent-child relationship continued to be perceived as "contented, affectionate, and easy-going." The baby functioned adequately both physically and psychologically at his 18-month evaluation.

Although *Theresa* was born into a family that already had four boys and three girls—spaced at yearly intervals—the caregiving environment, as observed during the mother's pregnancy, was apparently conducive to satisfactory adjustment and continued to be so during her early years. During her prenatal visit, the public health nurse found Theresa's mother to be a woman "who does not show any worry or undue apprehension of her (eighth) pregnancy. The children were playing in the yard with her when I arrived. They behaved well and seemed to be having a swell time. Mrs. S. expressed herself and looked as if she is happy."

Seen for her postpartum visit, Theresa's mother remarked, "I'm glad everything is all over, and happy she's a girl." The other children were described as "happy," and there was no evidence of jealousy from the younger ones. The husband was "doing all the work for the mother," and the older siblings helped take care of the younger ones.

This child-caretaker pattern was apparently continuing after 1 year, and the infant responded favorably to it. Theresa was described as "affectionate, easy to deal with, and very active." Her mother indicated that she was given a great deal of attention and, indeed, considered her "spoiled by the family. She wants someone to play with her all the time"—a request frequently and easily satisfied.

DISCUSSION

Susan Goldberg (1977) has offered a model of social competence and parent-infant interaction that dovetails with our findings on the characteristics of resilient infants and their early caretaking environment.

"An infant is competent," Goldberg argues, "to the extent that s/he is effective in eliciting attention and appropriate care from the environment" (ibid., p. 252). This the resilient babies on Kauai were able to do, even in conditions of poverty and crowding.

Parents' feelings of efficacy, according to Goldberg, are derived from their evaluations of interactions with their infants. She argues that parental perception of infant characteristics is probably a more powerful determinant of interaction than any other assessment of the infant. The responsiveness of the infant influences the caretaker's feeling of efficacy.

Most of the resilient infants on Kauai shared several characteristics of responsiveness. They were "cuddly" and "affectionate," i.e., they responded positively to social interaction; and they were "very active," i.e., they initiated contacts with both people and objects around them. Activity provides a sense of mastery and control, and it discharges energy generated in stressful situations (Gal & Lazarus, 1975). Being active, rather than remaining passive, appears to be a powerful coping tool even in the first year of life.

Responsive, active infants have the potential for capturing even an initially unresponsive parent into cycles of effective interactions. This has been noted in studies of the behavioral consequences of nutritional supplementation of infant diets in developing countries (Werner, 1979a). One of the first signs of improvement is usually a striking increase in the physical activity of the babies, which leads to an increase in their exploratory behavior. Caretakers then take a greater interest in them, which, in turn, is reinforced by the infants' tendency to smile more.

Thus a responsive infant can generate parental feelings of efficacy even among caretakers who have little formal education, such as the mothers of the resilient infants on Kauai.

These characteristics of resilient infants and their caretakers seem to cut across ethnic, cultural, and social class boundaries, as we can see from related evidence in the child development literature.

Spanning an age range similar to ours is a report by Heider (1966) on 31 infants who were part of the Coping Project of the Menninger Foundation. These were healthy white babies from middle-class, stable homes in metropolitan Topeka, Kansas. Thus, the sociocultural context in which these infants spent their first years of life was quite distinct from that of the Asian and Polynesian babies in the rural poverty of Kauai.

Yet Heider reports a number of findings, based on careful clinical assessment of the infants between the ages of 4 to 32 weeks, that are strikingly similar to ours. Vulnerability in her study shows an inverse relationship to good energy resources and easy vegetative functioning of the infants, and to positive mother-infant interaction in the first year of life. Heider (1966) argues from her findings that such physiological factors as energy as well as the early caretaking environment are most apt to affect the development of basic trust and a secure identity in the child.

With regard to critical time periods, it is a safe guess from cross-cultural studies by Ainsworth (1977) that for most infants attachment to a primary caretaker by the end of the first year is essential. Such early attachments between human infants and their caretakers are highly adaptive in evolutionary terms because it allows the subsequent development of autonomy in the newly mobile child to take place relatively unfettered by recurring dependency.

While the amount of attention an infant *elicits* appears to be related to his or her activity level, the amount of attention given by the mother depends to some extent on her workload, the presence of other care- takers in the home, and the presence of other children.

Birth-order studies (reviewed by Clausen, 1966) have shown that first-born children experience more social interaction with the mother, as compared with later-born children who must share their mother's attention, and that this affects their intellectual competence, their school achievement, and their social relationships with peers and el- ders.

Most of these studies have been done with healthy children, but Cohen and Beckwith (1977) have also investigated the effect of birth order on the stimulation received by low-birthweight (preterm) babies. They observed 54 preterm infants and their caregivers in the home at 1, 3, and 8 months. At 1 month of age the care of first-born and later-born preterm infants was similar in many ways. But as early as 3 months, and again at 8 months, first-born infants received more responsive care and more social stimulation from their mothers than later-born infants. By 8 months they also received more intellectual stimulation (through verbal and object exchange), a factor highly related to infant compe- tence in the second year of life (Clarke-Stewart, 1973). Furthermore, first-born infants received more social stimulation from everybody, in- cluding visitors and other members of the household.

Belmont (1977) has reviewed extensive evidence on the relation- ship between birth order, intellectual competence, and psychiatric status based on a population of 400,000 Dutch youth who were proc- essed for military service. Her data show that a first-born male, *from a family of any size,* enjoys a number of advantages later in life. First- born sons demonstrate greater intellectual competence, are less at risk of school failure, and are less likely than last-borns to develop serious mental health problems.

Our study indicates that being first born matters more for the psy- chological well-being and resiliency of boys than of girls. This finding is supported by observations of sex differences in the care of infant boys and girls in a number of other cultures.

Super (1977) has made a comparison of observational data from thirteen societies in Africa, Latin America, Europe, and the United States. Additional data on sex differences in the early care of infants are available from observations of mothers from West Bengal in a free- play situation with their 7- to 18-month-old infants (Graves, 1978).

When a mother shares the daytime care of her infants with others (as she does in many of the large households on Kauai), she is more likely to retain the primary caretaking role if the baby is male, and male babies also appear to receive more attention and physical stimulation from their mothers than do female infants. Mothers are more likely to turn over the daytime care of their infant daughters to someone else, such as an older sibling or a grandmother, if available.

Both Super and Graves suggest a number of reasons for the differential treatment of boy and girl infants across a great variety of cultures: Among them are (1) the greater biological vulnerability of male infants, which might call for greater maternal protectiveness; (2) early sex differences (favoring girls) in the infants' social interest and perceptiveness, which might require greater maternal stimulation of sons than daughters to elicit and sustain social interaction with them; (3) the higher value placed in all societies studied on male babies than on girl babies.

In sum: Certain characteristics appear to be shared by resilient infants across sociocultural boundaries:

1. They tend more often to be first-born, especially the males.
2. They may have survived some birth complications (such as moderate to marked perinatal stress or low birthweight), but they have few congenital defects and draw on generous reserves of energy.
3. They are perceived by their caretakers as very active and socially responsive infants.
4. They elicit and receive a great deal of attention during the first year of life.
5. They have rarely experienced prolonged separations from their primary caretaker during the critical time period for the development of attachment.

In short: They are robust, responsive, and have learned to trust.

CHAPTER 7

RESILIENT TODDLERS: EMERGING COMPETENCE

Our assessment of the resilient children and their caretaking environment in the second year of life is based on three sources of information:

1. Interviews with the primary caretaker, usually the mother, detailing stressful life events up to age 2;
2. Behavior observations, test scores, and clinical ratings of the toddlers during pediatric and psychologic examinations; and
3. Observations of parent-child interactions before, during, and after the developmental exams.

STRESSFUL LIFE EVENTS

Among the most commonly reported stressful events during this period in the lives of these high-risk families who lived in chronic poverty were: mother's pregnancy or birth of another sibling; mother's outside employment, part- or full-time; serious or repeated illnesses of the child that necessitated medical care; the absence of the father from the household; and serious illnesses experienced by the parents.

There were no significant differences between the resilient children and those who later developed serious coping problems in the total number of such stressful events recorded for each group up to age 2.

Among the girls, but not among the boys, there were *some* specific stressful life events that differentiated the resilient children from same-sex age mates who later developed problems.

There was a tendency for more parental mental health problems and parental conflict during the first 2 years of life among the high-risk girls who later developed serious coping problems.

A significantly higher proportion of resilient girls had grown into toddlerhood without a father present in the household since before their birth. A significantly lower proportion of resilient girls had experienced serious illnesses or accidents during the first 2 years of their lives.

Behavior Characteristics of the Toddlers

During a potentially stressful situation—the developmental exams at 20 months—resilient children met familiar adults and strangers on their own terms. In contrast, toddlers who developed serious coping

Table 14: Characteristics of the Females: Developmental Examination: Year 2 (1955 cohort, Kauai, low SES homes)

	High-Risk F Resilient % (N:42)		High-Risk F Problems at 10 % (N:39)		High-Risk F Problems at 18 % (N:43)	
Infant Behavior Patterns Observed by Examiner	*Mean*	*SD*	*Mean*	*SD*	*Mean*	*SD*
Proportion positive interactions with examiner	.58	.35	.43	.34	.50	.32
Proportion negative interactions with examiner	.33	.28	.49	.33	.42	.30
Mother/daughter interaction observed during 20-month exam						
Proportion positive	.62	.39	.37	.31	.40	.32
Proportion negative	.24	.29	.46	.29	.43	.31
Cattell IQ	95.40	8.83	85.43	17.25	91.80	13.32
Vineland SQ	118.63	12.90	108.81	22.93	113.81	14.56
	%		%		%	
Psychological status rated normal	84.2		60.0		70.3	
Physical status (rated by pediatrician) normal or superior	84.6		73.0		83.3	

Table 15: Characteristics of the Males: Developmental
Examination: Year 2 (1955 cohort, Kauai, low SES homes)

	High-Risk M Resilient % (N:30)		High-Risk M Problems at 10 % (N:51)		High-Risk M Problems at 18 % (N:49)	
Infant Behavior Patterns Observed by Examiner	*Mean*	*SD*	*Mean*	*SD*	*Mean*	*SD*
Proportion positive interactions with examiner	.55	.31	.36	.32	.42	.33
Proportion negative interactions with examiner	.38	.25	.55	.30	.53	.29
Mother/son interaction observed during 20-month exam						
Proportion positive	.56	.32	.51	.40	.51	.36
Proportion negative	.35	.28	.37	.37	.39	.34
Cattell IQ	97.15	14.24	85.45	16.43	90.26	13.08
Vineland SQ	113.46	16.08	103.90	20.21	110.83	13.32
	%		%		%	
Psychological status rated normal	82.1		67.3		76.6	
Physical status (rated by pediatrician) normal or superior	75.0		72.5		87.5	

problems in the first decade of life showed considerable defensive behavior in their interactions with pediatricians, psychologists, and parents.

Both resilient boys and girls were described with a significantly
greater number of adjectives that indicated *positive social orientation*
than children of the same sex who later developed problems. This was
especially true for the resilient girls.

Observers described them as "agreeable," "cheerful,"
"friendly," "relaxed," "responsive," "self-confident," and "sociable" in their interactions with both familiar caretakers and unfamiliar
examiners.

In contrast, high-risk children who later developed problems were
significantly more often characterized as "anxious," "bashful," "dis-

agreeable," "fearful," "hostile," "nervous," "suspicious," "withdrawn," or, at best, "ambivalent" in their approach to strangers.

Observers also noted significantly more signs of *autonomy and independence* among the resilient toddlers, both among the boys and the girls. Resilient boys were more often described by such adjectives as "aggressive," "deliberate," "determined," "dominating," "independent," "persevering," "stubborn"; resilient girls were less often characterized by such adjectives as "dependent," "frustrated," "impulsive," "indecisive," "insecure," or "vacillating" than high-risk children who developed problems by age 10.

Both resilient boys and girls were facile in *information processing*. Observers characterized significantly more resilient boys as "alert," "fluent," "intelligent," "quick," or "talkative," and significantly fewer resilient girls as "dull," "hesitant," "slow," or "uncommunicative" than same-sex control-group children.

These behavior observations were complemented by test results obtained on the Cattell Infant Intelligence Scale (at this age a measure of sensorimotor, adaptive, and emerging language skills) and on the Vineland Social Maturity Scale. On both examinations, resilient toddlers scored significantly higher than the control-group children: They were more advanced in communication, locomotion, and self-help skills, and tended to engage in more social play by age 2 than children who developed serious learning and/or behavior problems in the first decade of life.

No differences were noted between the resilient toddlers and control-group children in *physical status* and *activity displayed* during the 20-month examinations. The proportion of children rated below normal in physical status by the pediatricians was similar in all groups, and there were no significant differences between the groups in how frequently psychologists checked such adjectives as "active," "energetic," "excitable," or "restless."

The observers commented, however, on the *sex-appropriate behavior* of the resilient toddlers. They characterized resilient boys more often as "masculine" in their behavior and the resilient girls more often as "feminine" than same-sex control-group children.

Mother-Child Interactions During the Developmental Examinations

Mothers of high-risk resilient girls interacted more positively with them than mothers of high-risk girls who later developed problems, and significantly fewer negative interactions occurred between mothers and resilient daughters than between control-group dyads. Adjectives that differentiated mothers of resilient daughters from control-group mothers were "takes in stride," "kind, temperate," "affectionate," and "contented." In contrast, mothers of girls who later developed problems were more often characterized as "childlike" or "indifferent."

No such differences were noted among the boys: Mothers of all three groups, the resilient boys and those in the two comparison groups, interacted with their sons in a predominantly positive (i.e., accepting, responsive) fashion during the developmental examinations.

Here are some vignettes drawn from the records of two resilient children, Sam and Jenny, when they were 2 years old:

Sam, first-born son of part-Hawaiian and Japanese parents, had grown up in a poor, but stable home when he was seen by our study staff at 22 months. He performed adequately on both the Cattell Infant Intelligence Scale (IQ 105) and on the Vineland Social Maturity Scale (SQ 105). He was observed to "learn quickly," "to imitate well," and "with apparent pleasure." Although the psychologist commented that more play with other children and directed adult attention might be profitable for the toddler, she noted the "kind, temperate" quality of the mother's interaction with her son. Sam was perceived to be an "agreeable, sensitive" child who was usually "friendly with strangers." His physical and emotional development were considered normal by both the pediatrician and the psychologist.

Jenny, a slightly premature infant whose mother had had a difficult pregnancy and delivery, was at 20 months a small, frail-looking child, but appeared to be active and very alert to the examiners. Her score on the Cattell Infant Intelligence Scale was in the average range (IQ 97), but she demonstrated superior self-help skills (SQ 132). The examining psychologist felt that Jenny was probably above average in intelligence, but that she had a relatively low frustration tolerance. The little girl refused many of the test items, and was "inclined to throw things if not pleased or interested." During the developmental exam, Jenny's mother was "good-humored, affectionate, relaxed" and appeared to be quite indulgent with her daughter. Earlier home interviews had characterized the mother as "intelligent, responsible," and "sensibly permissive" and as "trying hard to be a good mother." Jenny, in turn, was perceived by her mother as an active, determined, and domineering little girl who could occasionally be disagreeable if she did not get

her way. Her independence and autonomy seemed to have contributed
to her resilience, in spite of her physical frailty and her exposure to
considerable perinatal stress.

DISCUSSION

The behavior characteristics observed among the resilient toddlers
who grew up in the rural poverty of Kauai are quite similar to the coping patterns noted in longitudinal studies of white preschool children
on the U.S. mainland, whether in the East (Halverson & Waldrup,
1974; White and Watts, 1973), in the Midwest (Murphy & Moriarty,
1976; Werner, 1961), or in California (Block & Block, 1977).

Murphy and Moriarty (1976) observed 32 healthy, middle-class,
preschool children in Topeka, Kansas, in situations similar to those in
our own study: that is, during the course of intelligence-testing and
medical examinations, and in response to stressful events at home,
such as illnesses, accidents, or parental loss. Characteristics of preschool resilience that correlated significantly with positive coping in
early childhood (and in puberty as well) included: a realistic evaluation
of people; insight into social situations; the ability to provide one's own
structure; the ability to ask for help when needed; speed of orientation;
clarity of perception; and a capacity for freewheeling attention.

White and Watts (1973) observed 3- to 5-year-old preschool children in their homes in eastern Massachusetts and at play in nursery
school and found the following behavioral skills discriminated between
the 13 children judged most competent, and the 13 children judged least
competent by their teachers: the ability to retain the attention of adults
in a socially acceptable way; the ability to use adults as resources; the
ability to carry out multistep activities; and the ability to attend to two
things simultaneously or in rapid succession.

In suburban Washington, D.C., Halverson and Waldrup (1974) observed 74 preschoolers (median age: 30 months), from white, upper-
middle class families, in experimental barrier situations in the nursery
school and again at age 7-1/2 years in test situations and free play at
grade school. Preschool features of successful coping with the barrier
situation were absence of fear, initiative, vigorous play, and ratings
that indicated that the children were socially at ease. These characteristics correlated positively with early school-age measures of coping,
imagination, and verbal development. Halverson and Waldrup noted
that behavior in barrier situations reflects something about the nature
of the assumptions that a child makes about the environment. A child

who can demonstrate at an early age that s/he is an agent capable of producing change in the environment appears to be active, and competent in the early school years as well.

Similar results were reported by Block and Block (1977) from their longitudinal study of 129 nursery school children at the University of California, Berkeley. The children were seen at ages 3, 4, and 5, and again in the early school years. Those youngsters judged most competent by their nursery school and elementary school teachers had good insight into social situations; were self-reliant and competent; were bright, fluent, and novelty seeking; and lacked fear.

All these studies dealt with the coping skills of relatively privileged children who were not subjected to poverty and family instability. Similar data, however, are available from observations of high-risk children who were exposed to chronic family stress or parental psychoses and who coped well in spite of such misfortune.

Werner (1961) conducted a follow-up of 79 nursery school children at the University of Minnesota's Institute of Child Development who were subjected to chronic family stress during their formative years. Among the longitudinal data were observations at home and in the nursery school when the children were between 2 and 5 years old.

The following characteristics differentiated the preschool boys who coped well from those who coped poorly: sociability, demonstrativeness, dominance, endurance, and a high activity level. The following dimensions differentiated the preschool girls who coped well from those who coped poorly: sociability, acceptance by peers, lack of timidity, lack of hostility, adaptability, and a high activity level.

We note here a similarity between the findings from Minnesota and from Kauai: The preschool boys who coped well were described more often by observers in positive terms (i.e., demonstrativeness, dominance, endurance); preschool girls who coped well were characterized more often by the *absence of negative* characteristics (i.e., lack of hostility, lack of timidity).

The high-risk offspring of psychotic parents who have been labeled "invulnerable" by Anthony (1974; 1978) and Garmezy (1974) were first seen at a later age than were the children of Kauai, but they share some salient behavior characteristics with our resilient preschoolers: They appear socially at ease; they know how to attract and use the support of adults; they actively try to master their environment; and they think for themselves and develop a high degree of autonomy early in life (Pines, 1979).

Let us now turn from an examination of shared behavior characteristics to characteristics of the caretaking environment that appear related to competence and resilience in young children.

In a sample comparable to ours in low SES status, Clarke-Stewart (1973) monitored the interactions between 36 mothers and their young children over a 9-month period, from age 9 months to 18 months. Her sample consisted of equal members of black and white mothers who were the primary caretakers of their (first-born) sons and daughters.

A highly significant relationship was found for both sexes between the young children's competence in all areas of development (cognitive, language, social—highly intercorrelated) and affectionate, responsive maternal care. This trend was observed in our data as well.

Her analysis of mother-child interactions over time, from year 1 to year 2, suggested that stimulating, responsive maternal behavior influenced the child's cognitive development, whereas in the area of social relations the child's behavior influenced the mother, a trend we already noted in infancy. Although in general all the children became less involved with their mothers over this time period, the boys' involvement decreased more than the girls'. Boys became more object-oriented with time and engaged in more exploratory play. Girls were more socially oriented, at least vis-à-vis their mothers, and their involvement with their mothers remained significantly higher across time than that of boys.

Other investigators have also observed a more intense attachment of girls to their mothers in the second year of life (e.g., Lewis, 1972). Lamb (1976) has reviewed the literature on mother-infant and father-infant attachment in the second year of life, and concludes that girls become more dependent than boys on closeness to and contact with their mother at this age.

This trend is observable in other cultures as well, and may reflect sex differences in security of attachment. Graves (1979), in a study of maternal interaction patterns with 7- to 18-month-old children in West Bengal (India), found that girls showed a heightened need for physical closeness to their mother and reduced exploratory behavior in free play during the second year of life.

We noted in our own observational data that the quality of the mother-child interaction in a potentially stressful situation—the 20-month examination—varied more among the girls than among the boys and was an indication of later behavior. Mothers of resilient girls in our sample interacted much more frequently in a supportive manner with their daughters than mothers of control girls who later developed serious coping problems.

The only other study that explored mother-child interactions in coping with stress at preschool age reports a finding similar to ours. Murphy and Moriarty (1976) observed that preschool-age girls were positively affected by the mother's support and by her encouragement of her daughter's coping style.

There is a hint from other studies of older children that girls may be more *directly* affected by the coping style of their mothers' (Haan, 1974); boys may be more *indirectly* affected by their mothers' encouragement of their autonomy (Rowland, 1969).

In sum: Both our own and related studies of competent preschool children indicate that resilient children, even in their early years, meet the world on their own terms, with little evidence of defensiveness and with skill in eliciting positive social responses. They appear to balance a strong social orientation and social competence with a great deal of independence, and they are quick and facile in information processing.

During the second year of life, resilient girls appear to be more affected by the quality of their interactions with their mothers than boys, especially in situations of acute stress, such as an examination.

Both resilient boys and girls appear to have more positive (accepting, supportive, stimulating) interactions with their mothers during the first two years of life and experience less bond disruption during this period than children who develop serious coping problems. Having established a secure attachment in infancy, resilient boys and girls venture into early childhood with a great deal of independence.

By the end of the second year of life, resilient boys and girls have evolved coping patterns that combine the ability to provide their own structure with the ability to ask for support when needed. At the same time, they display behavior judged by observers to be appropriate for their social sex roles. These characteristics of resiliency, observed in preschool boys and girls in a variety of sociocultural contexts, appear to be predictive of resiliency in later years as well.

CHAPTER 8

RESILIENT CHILDREN: FAMILY STRUCTURE AND SUPPORT

Material circumstances did not improve much for the families on Kauai during the early and middle childhood of the 1955 birth cohort. The economy of the island was somewhat depressed by the closing of several pineapple canneries and plantations after our follow-up at age 2, and more children had been born in the majority of the families by the time we began our follow-up at age 10.

With limited economic opportunities and an increase in family size, the general quality of family life deteriorated in many instances. Three out of four Kauai families were given a favorable rating in family stability when the children were 2; by the time our study group reached age 10, only the resilient boys and girls had a narrow margin of adequate emotional support. Most of the children who developed serious behavior problems received little emotional support in early and middle childhood. They had poorer relationships with their parents, fewer opportunities for satisfactory identification; and were exposed to more inconsistent methods of discipline than the resilient children.

By age 10, the families we studied contained on the average 7 to 8 persons, including 4 to 5 children, with fewer children in the households of the resilient ones. Resilient girls however tended to have a larger number of siblings than did resilient boys, and more persons lived in their households. This included adults other than parents.

STRESSFUL LIFE EVENTS BETWEEN YEARS 2 AND 10

Let us now examine some of the stressful life events that were recorded for these low SES families during the 2–10 year period. The most frequently reported stresses among these high-risk families included: mother's employment outside of the household on a long-term basis; childhood illnesses or accidents requiring medical treatment; chronic illnesses, handicaps, or death of a sibling; parental illnesses; the departure of a sibling from the household; the absence of the father; and chronic family discord during the early and middle childhood years.

The proportion of mothers who were employed outside the household rose dramatically from one out of four at age 2 to one out of two by age 10. This is a nationwide trend, reported for a similar time period in reviews by Clausen (1966) and Hoffman (1974) as well. There were some interesting sex differentiations among the resilient children and between the resilient children and their control-group peers in the proportion of mothers who were gainfully employed.

By the time they were in grade school, a larger proportion of resilient girls (1:2) had mothers who were employed on a long-term (greater than 12-month) basis than girls who developed serious coping problems. Other mothers worked on a seasonal basis in the canneries, so that, all together, four out of five mothers of resilient girls had some full- or part-time employment outside the household by the time their daughters were 10 years old.

In contrast, the resilient boys had the smallest proportion (1:3) of mothers who worked outside the household for extended periods of time. The proportion of working mothers was higher among the boys who developed serious learning and/or behavior problems.

An examination of specific stressful life events in the period between 2 and 10 years reveals a distinct pattern that differentiated the resilient girls from the resilient boys, and resilient children from same-sex comparison groups who developed behavior problems at age 10 and age 18 (see Tables 16 and 17).

Resilient girls, as a group, experienced a significantly larger number of stressful life events than resilient boys during early and middle childhood. Significantly more resilient girls than girls with serious coping problems at age 10 and at age 18 grew up in homes where the father was permanently absent, either since before their birth or since early childhood. More resilient girls had older siblings who left home during childhood, but, in contrast to the control-group girls who developed serious learning and/or behavior problems, they did *not* experience the death of a sibling during that period.

The resilient boys, in turn, were exposed to fewer stressful life events during their childhood years than control-group boys who developed serious problems by age 10 or by age 18.

They came from families with fewer children and less crowding in the household than the boys who developed serious learning or behavior problems by age 10 or by age 18. They were also more often first-born sons. A smaller proportion of resilient boys than control boys with problems at 10 or 18 was exposed to serious conflict between family members during childhood and none of the resilient boys experienced the ill effects of sporadic father absence.

Table 16: Childhood Characteristics that Differentiated Resilient F from F with Problems (1955 cohort, Kauai, low SES homes)

Stressful Life Events (2–10 years)	High-Risk Resilient F % (N:42)		High-Risk F Problems at 10 % (N:39)		High-Risk F Problems at 18 % (N:43)	
Mother worked (> 12 months)	47.6		35.9		37.2	
Sibling left home	33.3		12.8		18.6	
Father permanently absent	19.0		5.1		7.0	
Sibling (brother) died	0		10.3		4.7	
Emotional Support Rating (2–10 years)						
Adequate or better	57.1		25.6		25.6	
	Mean	*SD*	*Mean*	*SD*	*Mean*	*SD*
N of children in household by age 10	5.40	2.15	5.54	1.99	5.48	1.84
N of persons in household by age 10	7.74	2.07	7.85	2.16	7.81	2.10
Primary Mental Abilities test scores (at age 10)						
PMA IQ	104.60	9.31	87.57	9.02	92.14	9.85
PMA Reasoning Factor	109.19	13.40	97.92	14.43	92.93	15.43
PMA Verbal Factor	101.57	12.25	85.84	8.22	89.95	8.98
Bender-Gestalt error score	1.86	1.72	3.30	2.32	2.83	2.32

Table 17: Childhood Characteristics that Differentiated Resilient
M from M with Problems (1955 cohort, Kauai, low SES homes)

Stressful Life Events (2–10 years)	High-Risk Resilient M % (N:30)	High-Risk M Problems at 10 % (N:51)	High-Risk M Problems at 18 % (N:49)
Mother worked (> 12 months)	33.3	48.1	40.8
Conflict in family	6.7	17.7	24.5
Father absent temporarily	0	7.9	12.3
Emotional Support Rating (2–10 years) Adequate or better	53.3	43.1	40.8

	Mean	SD	Mean	SD	Mean	SD
N of children in household by age 10	4.53	2.00	5.33	2.26	5.78	1.97
N of persons in household by age 10	6.73	2.03	7.80	2.42	8.27	2.06
Primary Mental Abilities test scores (at age 10)						
PMA IQ	101.13	10.01	86.31	8.98	91.29	10.24
PMA Reasoning Factor	103.43	14.81	86.41	13.74	92.85	15.29
PMA Verbal Factor	99.83	11.41	86.35	9.33	89.69	10.60
Bender-Gestalt error score	1.70	1.95	3.75	2.81	3.06	2.79

CHARACTERISTICS OF RESILIENT CHILDREN BY AGE 10

By age 10, resilient children of both sexes had significantly higher mean scores on the Primary Mental Abilities Test (PMA) than the children who developed serious problems in childhood or adolescence.

The difference between the resilient children and control-group children with coping problems in childhood and adolescence was most pronounced on the Verbal Comprehension (V) factor and on the Reasoning (R) factor, a nonverbal measure of problem-solving ability. At age 10, resilient girls tended to have higher mean scores on factor R than resilient boys. Resilient children displayed better perceptual-motor coordination on the Bender-Gestalt test as well. They made significantly fewer errors (reversals, rotations) than control-group children of the same sex who developed problems at age 10 or age 18.

There were no significant differences between the resilient children and control groups in the proportion of children with moderate to marked physical handicaps who required continuous medical care.

Before we turn to a discussion of our findings, let us take a look at the households of four resilient children: Theresa, Martin, and twins Ellen and Darlene.

The case of *Theresa*, whose development we followed from birth through infancy in Chapter 6 summarizes many of the positive aspects in the family lives of the resilient children in early and middle childhood.

Between age 2 and age 10, Theresa's family continued to live in strained financial circumstances, but Theresa received plenty of emotional support from her parents and older siblings. Another baby was born shortly after Theresa's second birthday. The mother remained at home, but a family of 11 gave Theresa plenty of opportunity to help with the care of her younger brother and the many other household jobs. Her mother said, "I've taught my children to help work. I've taught them what's good and what is bad and trained them when they were little, and so they are good when they get older. I spank Theresa if she needs it. Not often though. I prefer to tell her she can't go out to play." The older children were seen to work together and to help each other. Household rules were related to finishing homework before playing. Chores were assigned to all. "The children rotate jobs. Theresa makes her own bed and cares for her play clothes, washes and irons them."

There was little conflict between family members. The family was devout, and many of their activities centered around church. A warm relationship was reported between father and daughter as well as mother and daughter. "The father plays with the children—acrobatics and everything. They enjoy each other. Theresa likes to tell him about school and what she does—she tells me, too. There is nothing false in her. She likes to be loved." Questioned as to how this was shown, her mother said, "We praise her about her work and what she does. She likes attention. I give them all attention. The father, he always tickles her and plays with her. . . . She is not a problem child."

Apparently the attention that her mother provided in response to Theresa's "requests" in infancy had not only become a well-established practice, but had also paid off in the positive reinforcement the mother received.

Martin's early developmental history revealed numerous features that could be expected to induce stress and difficulty in coping with the demands of school. He had some congenital defects that included visual difficulties and the absence of teeth, and he functioned only on the "borderline"–"dull normal" level in early childhood (Cattell IQ: 68; Vineland SQ: 88).

By the time of the 10-year follow-up Martin had made significant strides. He was considered by his teachers to be an average student, although some of his work was slightly below grade level. No significant learning or behavior problems were identified. He received a PMA IQ of 98 and an age-appropriate score on the Bender-Gestalt. School grades had been "satisfactory" for the previous two years.

Martin was the eldest of eight children in a family whose socioeconomic status was rated low, but in which educational stimulation and emotional support were considered average. His father was a heavy-equipment operator for one of the plantations, and his mother worked part-time (in summer) at a pineapple cannery. Although neither parent had graduated from high school, they supported the children's education by reading to them often, reading considerably themselves, and encouraging their participation in extra-curricular activities. They helped Martin with his homework and attended parent-teacher conferences. Their goal for Martin was placement in Kamehameha School—a private school on Oahu for part-Hawaiian youngsters.

Martin had regular daily chores and shared in the responsibility for his younger siblings. The family was quite close-knit: "almost everything we do, we do as a family—hunting, picnicking, family gatherings. And the father takes the boys lots of places with him." Martin's paternal grandparents gave additional support—"Sometimes he doesn't even want to come home." His mother described 10-year-old Martin as a youngster of whom she was proud. She especially liked the way he took care of his siblings and showed concern for them. She noted, "He listens to me. I explain to him and he does what I ask. He never complains." Both parents were open in their expressions of approval.

Ellen and Darlene—the early years:
High-risk twin daughters of a 24-year-old mother and 35-year-old father, Ellen and Darlene remained in the hospital for their first weeks

of life. The mother was "very happy, especially that they were girls," and the other children were disappointed when she came home without the babies. The eldest child, a daughter of 9, was considered particularly helpful in the care of the infants and in other household tasks when the twins came home, an additional support throughout their early years.

When they were 1 year old, their mother's response to both was described as resourceful, good-humored, energetic, affectionate, responsible, and patient. The babies were considered "very active, good-natured, and easy to deal with," with Darlene viewed as the more "aggressive" twin. The visiting nurse found them both "happy, healthy, and alert."

At 2 years of age the twins received similar scores on the Vineland Social Maturity Scale (SQ's 116). The mother reported no difference in their activities and self-help skills. On the Cattell Infant Intelligence Scale, Ellen received an IQ of 95, and Darlene's IQ was 100. Darlene was considered slightly more responsive than her twin sister by the psychologist. Both children were considered agreeable, feminine, and healthy, but Ellen was considered more "solemn."

Maternal response to the girls was kind, temperate, and contented—from a mother who "takes things in stride." Although the socioeconomic status of the family was low and the parents' education at only the eighth grade level, family stability was rated high. Conflict between the parents was minimal, and there were no apparent mental health problems.

The childhood years: The twins continued their pattern of successful coping during their childhood years. At age 10 they were both doing well in school (receiving grades of A's and B's and PMA IQ's of 107 and 105; their perceptual-motor development was age appropriate and no behavior difficulties were noted).

The socioeconomic status of the family continued to be below average, but emotional support within the family was rated satisfactory. The father had worked steadily for the plantation during the period, and the mother had worked intermittently until the girls were 7 and then went to work on a full-time basis. In her absence an older sister took responsibility for the primary care of the children. Not only was the older sister important in the twins' world, but "the older brothers help with their homework" and participated in activities with them. The environment provided support and the opportunity for the girls to draw on their own skills and resources: "They usually can do most of their school work by themselves; they can cook their own food and do occasionally; they help clean house and wash dishes—they know I work, so they'll help.''

Their life during this period provided little out of the ordinary and chiefly involved the day-to-day existence of home, school, and outings in a rural community. But the emotional support they received from their older siblings and the model of a gainfully employed mother seems to have contributed to their independence, competence, and autonomy—characteristics the twins shared with the other resilient children in the study.

DISCUSSION

Our findings highlight the need to consider how the family structure makes a difference for the developing boy or girl.

Household composition

The importance of household composition is obvious when we consider that it defines *both* the number of persons with whom the child interacts and the physical nature of the setting, the space in which s/he is socialized. This is a point often overlooked in studies of middle-class children who grow up in small, nuclear families with ample space and whose investigators tend to focus mainly on mother-child interactions.

Sociologists and anthropologists remind us that the amount of attention mothers can give their children depends on her workload, the presence of siblings, and the presence of other adult caretakers in the household. We know relatively little about the specific effects of auxiliary caretakers, varying in age and status, on the development of the child, but we do know that the effects of caregivers on child behavior depends on the ratio of adults to children.

In each culture of the study conducted in India, Okinawa, the Philippines, Mexico, East Africa, and New England (Minturn & Lambert, 1964), a mother's emotional stability and warmth toward her children was greater when other adults were around to help with the children (as in the case of the resilient girls in our study), or when she had fewer of her own children to handle (as in the case of the resilient boys).

Alternate caregivers

A second or third adult in the household appears to make a critical difference. When other adults are present in the household as child-rearing agents, children the world over tend to receive a fair amount of warmth. A worldwide study of the antecedents and correlates of parental acceptance and rejection was undertaken by Rohner (1975), based on an intensive analysis of ethnographies of some 101 societies. Both acceptance and rejection were rated on a 5-point scale, ranging from warm and accepting parent-child relationships characterized by much cuddling and demonstrations of love through parental words and actions, to rejection that either took the form of indifference to the child's development or frequent and severe physical punishment and withdrawal of emotional support.

One of Rohner's principal hypotheses explaining the worldwide variability of parental acceptance and rejection relates to the intensity of interaction between parents and children. Mothers or other major caretakers are likely to reject their children when they are unable to break continuous interactions with them. Rohner found a significant, worldwide relationship between parental behavior and household composition. Mothers who were home alone all day with their children were more likely to reject them than mothers who had someone else in the household (grandparent and/or father) to help assume the burden of child care.

Accepted children, throughout the world, tended to be more self-reliant than rejected children and to draw on their own resources to meet their physical and emotional needs—a trend we observed among the resilient children in our own study. They also appear to form warmer and less hostile peer relations and to grow into more caring and responsible adults than rejected children.

On the U.S. mainland, some recent studies of black children living in poverty have begun to take a look at the relationship between family structure, social adaptation, and psychological well-being in school-age children. Kellam, Ensminger, and Turner (1977) examined some of the relationships between family types and the mental health of children in a black, urban community on the south side of Chicago. Family types were defined in terms of adults present in the home. Family composition was strongly related concurrently (in first grade) and over time (from first to third grade) to the child's competence and social adaptation in school, and was predictive of his or her later psychological well-being in grade 3 (judged by the presence or absence of psychiatric symptoms). Their results suggest that: (1) an absent father was less important, in relation to risk, than the aloneness of the mother; and (2) the presence of certain second adults had important ameliorative functions—mother/grandmother families being nearly as supportive as mother/father families.

Sibling caretakers

Alternative caregivers who share child-rearing responsibilities are not exclusively adults. Worldwide, especially in developing countries, they are usually older siblings, often an older sister (Weisner & Gallimore, 1977; Werner 1979a).

Anthropologists report that a domestic group with a large number of kin present, a mother with many offspring, and a daily routine keeping siblings and adults available for caretaking appears to be *the* optimal situation for the development of sibling caretaking (Minturn, 1969). This is a common situation in families on Kauai.

We noted that a significantly higher proportion of resilient girls than control-group girls had older siblings who left home during the period our sample reached middle childhood. The resilient girls tended to assume the care of yet younger children, and with it a greater sense of responsibility and competence. We know from cross-cultural surveys (Rogoff, et al., 1975) that there is a pan-cultural trend to assign child-care roles to girls when they reach the 5–7-year period. We also know that the caretaking of siblings is a prominent feature in Hawaiian-American families (Gallimore, Boggs, & Jordan, 1974).

Conversely, the death of a sibling, especially a brother, occurred significantly more often in this age period in the families of girls who developed serious coping problems. We can only speculate that this loss of an alternative caregiver may have added to their vulnerability, especially at a time when a child begins to ponder the meaning of death.

There is a great need for additional data that document the possible effect on a child of either providing or receiving child care. It may be that children reared in a sibling caretaking system develop psychological and behavioral characteristics that are adaptive in some settings and not in others. Sibling caretaking in extended families anywhere in the world, as among the rural poor of Kauai, may be a functional adaptation of low-income groups that allows these families flexibility in crisis and increases the number of potential resource contributors.

Maternal employment

We noted that the mother's employment outside the household during childhood had no negative effects on the resilient children, and may actually have contributed to the competence and independence of the resilient girls.

Let us turn to a brief review of recent literature on maternal employment to get some additional clues that might help us in the interpretation of our findings. Lynn (1979) has reviewed the literature on working mothers and their daughters. Most of the studies appear to support the positive relationship between maternal employment and competence in girls that we observed in our own investigation.

The effect of maternal employment appears to raise the daughter's estimate of her own sex, so that she can see women as competent and effective (Vogel, et al., 1970).

Miller (1975) discovered that kindergarten-age daughters of working mothers were more assertive than daughters of nonworking mothers. Evidence from a longitudinal study by Rees and Palmer (1970) indicates that daughters of working mothers obtain higher intelligence test scores at 6 and 15 years of age.

Lois Hoffman (1974) found some support for her proposition that daughters of working mothers are more independent because they model independent mothers. A basic theme that runs through her review is that the context within which maternal employment takes place determines its effect (see also Cherry & Eaton, 1977).

Working mothers who had not gone to college, like the mothers in our study on Kauai, are more likely to stress independence training and to assign to their children, especially the girls, a greater share of household responsibilities than middle-class, better-educated women (Douvan, 1963).

Woods' (1972) study, which included results of psychological tests, information gathered from teachers, and school and community records, found that a full-time working mother in low-income families seemed to be a positive factor in a child's social adjustment. Consistent with Woods' interpretation is the fact that children who were given extensive responsibility for household tasks and the care of siblings showed higher school achievement than those who were not. The author is aware that the causality might be reversed: Mothers may give competent children more responsibility. This seems to have been the case in our sample, judging by the demonstrated competence of the resilient children in both early and middle childhood.

However, sons of working mothers who remain unsupervised in their mother's absence during childhood may not fare so well. In their longitudinal study of lower-class boys, McCord, McCord, and Thurber (1963) found no tendency for maternal employment to be associated with delinquency when the family was stable, but sons of working mothers in unstable families had a higher delinquency rate. We noted the same trend among the boys in our cohort who were exposed to a higher frequency of family discord and maternal employment and who became delinquent in adolescence.

In sum: The effects of maternal employment on sons and daughters have to be seen *in context.* Available evidence suggests that full-time maternal employment in the very low social class groups represents a realistic response to economic stress, and thus may be correlated with more socially desirable characteristics in the children, especially girls. It may give children an opportunity to identify with resilient adult models, a trend also noted by Murphy and Moriarty (1976) among middle-class families.

Absence of the father

The effect of the absence of the father has to be seen in the context of the total family structure as well.

On Kauai, a higher proportion of resilient girls than girls with serious coping problems grew up in homes in which their father was permanently absent, either because he was dead, or their mothers had not been married before their birth, or because their parents separated during their early childhood.

Among the boys the situation was reversed: None of the resilient boys, but a significant proportion of boys who developed serious coping problems in adolescence, had lived in families in which their father was absent temporarily, either because of family discord or work.

In reviewing the literature on paternal absence and daughters, Lynn (1979) notes that negative associations with paternal absence are more consistent and stronger for sons than for daughters. Females rarely lack for a same-sex adult in the critical early years, and it is therefore predictable that they would display fewer problems of sex typing than males. There are few studies on the effects of paternal absence on sex-role development in females, but their results do not indicate any detrimental influence.

The opposite effects have been consistently noted for boys. Lynn (1974) and Rutter (1970) have reviewed research evidence that point to the greater vulnerability of boys to paternal absence and to family discord. *Both* occurred in significantly higher proportions among the boys in our study who became delinquent or developed serious mental health problems in adolescence.

The predominantly negative consequences of paternal absence in early childhood on boys found in the Western world have been confirmed in cross-cultural studies. Bacon, Child, and Barry (1963) surveyed a sample of 48 nonliterate societies in the Human Areas Relation Files (HRAF) and found that a lack of contact with the father and the consequently limited opportunity for the young boy to form an identification with him was associated in these societies with both frequency of theft and personal crime.

Family discord

Prospective studies by Rutter (1977, 1978) in England, have shown that all varieties of family discord and bond disruption—whether between the mother and father, or between a parent and child—were strongly associated with antisocial disorders in boys, but not in girls. From his review of European studies with Caucasian samples, Rutter (1970) concluded that the available evidence points to a general tendency for boys to be more susceptible to the ill effects of family stress than girls. Our study with Asian and Polynesian children offers cross-cultural evidence in support of his conclusions.

SUMMARY

Our data on the resilient children of Kauai give us some tantalizing clues about the role of ecological factors and household structure in child development. Cross-cultural studies of traditional societies have noted the constraints these factors exert on the members of a household, but their impact on parents and children needs to be studied more systematically in the modern American family.

These factors appear to affect boys and girls in different ways, most likely because the sexes mature at different physical and cognitive rates, and because they differ in their need for close physical contact, in range of exploratory play, and in their expression of aggression.

The resilient girls seem to be pushed into greater autonomy, independence, and competence by life events that might be more "stressful" for boys. Long-term maternal employment outside the household, the permanent absence of the father from the family, responsibility for sibling caretaking, all appear to have a maturing effect on girls when they occur in a family context where some emotional support is provided by at least one other person besides the mother, for example, a grandmother or an older sibling.

Resilient boys, on the other hand, thrive even in poor homes, if there is some structure, little crowding, and little family discord, and if the father is present in the household.

In short: Resilient children appear to derive from life events and the available models in their household those attributes that complement each sex: autonomy and independence for the resilient girls; caring and nurturance for the resilient boys; competence for both.

CHAPTER 9

RESILIENT ADOLESCENTS: APTITUDES, PERSONALITY ATTRIBUTES, AND LOCUS OF CONTROL

Our information on the resilient adolescents is based on a variety of data: group tests of scholastic aptitude and achievement, routinely administered in the Kauai high schools during grades 8–10 and grade 12; scores on the California Psychological Inventory (CPI) (Gough, 1969) and the Nowicki Locus of Control Scale (Nowicki & Duke, 1972); agency records; and interviews with the youth around age 18.

In the present chapter we shall focus on personality attributes of the resilient adolescents as they revealed themselves on the group tests, and in the next chapter we shall present the youths' own perspectives on coping and sources of support.

Tables 18 and 19 show the mid-percentile scores and standard deviations for resilient males and females and same-sex comparison groups with serious problems in the second decade of life (i.e., delinquencies and/or mental health problems) on the Cooperative School and College Ability Tests (SCAT, 1966) and on the Sequential Tests of Educational Progress (STEP, 1966).

The mean scores of resilient males and females fell within the average range on the scholastic aptitude and achievement tests in grades 8–10 and grade 12. The resilient females, however, obtained significantly higher scores than the resilient males on the verbal communication skills tests (SCAT Verbal, STEP Reading and Writing). Resilient

Table 18: Mean Percentile Scores and Standard Deviations on the SCAT and STEP: Females (1955 cohort, Kauai, low SES homes)

	High-Risk Resilient F % (N:28)		High-Risk F Problems at 18 % (N:27)	
	Mean	SD	Mean	SD
SCAT: GRADES 8–10				
Verbal	50.39	23.82	21.44	12.45
Quantitative	51.11	28.92	18.22	12.36
Total	50.29	25.64	16.26	10.63
STEP: GRADES 8–10				
Reading	51.93	28.13	20.29	14.85
Mathematics	38.21	23.52	25.04	17.76
Writing	63.00	25.09	37.67	22.70
SCAT: GRADE 12				
Verbal	42.63	26.37	12.42	10.13
Quantitative	46.71	28.17	13.75	17.47
Total	44.17	27.56	10.58	11.32
STEP: GRADE 12				
Reading	51.56	30.77	17.65	14.23
Mathematics	41.54	20.23	16.95	12.13
Writing	55.33	28.46	18.63	16.24

females also scored significantly higher than the other females on the SCAT Total scales in grades 8–10 and in grade 12, and on the STEP Reading and Writing scales in grade 12. Resilient males scored significantly higher than the other males on the SCAT Total scale, and on the STEP Reading and Writing scales in grade 12.

In short, both resilient males and females, though within the average range of intelligence, had better verbal communication skills than did same-sex control groups who developed serious behavior problems in adolescence.

Let us now take a look at some of the personality attributes that differentiated resilient adolescents from those with delinquency records and/or mental health problems.

The CPI is a well established, reliable, and widely validated instrument that has been used in longitudinal research with white youth at the University of California (Block, 1971; Haan, 1977) and the Univer-

Table 19: Mean Percentile Scores and Standard Deviations on
the SCAT and STEP: Males (1955 cohort, Kauai, low SES
homes)

	High-Risk Resilient M % (N:25)		High-Risk M Problems at 18 % (N:37)	
	Mean	SD	Mean	SD
SCAT: GRADES 8–10				
Verbal	35.40	20.69	19.41	16.19
Quantitative	43.48	25.21	23.03	20.21
Total	36.88	22.22	18.51	17.03
STEP: GRADES 8–10				
Reading	36.80	23.53	23.32	17.91
Mathematics	39.96	24.92	30.32	18.46
Writing	39.36	23.07	24.97	20.08
SCAT: GRADE 12				
Verbal	34.36	19.34	19.03	16.21
Quantitative	39.91	25.90	25.22	23.84
Total	35.73	21.77	19.37	17.57
STEP: GRADE 12				
Reading	36.39	25.05	16.50	11.57
Mathematics	44.65	29.50	31.03	18.39
Writing	34.39	25.48	13.26	12.98

sity of Minnesota (Werner, 1961); and in studies of black, Hawaiian, Japanese, Native American and, Mexican-American high school students (Megargee, 1972).

In their handbook on cross-cultural research methods, Brislin, Lonner, and Thorndike note that (1973) "By any reasonable cross-cultural criteria the CPI ranks as the most well-known and prolifically used objective personality test."

The 18 CPI subscales cluster in four classes: (1) measures of poise, ascendency, self-assurance, and interpersonal adequacy; (2) measures of socialization, maturity, responsibility, and interpersonal structuring of values; (3) measures of achievement potential and intellectual efficiency; and (4) measures of intellectual and interest modes.

The Nowicki Locus of Control Scale (I-E) measures the degree to which a person believes that a "behavioral" event is contingent upon his or her own action. Those who believe that events happen to them as a result of fate, luck, or other factors beyond their control are called "externals"; "internals" believe that their own action determines the positive or negative reinforcement they receive.

The Locus of Control Scale has stimulated a great deal of research, some of it cross-cultural. In all reported ethnic studies, groups without power, either by virtue of social class or race, tend to score higher in the external control direction.

Accumulating evidence indicates that the concept of internal-external control is not as unitary as it was once hoped it might be (Lefcourt, 1976). Nevertheless, the concept of control from "within" or from "without" has remained a focal point for studies of minority groups (Coleman, 1966) and for inquiries into the ways people deal with stressful life situations and challenges (Bryant & Trockel, 1976; Lefcourt, 1976; Lefcourt & Hogg, 1978).

Tables 20 and 21 show the means and standard deviations of resil-

Table 20: Means and Standard Deviations on the CPI and the Nowicki Locus of Control Scale: Females (1955 cohort, Kauai, low SES homes)

CPI Subscales	High-Risk Resilient F % (N:26) Mean	SD	High-Risk F Problems at 18 % (N:23) Mean	SD
Dominance	24.35	6.44	20.13	6.23
Capacity for Status	14.31	4.25	11.87	3.02
Sociability	22.08	4.72	18.65	4.16
Social Presence	31.88	5.95	29.30	4.36
Self-Acceptance	19.88	4.05	18.09	3.59
Sense of Well-Being	28.81	5.85	23.65	7.41
Responsibility	25.23	5.49	19.93	5.76
Socialization	36.27	4.70	27.96	6.63
Self-Control	22.35	7.59	21.35	7.24
Tolerance	13.73	5.14	11.61	5.15
Good Impression	12.81	4.61	13.00	4.38
Communality	25.42	1.86	20.22	5.32
Achievement via Conformance	23.00	4.78	17.52	4.93
Achievement via Independence	14.54	3.55	11.48	3.75
Intellectual Efficiency	30.15	5.79	22.87	7.12
Psychological Mindedness	7.81	2.80	7.52	2.57
Flexibility	6.96	3.11	6.78	3.54
Femininity	23.48	3.69	21.39	3.64
Locus of Control (I-E)	12.00	3.94	16.17	5.85

Table 21: Means and Standard Deviations on the CPI and the
Nowicki Locus of Control Scale: Males (1955 cohort, Kauai, low
SES homes)

CPI Subscales	High-Risk Resilient M % (N:21)		High-Risk M Problems at 18 % (N:26)	
	Mean	SD	Mean	SD
Dominance	21.81	5.50	21.23	4.10
Capacity for Status	14.52	3.74	12.96	3.33
Sociability	19.90	5.38	19.69	4.10
Social Presence	29.52	5.96	29.85	4.92
Self-Acceptance	18.05	4.17	18.19	2.91
Sense of Well-Being	25.19	6.28	22.27	6.05
Responsibility	22.71	4.04	19.96	3.46
Socialization	30.71	5.14	26.62	4.99
Self-Control	23.76	5.77	22.00	5.31
Tolerance	13.33	3.98	13.00	3.63
Good Impression	16.05	4.83	15.35	3.69
Communality	21.19	4.56	15.92	4.79
Achievement via Conformance	21.19	4.18	18.54	3.40
Achievement via Independence	13.57	3.12	13.19	3.25
Intellectual Efficiency	26.85	5.71	25.96	5.29
Psychological Mindedness	8.57	2.73	8.77	2.32
Flexibility	8.57	3.61	8.92	3.26
Femininity	17.52	3.59	15.23	3.22
Locus of Control (I-E)	13.10	5.01	14.79	4.80

ient males and females and same-sex comparison groups with serious
coping problems in adolescence on the 18 subscales of the CPI and on
the Nowicki Locus of Control Scale.

Both resilient males and females scored significantly higher than
youth with serious coping problems in adolescence on the following
CPI dimensions: Responsibility, Socialization, Communality,
Achievement via Conformance, and Femininity.

The Responsibility scale identifies persons of conscientious, responsible, and dependable disposition; the Socialization scale measures the degree to which values are internalized and made useful in a
person's life, that is the degree of social maturity a person has
achieved; the Communality scale indicates the degree to which a person's response corresponds to the common pattern established in the
CPI; the Achievement via Conformance scale identifies motivational
and personality factors associated with academic achievement in high

school; the Femininity scale identifies persons with emotional responsiveness, social perceptiveness, and sensitivity.

Adjectives that characterize high-scoring men and women on these scales are: adaptable, efficient, organized, sincere, unassuming, enterprising, idealistic, intelligent, resourceful, confident, energetic, humorous, rational, realistic, strong, emotionally responsive, gentle, nurturant, and sensitive.

High-risk resilient females differed significantly from high-risk females with serious coping problems by age 18 on a number of additional CPI dimensions.

The resilient girls scored significantly higher on Dominance, Capacity for Status, Sociability, Sense of Well-Being, Achievement via Independence, and Intellectual Efficiency.

The Dominance scale identifies strong, dominant, and ascendant individuals who are able to take the initiative; the Capacity for Status scale measures the personal qualities that underlie and lead to status and upward social mobility; the Sociability scale identifies persons of outgoing, sociable, and participative temperament; the Sense of Well-Being scale reflects differences in feelings of both physical and psychological well-being; the Achievement via Independence scale identifies those factors of interest and motivation that facilitate achievement in settings where autonomy, independence, and originality are valued; the Intellectual Efficiency scale indicates the degree to which an individual effectively utilizes whatever abilities s/he has.

Adjectives that characterize high-scoring women on these dimensions are: adventurous, alert, assertive, capable, confident, clear-thinking, daring, dominant, energetic, fair-minded, informal, ingenious, individualistic, insightful, intelligent, mischievous, original, outgoing, reflective, self-controlled, sociable, spontaneous, tactful, understanding, versatile, wise, witty.

There was a highly significant difference between the resilient females and the other high-risk females on the Nowicki Locus of Control Scale. The resilient girls had the most "internal" scores of all groups. Among the boys, there was a similar, but nonsignificant trend: The resilient boys had more "internal" scores on the Nowicki Locus of Control Scale, the boys with serious coping problems by age 18 had more "external" scores.

In short, the resilient adolescents, especially girls, had greater faith in their own control of the environment than adolescents with serious coping problems. Achievement and psychological well-being appeared to be closely related to what the youth believed about their environment—whether they believed, as the resilient ones did, that the environment would respond to reasonable efforts, or whether they believed as the youth with serious coping problems did, that it was random and immovable.

DISCUSSION

The resilient adolescents in our study were not unusually gifted, nor did they possess outstanding scholastic aptitudes. What attributes they had, however, they put to good use. They were responsible, had internalized a set of values and made them useful in their lives, and had attained a greater degree of social maturity than many of their agemates who grew up under more favorable circumstances. They displayed a strong need for achievement as well, with an internalized appreciation for the need for some structure in their lives.

Resilient youth also shared a greater interest in matters that are labelled in conventional wisdom as "feminine"; they were more appreciative, gentle, nurturant, sensitive, and more socially perceptive than the young men and women who had difficulties coping with the world around them.

Paul displayed a sensitivity to interpersonal relationships that was seen in many of these youth. Describing himself at adolescence, he said, "I'm quiet." An affectionate baby, only mildly active but easy to deal with, and later a bashful, quiet 2-year-old who received average scores on developmental measures, Paul continued into childhood presenting much the same picture. The middle child of nine, he received adequate emotional support from his family (10-year rating), in spite of very low socioeconomic status.

His adolescence differed significantly from that of the other youngsters in our study, in that he spent his school years from seventh grade on, boarding at Kamehameha School (for students of part-Hawaiian ancestry) in Honolulu. He reported that he liked it with the exception of his seventh and eighth grades, when he was very homesick.

Paul found a number of his supports within the boarding community. He turned to his friends, "only my friends," for help with his problems, which related primarily to getting along with the rest of the group and with other people.

Although he described both parents as "quiet" and indicated that he "guessed he got along with them so-so," he was clear in stating that his parents understood him "kind of good." Indeed he felt that his mother's quietness had made her even more understanding. Several times during the course of the interview he referred to his "respect" for his parents. Their integrity and honesty and his father's respect for people were values that Paul had clearly internalized. One of the goals Paul most wanted to achieve in life "to take care of my parents." He was a sensitive youth who had been able to develop some of the "feminine" personality characteristics associated with nurturance and concern for people.

While the gentle, emotionally responsive aspects of human nature were allowed expression in the resilient men, the resilient women possessed a number of personality attributes that enabled them to take the instrumental as well as the expressive role, depending on the demands of a situation.

Resilient girls were more assertive, autonomous, independent, poised, self-assured, and vigorous than adolescent girls with serious coping problems, and made good use of whatever abilities they had. They thrived in situations where independent efforts and thinking were rewarded, and where autonomy and originality were valued.

Above all, they believed in a concept of control from "within"; they felt strongly that their own actions determined the positive or negative reinforcement they received in their lives.

Susan, in adolescence, clearly exemplified these points. Speaking of school she said, "Senior year is exciting . . . I've enjoyed it, I'm quite popular . . . I like to get good grades, too. School is very important." She was a youngster of average ability (PMA IQ at year 10 was 104, SCAT and STEP scores were in the 30–40 percentile range), but had used her capacities well, school grades in tenth through twelfth grades being primarily B's with occasional A's. On the CPI she scored especially high in the dimensions of self-control and socialization, and her score on the Nowicki Locus of Control was in the internal direction. She was rated by the interviewer as having a "very high" degree of self-insight and a "very great" extent of goal and value differentiation. Self-esteem was high and she displayed little in the way of conflictive feelings.

Susan's future included plans to go to Honolulu for school: "I plan to go to a 2-year college. When I graduate from there, I'll see. I might change my mind and continue on. It depends. I think I can make it. I don't plan to get married till I'm 24 or so—too many people get married too young and don't make it . . . I'll work after my kids are in school; a parent should be with a child until they're in school at least." Clearly she had been thinking about her future and how she would handle it. Asked to describe herself, she said, "My personality is good enough for people to like me. I can control myself pretty well . . . I try to think things out calmly and try to think of a solution to things. I feel I want to do something important and get the most out of life."

Many of the personality attributes of the resilient adolescents in our study were shared by youth from different sociocultural backgrounds who coped successfully with academic hurdles, familial stress, and poverty.

The pattern of responses of the Asian and Polynesian youth on rural Kauai show striking similarity to the CPI scores of academically successful black high school students from a mid-western ghetto community (Benjamin, 1970). Academically successful blacks, both males and females, had significantly higher mean scores than unsuccessful black high school students from the same SES background on the following CPI dimensions: Responsibility, Socialization, Achievement via Conformance, and Communality.

Similar results have been reported by Gill and Spilke (1962) and by Mason (1967) among academically successful Mexican American high school students whose families relied for economic support on the success of their sons.

Born a generation earlier, the 171 participants of a longitudinal study of personality development at the University of California's Institute of Human Development were middle-class whites who had experienced the Great Depression (Elder, 1974). Like the minority students who succeeded against many odds, the ego-resilient males in the Berkeley study had higher scores than other males on the CPI dimensions of Responsibility, Socialization, and Achievement via Conformance (Block, 1971; Haan, 1972).

While economic deprivation in childhood (during the Great Depression) was correlated with self-consciousness, emotional sensitivity, and emotionality in *both* boys and girls, the long-term consequences of economic deprivation among middle-class adolescents were generally positive. As adults, they were rated high on ego strength, integration of impulses, and utilization of personal resources. They were more resilient, more self-confident, and less defensive than control groups who had not suffered economic deprivation (Elder, 1974). For both sexes, coping functions in adulthood correlated positively with intelligence test scores in adolescence and with a belief in an internal locus of control (Haan, 1963, 1977). For females, but not for males, autonomy and achievement in adolescence were positively linked with adult coping (Haan, 1974).

Women who coped well under difficult circumstances, whether they came of age in California in the late 1940s or early 1950s, or in Hawaii in the 1970s, valued independence, were socially poised, and not awed by parental authority. Haan (1974) suggests that females who rate high on these variables may possess coping skills that help them reject sex-stereotyped behavior.

Similar results come from the Longitudinal Coping Project at the Menninger Foundation in Topeka, Kansas. Among the 54 contemporary youth followed through adolescence, were fourteen "passionate renewers," who appeared to have a maximum capacity for basing their ego integrity on inner resources (Moriarty & Toussieng, 1976). Both boys and girls in this group were articulate and expressed a wide range of feelings. Among their outstanding characteristics were a great deal of self-reliance and autonomy, high sensitivity, and a strong desire to find out about people, things, and ideas. Their curiosity cut across "typical" masculine and feminine interest areas. Girls were as interested in politics, social issues, and sports as boys, and boys as interested in the arts and homemaking as girls.

These youth had been described as "lively," "curious," and "self-assertive" as preschoolers. Observers noted that they were vigorous and self-confident children who showed a high degree of autonomy and "could always do the impossible." Such assertiveness and autonomy appeared to rest on a solid foundation of basic trust, as we have noted among the resilient children of Kauai.

Crandall (1975) examined familial antecedents of perceptions of internal-external control among the participants of the Fels Longitudinal Study and found that an internal locus of control in young adulthood was facilitated by some degree of stress or a maternal push from the nest in childhood. This allowed children more opportunity to observe the connections between their actions and ensuing events.

Lefcourt and Hogg (1978) provide additional evidence on the link between encountering hurdles in achievement of affiliation in childhood and a more internal locus of control in young adulthood. Among both undergraduate men and women, those who recalled having to cope with academic hurdles in childhood were more internal with regard to achievement in young adulthood than those who did not recall such obstacles. For young women, but not for men, there was also a significant relationship between recall of having to cope with social hurdles (including loneliness) and a more internal locus of control in the affiliation area.

Studies of high-risk children at the University of Minnesota report similar findings. Reviews by Neuchterlein (1970) and Garmezy and Neuchterlein (1972) suggest that competent, disadvantaged children and the resilient offspring of psychotic parents share certain personality attributes. Among them are the regulation of impulsive drives; the ability to delay gratification and to maintain future orientation; a healthy expectation that positive outcomes will follow from their efforts; and an internal as opposed to an external locus of control.

And in a follow-up at adulthood of former nursery school children who experienced chronic family stress in their formative years, Werner (1961) found that the resilient ones in this group tended to be more spontaneous, less conforming, and more "inner directed" as adults than peers who developed mental health problems under the strain of family discord or children who grew up in a more protective environment. The resilient women in the Minnesota studies shared with the resilient men a sense of personal worth and capacity for independent thinking and action, as well as spontaneity and self-confidence in personal and social interaction.

One cannot help but note a striking consistency in the findings of these longitudinal studies, whether their participants are middle-class whites exposed to deprivation or family stress, or minority children growing up in poverty; whether they live in the cities, suburbs, or in rural areas; whether they came of age in California or Minnesota in the 1950s, or in Kansas or Kauai in the 1970s.

Resilient men and women have developed an alternative to the extremes of masculinity and femininity, a blending of the qualities of both. They are both assertive and yielding, instrumental and expressive, concerned for themselves as individuals and caring in their relationships with others, depending on the appropriateness of these attributes in a particular situation.

In sum: The resilient youth in our longitudinal study, and in others as well, appear to have come as close as any people we know of to a healthy androgyny. This goal still eludes most of their peers and many of their elders who try to live within the constraints of societal stereotypes that define men and women. The resilient ones have become whole persons instead, their own persons, and they were well on the road to that wholeness and individuality as infants and young children.

CHAPTER 10

RESILIENT YOUTH: PERSPECTIVES ON COPING AND SOURCES OF SECURITY

One wonders if any other generation among Kauai's children was exposed to so many and such rapid changes as those witnessed by the youth in our study during the second decade of their lives (see Chapter 2). Against a backdrop of unprecedented social change in the community, other, more personal life stresses tested the coping skills of Kauai's adolescents. Among the most frequently recorded stressful life events between ages 10 and 18 were

Problems in family relationships; with the father; with the mother; Parental, especially maternal mental health problems; Absence of the father; Absence of the mother; Financial problems; Serious illnesses or accidents during adolescence; and For the girls, problems associated with teenage pregnancy and marriage.

We need to keep in mind that we are dealing here only with stressful events that could be verified by some record, whether in the interview with the youth at age 18, or in the diagnostic work-ups of the community agencies that served these youth. Thus we do not have an exhaustive list of all the stressful events in the lives of the adolescents, only a report of what was considered traumatic by the youth themselves or by the agencies to whom they turned for support (see Table 22).

Both resilient men and resilient women reported a significantly smaller number of cumulative life stresses during adolescence than did

Table 22: Stressful Life Events that Differentiated between
Resilient Youth and Youth with Coping Problems in
Adolescence (1955 births, Kauai, low SES homes)

	High-Risk Resilient M % (N:30)	High-Risk M with Problems at 18 % (N:49)
MALES		
Problems in relationship with mother	0	10.2
Problems in relationship with father	3.3	22.4
Maternal mental health problems	3.3	18.4

	High-Risk Resilient F (N:42)	High-Risk F with Problems at 18 (N:43)
FEMALES		
Problems in family relationships	7.1	58.1
Teenage Pregnancy	2.4	34.9
Financial problems	7.1	39.5
Problems in relationship with father	0	32.6
Problems in relationship with mother	4.8	32.6
Serious illness or accident during adolescence	0	20.0
Maternal mental health problem	2.4	18.6
Permanent absence of father	0	9.3
Permanent absence of mother	2.4	16.3
Teenage marriage	0	11.6

the young men and women who developed serious coping problems in
their teens. Among these latter youth, fewer stressful life events were
reported by the young men than by the young women. A smaller proportion of resilient males than males with records of serious delinquency and/or mental health problems in adolescence had poor rela-

tionships with their parents or had mothers with mental health problems.

In comparison with the young women who developed serious behavior problems in adolescence, a significantly lower proportion of resilient women experienced parental conflict or problems in their relationship with their family during adolescence. A smaller proportion of resilient women had poor relationships with their fathers or with their mothers during their teen years. Fewer resilient women than control-group women had mothers with serious mental health problems or parents requiring psychiatric treatment.

Significantly more women with serious coping problems by age 18 had suffered from illnesses or accidents requiring medical care, or became pregnant and were married during their teens. More women with serious coping problems by 18 reported financial problems during adolescence, more had been separated from their fathers (including some whose fathers served time in jail), and more had mothers who were permanently absent from the home.

SOURCES OF SUPPORT

In comparison with other communities of similar size on the mainland, the island of Kauai is fortunate in having a great variety of community agencies and voluntary organizations that concern themselves with the needs of children and youth. They are well staffed, easily accessible, and open their doors to all, regardless of race, sex, or socioeconomic status.

Community agencies

We examined the records of these community agencies to determine the extent to which the children and their families availed themselves of these services.

Only a small proportion of resilient children and youth had contacts with social, educational, or health service agencies during the first and second decades of their lives. These contacts were less frequent and involved a smaller number of agencies than those of youngsters with serious coping problems. Overall, only one out of five among the resilient youth had any agency contacts; among them a higher proportion of resilient boys (1:4) than girls (1:10). In contrast, three out of four of the high-risk youth with problems had some contacts with community agencies during the first or second decades of their lives.

Among these youth as many as seven different agencies were involved in providing some service.

Most of the contacts (13%) of the resilient youth were with one agency—the Division of Public Welfare of the Department of Social Services and Housing—for some temporary financial assistance or food stamps in the case of a family emergency (such as divorce or separation of parents; breadwinner in a prolonged strike; work-study support; or medical aid for dependent children).

In addition, three resilient children received some medical attention through the Division of Public Health Nursing of the Department of Health and the Division of Vocational Rehabilitation of the Department of Social Services and Housing—one with an orthopedic problem, the second with a cardiac malfunction, and the third with a vision problem.

Finally, there was one joint action between the Department of Education and the Social Services Department in the case of a child whose parents were suspected of child neglect. None of the resilient youth had obtained any help from such mental health professionals as counselors, psychologists, psychiatrists, or social workers up to the time of our interviews at age 18.

Informal sources of support

The resilient youth, however, sought and received help from a great number of informal sources of support. Peer friends (35%), including siblings and cousins; and older friends (30%), including older relatives and parents of boy- or girlfriends, were the primary sources of support for the majority of resilient youth, more so for the resilient girls than the resilient boys. Parents ranked next (25%), followed by ministers (11.5%) and teachers (11.5%), more so for the resilient boys than the resilient girls.

Comments like, "I got help from my brother"; "sometimes I solve my problem alone, but mostly I get help from my mother"; "the lady I was babysitting for was a lot of help"; or, "I'd talk to the school staff sometimes but mostly to my sisters and my friends" were commonly heard from our resilient youth.

Peers ranked also first as source of support for high-risk youth with serious coping problems. These youth turned less often to their elders, whether friends of the family, parents, or teachers, because the family or school were often the major source of their problems. A significantly higher proportion of the problem youth sought professional help instead, from counselors in the schools or from members of the mental health profession.[1]

Overall, there was no significant difference between the youth who had received professional assistance during adolescence and youth who relied exclusively on the counsel of their friends, in their judgment of the effectiveness of the help they received.

Among those interviewed, the overwhelming majority of the resilient youth (80%) felt that the support and counsel from friends and parent figures helped a lot. They also felt they could draw on a greater number of such informal sources of support than did youth with serious coping problems.

PERSPECTIVES OF THE YOUTH IN THE 18-YEAR INTERVIEW

Judging by their responses in their interviews, resilient youth, though poor by material standards, derived a greater feeling of security from their family than did youth with serious coping problems in adolescence.

In comparison with high-risk youth from equally poor homes who developed a record of delinquency or serious mental health problems in adolescence, more resilient youth lived in families that had consistently enforced rules.

A higher proportion of high-risk resilient youth identified with their fathers and a higher proportion perceived their mothers as understanding, as someone who treated them as individuals worthy of respect. Mothers were generally viewed as somewhat more supportive than fathers.

There were some differences between the resilient men and women in their perceptions of their parents: The overwhelming majority of the resilient men (86.0%) identified strongly with *both* their mothers and their fathers, and wanted to emulate some of the positive attributes of both. Among the resilient women, a larger proportion identified with their fathers than with their mothers (78% vs. 62%). The choice of parental models may thus enhance the trend toward androgyny that we have noticed among the resilient men and women in their responses to personality inventories.

---

[1]For a detailed discussion of the community agencies' responses to children and youth with learning and behavior problems, see Chapter 9 in *Kauai's Children Come of Age* (Werner & Smith, 1977).

Resilient men and women also differed in which parent they chose to discuss personal problems with. The overwhelming majority of the resilient women (70%) preferred to turn to their mothers first, a preference that may reflect a continuation of the strong mother-daughter bond noted throughout the first decade in the lives of the girls. The resilient men were willing to turn equally to either mother or father for counsel, depending on which parent was available at the time they needed support.

Andrew commented in his 18-year interview on some of the informal support he had received throughout childhood and adolescence.

No family discord had been noted in Andrew's first 2 years, though he grew up in chronic poverty, as had the other resilient children. He was the youngest of four children. At the time of his birth his father was 41 years of age and his mother 27. Although the family's socioeconomic level was below average, Andrew's father had worked steadily since his birth.

The mother's outside employment had not started until he was 6 years old and she only worked at nights, thus permitting continuity in his care by the primary caretakers. In addition, two sisters 5 and 6 years older than Andrew were active as "homework helpers" and supportive companions. Andrew had a particularly good relationship with the family minister and enjoyed spending time with him.

His parents apparently made special efforts to spend meaningful time with Andrew: "A time is set aside for the children. We do something special together every week—go out to dinner, or hiking." Andrew reported that he felt "really close" to both parents, although he had more contact with his mother. "My father works hard, he doesn't talk that much but he explains things to me. Every time when my mother used to lick me, father would come to me and tell me about it and explain. The talk really meant something, not the licking. Then my mother would talk and everything would be OK." Though the mother was the source of immediate early discipline, Andrew perceived her as "soft . . . she's not going to force you to do something. . . . I wouldn't do anything to hurt her." Andrew himself was able to say of his parents, "They're proud of me—and now we get along good."

Structure and rules were an important part of his environment. As Andrew said, "Whatever they say is law—but they do ask our opinion about things. There isn't much arguing. I can talk to them, and I do not like to hurt their feelings."

Andrew received support from other members of his family. An older, married sister played a particularly important role: "She takes care of me. Me and her are really close. Sometimes when I get tired of school and things, I go to her house. My friends have influenced me, too. Now sometimes maybe they're more important than my family—I mean I stay with them more and do more things with them."

The generally positive attitude of the resilient youth toward their family (which included positive relations with their siblings) carried over to their evaluation of their school experience.

An overwhelming majority of the resilient youth, but only a minority of the youth with serious coping problems in adolescence, expressed a favorable attitude toward their school experience. Typical of the comments made by the resilient youth were: "I got a good education there. I liked the teachers. We had good group discussions"; "Senior year was exciting"; "I've enjoyed it even though I've had lots of problems with girlfriends"; "From grade school time, I always thought getting good grades and doing well was a goal I had to reach for . . . I was well satisfied, I did pretty good."

Among the women, but not among the men, there was a significant difference in achievement motivation and level of aspiration between the resilient youth and those with serious coping problems.

Resilient girls also reported being more active in their social life, and resilient boys had participated more extensively in extracurricular school activities, than the girls and boys in the comparison groups. The resilient youth managed this in spite of limited finances in the home, which was perceived to be a burden by the high-risk youth with problems.

By the time they reached the threshold of adulthood a larger proportion of the resilient men and women had a positive self-concept and higher degree of self-esteem than the men and women who developed serious coping problems in the second decade of their lives. Yet the resilient youth anticipated more changes in themselves in the future and saw more need for improvement; in other words, they reflected a greater concern with continued psychological growth.

Before we turn to a discussion of our findings, let us briefly consider *Delia,* whose story illustrates many of the points made in the interview.

Delia, born to an unwed 17-year-old mother who was described during the infant's early years as being indifferent, withdrawn, childlike, and discontented, went to live with her grandparents shortly after her first birthday, and was eventually adopted by them at age 7, along with her younger brother.

While this environment was below average in both socioeconomic status and educational stimulation, it provided at the time of the 10-year follow-up adequate emotional support for the girl. She had only fleeting contacts with her mother (her father had died when she was 5 years old) prior to going to live with her grandparents.

The structure in the grandparents' home, and the grandparents' expectations of Delia's behavior, were consistently clear. Although they encouraged self-discipline, they had specific rules. "Not to stay out late, ask to use the car, get permission before going out, clean our rooms . . . and they'd come out and say it; whatever they say goes; I lose the argument."

Delia considered them both "strict," but she felt they had "complete understanding" of her, and that she could talk to both of them. She was closer to the grandfather than grandmother, however, and believed he had had the greatest influence on her, particularly in relation to future educational goals.

She felt her own strong points included the fact that she "tried to understand people and that anybody can talk to me freely." No "generation gap" interfered with her accepting the modelling provided by these older caregivers. Indeed, the kind of person she looked up to was "somebody who's older, somebody who respects me."

Additional environmental supports had been provided by her extracurricular activities. She believed that one of the most important experiences in her life had been her membership in the Y-Teens Club. "I was secretary, I learned about responsibility, to be on time." Similarly as a cheerleader, "I learned to be closer to people, to have fun."

In a caregiving environment marked by significant life stresses in the early years, Delia grew into a young adult with a fair degree of self-insight, adequate self-esteem, high achievement-motivation, and realistic plans for the future. While our data do not permit us to be specific about the degree to which various aspects of her life experience contributed to her resiliency, we see in Delia's second decade of life (and to some extent in part of her earlier years) many of the characteristics found in the resilient youth in this cohort: structure and rule in the home during adolescence, few problems in the relationship with her primary caretakers, stable mental health of her primary caregivers, and adequate sources of emotional support. The interaction of these environmental characteristics with the qualities of the young woman herself—her positive self-concept, her identification with her adopted mother and father (more so with the father), her educational and vocational aspirations, her active social life, and, possibly above all, a set of values involving respect for self and others—made effective coping possible, in spite of significant early risks.

As we reviewed the life stories of these resilient youth we were struck by the ordinariness of their existence. We did not see any exceptional quality to the characteristics of the caregiving environment except for a certain *steadiness* in the availability of caring, and we were struck by the youngsters' ability to elicit and respond to this caring. For Delia, Andrew, and the other resilient youth in our study, this seemed to be a crucial catalyst that mobilized their inner resources and that provided the basis for their self-esteem.

DISCUSSION

Our findings on Kauai dovetail with the results of some major prospective studies of the mental health of working-class children and youth in Great Britain (Rutter, 1978; Shepherd, Oppenheim & Mitchell, 1971) and with reports on adolescent coping from studies of white, middle-class children on the U.S. mainland, notably the Berkeley longitudinal studies (Haan, 1974; Weinstock, 1967a,b) and the Menninger Coping Project (Murphy & Moriarty, 1976).

We noted that resilient youth on Kauai were subjected to fewer cumulative life stresses in their family environment than youth who developed serious coping problems in adolescence, especially the young women. This trend was also reported by Rutter (1978, and cited in Pines, 1979), who sorted out the cumulative stresses to which children from poor neighborhoods in inner London and the Isle of Wight were subjected. He found that six risk factors were strongly related to psychiatric disorders: severe marital discord, low social status, overcrowding in the home, psychiatric disorder in the mother, a father with a criminal record, and admission into foster care or institutions.

A number of these risk factors discriminated significantly between resilient youth and youth with serious coping problems on Kauai as well, although we deal here with a population from an entirely different ethnic background. Maternal mental health problems; difficulties in family relationships; financial problems; permanent separation from the mother because of placement of the child in foster care or of the mother in a mental institution; and temporary separation from the father, including time served by him in jail, were among significant discriminators in this birth cohort.

We noted, as Rutter did, that youth with just one of these risk factors were less vulnerable than those with an increasing number of cumulative stresses. This trend was especially noticeable among the girls in adolescence and confirms Gove's (1979) notion, based on nationwide mental health statistics, that the second decade of life may generally be more stressful for women than for men.

While the impact of community services was relatively insignificant, parental attitudes (i.e., their understanding and support) played an important role in contributing to the psychological well-being of the teenagers on Kauai, a finding supported by a British mental health survey conducted by Shepherd et al. (1971) in Buckinghamshire County in England, and by Masterson's (1967) study of adolescents in the United States.

In his 1974 book, Lynn provides an excellent review of the contribution of the father to the psychological well-being of his offspring. The quality of the relationship with the father and the degree of identification with him discriminated significantly between our resilient men and women and youth with coping problems in adolescence. This trend was especially pronounced for the resilient women, who tended to choose their fathers more often as models for identification than their mothers. The modeling of fathers by daughters has been noted in other studies of women who were high in achievement motivation, independence, and originality (Lynn, 1979). However, a special mother-daughter bond persisted well into the second decade, which was noted in the responses of the women in our study who were more willing to confide in their mothers than in their fathers. Other studies dealing with youth (e.g. Diamond & Hellkamp, 1969; Rivenbark, 1971; and Weibe & Williams, 1972) have also reported that adolescent daughters generally disclose more personal problems to their mothers and share more intimately their concerns with them than with their fathers.

Family closeness and respect for individuality bolstered the self-esteem of teenagers in urban Kansas as well as on rural Kauai. Murphy and Moriarty (1976) found, as we did, that clear limits and expected rules and discipline were generally welcomed by adolescents and contributed to the psychological well-being of the resilient ones, as did a family faith that "God helps those who help themselves." This faith supported successful problem solving and coping with stress.

Haan (1974) and Weinstock (1967a,b) examined the relationship of ego functioning to the family environment at ages 2 and 11, and in adolescence, among the participants in the Oakland Growth and the Berkeley Guidance study. Coping parents tended to have coping adolescents, and defensive parents produced defensive adolescents, but these trends were more salient for the boys than the girls in the Berkeley longitudinal studies. Adolescent girls appear to be able to cope even in the presence of relatively ineffective fathers if there is a strong mother-daughter bond and the mother provides a competent model.

Resilient children and youth appear to be skillful in selecting and identifying with resilient models and sources of support, as was noted by Murphy and Moriarty (1976) and by investigators who have studied competent children of psychotic parents (Pines, 1979). In our study, the resilient youth, in spite of their poverty, felt they were able to rely on a greater number of sources of support than youth with serious coping problems. They did not seek any professional help, but preferred instead a network of informal relationships that included peer friends, older friends, ministers, and some trusted teachers.

Other students of the Hawaiian culture, such as Gallimore and his associates (1974) have commented on the Hawaiian preference for personal as opposed to impersonal, "professional" relationships. To operate in the context of such personal relationships and in the spirit of "kokua" (mutual cooperation) is familiar and comfortable for many of the youth and families of Asian and Polynesian descent on the island. Of all sources of acknowledged help, peer friends and older friends surpassed parents and professionals in acceptability among the youth on Kauai.

Offer (1969) noted a similar trend among a group of 106 high school boys who were followed from their freshman to their senior year, and who represented a "modal" group, ranging between psychopathology and superior adjustment. The boys sought reassurance about themselves among their peers and searched for an interpretation of their behavior. Offer comments that these adolescents were good amateur psychologists.

A related series of coping studies on the transition from high school to college was conducted at the National Institute of Mental Health (Hamburg & Adams, 1967; Hamburg et al., 1974): A group of highly competent high school students from middle-class urban homes in Washington, D.C., was selected by screening an entire senior class and selecting students who demonstrated interpersonal and academic effectiveness during the high school years. Comparison groups included freshmen who required psychiatric hospitalization after they had left home for school, and, for cross-cultural replication, a similar urban middle-class sample in San Juan, Puerto Rico.

The following characteristics differentiated the highly competent youth in Washington, D.C., and Puerto Rico from youth who developed psychiatric symptoms during a time of major psychosocial transition: The competent youth sought information about the new situation, mostly from older siblings and friends. They utilized friendship to clarify self-definitions and career possibilities; to learn through pooling of information and of coping skills; and to help each other in their respective areas of strength. They used friends as a support in dealing with academic and interpersonal difficulties and as a sounding board for other possible points of view.

Youth who successfully negotiated the transition from high school to young adulthood presented a striking contrast to youth with serious coping problems in their ability to seek and utilize information in times of major psychosocial transitions and when exposed to stressful life events. The implication for a constructive use of peer counselors is clear. Its effectiveness has already been demonstrated in hard-core, black, poverty-stricken areas on the mainland and in the helpfulness of student companions for children at risk for learning or behavior problems (Cowen, 1973).

The presence of such an informal network of support may be a crucial factor in increasing the coping skills of low-income families. In a study of child neglect among low-income families, Giovannini and Billingsley (1970) sought to identify the environmental circumstances associated with the parent's treatment of the child. Among other conditions (such as inadequate housing and absence of a telephone), differentiating factors included the existence of a network of kin and friends, as well as church attendance.

The resilient poor on Kauai were able to draw on all of these supports: advice and counsel by older siblings, cousins, relatives, and refuge in a strong faith, whether Buddhist, Catholic, Mormon, or other Protestant. Religious mentors, ministers, and members of church youth organizations gave significant support in times of stress to the resilient youth on Kauai. Religion provided stability in the midst of change as it did to their middle-class contemporaries in Topeka, Kansas (Murphy & Moriarty, 1976; Stewart, 1967), and to many of the blacks, Chicanos, and poor whites in the South, North, and far West interviewed by Coles (1972) who rely on "the Lord in our Cities" to give meaning and coherence to their lives. One summed it up for all: "My mother believed that there is a lot of evil in the world, but she believed in love, God's love and our own kind, the kind I grew up with, the kind she showed us during all those grey and cloudy days."

CHAPTER 11

RESILIENT OFFSPRING OF PARENTS WITH PSYCHIATRIC PROBLEMS

So far we have examined the roots of resilience among children and youth who grew up in chronic poverty. Some in the 1955 cohort were also reared in families in which serious mental health problems incapacitated the mother or father over an extended period of time.

Other investigators, such as Anthony and his associates (1974, 1978) and Garmezy and his collaborators (1974, 1976), have undertaken prospective studies of the development of children of psychotic parents (beginning at school age). And they have noted that some "invulnerables" appear to escape the devastating effects of parental psychosis.

Most studies of such high-risk children—including those by Bleuler (1972, 1974), who followed some 184 offspring of schizophrenic parents in Zurich, Switzerland, over a 20-year period, and the longitudinal research by Mednick and associates (1968, 1971) in Denmark, are based on white children living in urban areas. In this context Bleuler observed "the steeling effect of pain and suffering" that rendered some children of psychotic parents capable of mastering life with all its obstacles, "just to spite their inherent disadvantage" (1974).

Our data from the island of Kauai provide a useful cross-cultural perspective on some of the characteristics of resilient children that enabled them to cope successfully with the hardships of parental psychosis. Our setting is quite distinct from that of other investigations in the metropolitan areas of the U.S. mainland and in Europe, and so is the ethnic make-up of our population. In addition, our data base extends now over nearly a quarter of a century, from the perinatal period to recent entries in the statewide Mental Health Register at age 24 (1955–1979).

Among the 1955 birth cohort, we were able to locate 29 children whose parents received treatment for serious psychiatric problems (this constitutes about 4% of the total cohort). We make no claim that this was an exhaustive list of all the parents *in need of* mental health care. We can only say that in these 28 families (one with a set of male twins) one or the other parent received mental health care, either on an in- or out-patient basis.

The children were identified through several screening procedures. The first screen was a review of the case files of the 1955 birth cohort. In an effort to ensure a complete evaluative file on each child, reports of contacts with various community service agencies, such as the Department of Health, Division of Mental Health, and the Department of Social Services and Housing, were examined for all family members. A number of parental mental health problems were identified in this manner and were verified through reports of psychiatric problems in interviews with family members (usually the mother) in the postpartum period and at ages 1, 2, and 10 years.

In addition, the Mental Health Register of the State of Hawaii, established in 1972, was reviewed. Safeguarding the privacy of the individuals with the help of code numbers, we were able to match codes and diagnoses of cohort parents who had obtained mental health care. The list included parents who had been seen for the first time since the establishment of the register (from 1972 to 1979), and parents whose initial contacts with mental health services had been earlier, but who were still being treated at the time their offspring were adolescents or entered young adulthood.

From these screening procedures, 29 children with parents who received a diagnosis of schizophrenia (paranoid, chronic undifferentiated, residual, catatonic, simple, or latent) or depression (psychotic depressive reaction, depressive neurosis, manic-depressive psychosis) were selected for study. Each index child was matched with a control child of the same sex, socioeconomic status at birth, and ethnicity. An attempt was made to match the ethnicity of both parents; in the few cases where this was not possible, however, the ethnicity of the parent who had received treatment for the mental health problem was of primary consideration.

The socioeconomic status distribution of these children resembled that of the 1955 cohort as a whole. For the most part, the ethnicity of the parents with treated mental health problems was also similar to the ethnic make-up of the island's population. The exceptions were a slight underrepresentation of the Japanese, and a slight overrepresentation of part-Hawaiian mixtures.

There were more boys (N:18) than girls (N:11) among the children whose parents had received treatment for psychiatric problems. Eleven children, including one set of male twins, had mothers whose primary diagnosis was depression; eight children had mothers who were diagnosed schizophrenics; five had schizophrenic fathers; and five had depressed fathers (see Appendix Table A-0).

By the time they reached age 10, 12 of the 29 offspring of these parents (some 40%) had developed serious learning and/or behavior problems; by the time they reached age 18, 16 of 29 (or 55%) of the youth showed evidence of antisocial behavior or mental health problems. Twice as many were boys as girls. The overwhelming majority had mothers with serious mental health problems, most with a diagnosis of schizophrenia.

Among the resilient offspring who had not developed any coping problems during the first two decades of life, the majority were offspring of depressed parents, mostly mothers with a diagnosis of uni- or bipolar affective disorders (depression, manic-depressive psychosis).

The resilient children among the offspring of psychotic parents had about the same proportion of moderate to marked perinatal complications as those who developed serious coping problems, a rate double that of the cohort as a whole (24% vs. 12%). But they differed from the more vulnerable offspring of psychotic parents in having fewer congenital defects (12% vs. 42%).

A number of behavior characteristics significantly differentiated the resilient offspring of parents with mental health problems from offspring of such parents who developed serious coping problems during the first two decades of life. The case of Mary, presented in Chapter 13, details the story of one of these resilient youngsters.[1]

The resilient offspring were more often perceived by their mothers as "good-natured" and "easy to deal with" when they were infants than were the others, and home observers noted that the mothers' way of coping with their babies during the first year of life was characterized by predominantly positive interactions.

During the 20-month developmental examinations, psychologists rated the resilient offspring of psychotic parents higher on social orientation, autonomy, and independence than children who later developed

[1]See Appendix Table A-8 for the results of t-tests and Fisher's exact probability tests.

serious coping problems. The informal observations of the toddler's behavior before, during, and after the psychological examinations were supported by the scores obtained on the Cattell Infant Intelligence Scale and the Vineland Social Maturity Scale at 20 months. The resilient offspring of parents with serious mental health problems received significantly higher mean scores on these two tests of adaptive and self-help skills than offspring in the control groups. Equally impressive was the difference between the two groups on the psychologists' rating of emotional status: Significantly more resilient children were rated as emotionally stable at age 20 months on the basis of the combined results of the developmental screening examinations and informal behavior observations.

At age 10, several independent sources of information discriminated significantly between the resilient offspring of psychotic parents and offspring who developed coping problems. More resilient children had higher scores on the PMA factor R, a nonverbal measure of problem-solving skills, and on factor V, a measure of verbal comprehension skills. They showed no impairment in perceptual-motor skills on the Bender-Gestalt test.

Teachers observed less disturbed behavior in the classroom among the resilient children at age 10. They got along better with their classmates and concentrated more on their school work. Parents noted independently that their resilient offspring had better emotional control at home and displayed fewer chronic nervous habits than children who developed serious coping problems.

In late adolescence, there was a significant difference in Locus of Control orientation between the resilient offspring of psychotic parents and youth who developed serious coping problems. More resilient youth had faith in the control of their own fate.

Since most of the "problem" youth were offspring of schizophrenic mothers, and most of the resilient children and youth were offspring of depressed mothers, we compared these two groups directly with each other, and with their respective control groups (i.e., children of normal parents), matched by age, sex, SES, and ethnicity. (For a detailed report on this part of the study see Johnston, 1981).

Offspring of schizophrenic mothers differed significantly from offspring of depressed mothers on a number of cognitive, social, and emotional variables at 20 months and at 10 years, and in their need for mental health care at ages 10, 18, and 24 years. The offspring of depressed mothers generally had higher Cattell IQ and SQ scores at age 2, indicative of greater adaptive, language, and self-help skills, and a higher proportion was rated as "emotionally stable" by the psychologists.[2]

At age 10, teachers noted less problem behavior in the classroom for the offspring of depressed mothers than for the offspring of schizophrenic mothers. Offspring of schizophrenic mothers had more difficulty paying attention and displayed more nervous habits in the classroom than children of depressed mothers. The parents differentiated significantly in the behaviors of their offspring at home: More offspring of schizophrenic mothers were perceived as showing little emotional control at home, while less problem behavior was noted at home among the children of depressed mothers. And finally, at three ages— middle childhood (age 10), late adolescence (age 18), and young adulthood (age 24)—the offspring of depressed mothers were judged to be less in need of mental health care and utilized it less often than offspring of schizophrenic mothers.

To rule out any differences that might be associated with the socioeconomic status of the children of psychotic parents, we also compared each index group (the children of schizophrenic mothers and the children of depressed mothers) with age-, sex-, and SES-matched controls.

In spite of a wide range of tests (chi-square, Fisher exact probability and t-tests for matched pairs) on some 35 biological, cognitive, and social variables gathered in infancy, childhood, and late adolescence, we found only *one* significant difference between the offspring of depressed mothers and their matched controls, a difference that could have occurred by chance alone: At age 10, teachers noted a slightly larger number of behavior problems in the classroom for the offspring of depressed mothers than for their controls. In contrast, there were a number of significant differences between the offspring of schizophrenic mothers and their matched controls at age 20 months and at 10 years.

In comparison with controls of the same age, sex, SES, and ethnicity, the offspring of schizophrenic mothers had significantly lower Cattell IQ and Vineland SQ scores at age 20 months and lower ratings of psychological status. At age 10, they had significantly lower mean scores on the PMA IQ, especially on factor R, a nonverbal measure of problem-solving ability, and on factor P, a measure of perceptual acuity and speed.

Children of schizophrenic mothers were considered more often to

[2]See Appendix Table A-9 for the results of the statistical analyses.

have behavior problems at home than children of normal parents. A significant discriminator was their lack of emotional control. The validity of the parental judgment was confirmed by the independent evaluation of an interdisciplinary panel consisting of a pediatrician, a clinical psychologist, and a public health nurse: A higher proportion of the children of schizophrenic mothers than of control-group mothers were considered in need of special mental health care by age 10.

In sum: Significant differences between the resilient offspring of psychotic parents and offspring who developed serious coping problems by age 10 or age 18 were apparent in adaptive, social, and self-help skills in early childhood; in cognitive and perceptual-motor skills in middle childhood; and in impulse control and focus of attention. The two groups also differed in late adolescence in their locus of control orientation (internal vs. external). These differences were confirmed by a number of independent sources of information: test results, behavior observations during psychological examinations, teacher observations in the classroom, and behavior checklists filled out independently by the parents.

There were no differences, however, between the index and control groups in physical status in early childhood or in rates of moderate to marked physical handicaps requiring continued medical care in middle childhood and adolescence.

There was a significant difference in *total* cumulative life stresses reported in childhood between the resilient offspring of psychotic parents and the offspring who developed serious coping problems. A key factor that accentuated any family distress was the likelihood of a progressive withdrawal and detachment of the primary caregiver among the schizophrenic mothers.

Before we turn to a discussion of our findings let us briefly contrast the records and views of some of the offspring of schizophrenic mothers with the daughter of a mother who suffered from major depressions and a father who was an alcoholic.

Donna's mother had been diagnosed as schizophrenic prior to Donna's premature birth. Her "spasmodic, disruptive" behavior continued through most of Donna's childhood years, and Donna, seen for her adolescent interview, described her mother as "nervous, overwrought . . . nervous, overwrought. I guess that's about it." She felt that her mother had trouble understanding her, that she "pushes me a lot." She was in considerable conflict with her mother, but strongly identified with her father, whom she perceived as closer to her, more understanding. "I'd like to be like my father."

Her relationship with her mother had already been difficult in her early life. Her mother was considered by home observers to be "careless and erratic" in the treatment of her infant daughter at year 1. The psychologist described the mother as "careless, punitive, and matter of fact" in her handling of Donna when she accompanied her for the 2-year examination. Throughout her early and middle childhood, Donna's home was rated very low in socioeconomic status, educational stimulation, and emotional support.

Donna received a Cattell IQ of 87 at age 2. By age 10 she was one year below chronological age expectancy in her grade placement and received D's in reading, writing, and arithmetic. At that time she attained a PMA IQ of 91 with a noticeably low perceptual factor score. She was described by the teacher as unable to sit still in class, very easily distracted, provoking quarrels continuously, negativistic, and frequently distorting facts. The mother noted similar behavior at home. By high school she was receiving C's and D's with an occasional F or B, and was often truant from school. She was "known to consume alcoholic beverages and smokes too much (agency report), but claims it is not a problem."

Her own interests centered around sports. While not enthusiastic about school, at age 18 she did acknowledge that it was "very important" to do well in school, that "nowadays you need an education to get a good job." She had vague plans about working for a while, then perhaps joining the Army and perhaps even attending a four-year college. She said, "No marriage for me. I guess I'm not ready and don't know when I'll be ready." She was considered by the interviewer to have unrealistic plans beyond high school. Her self-esteem was only fair and she could think of few strong points in herself.

Shirley's mother had frequent emotional disturbances from the time of Shirley's infancy. She had been diagnosed alternately as suffering from major depression and/or personality disorder. Additionally, Shirley's father had problems with alcohol in her early years, and later history suggests that both parents often turned to this as a solution to their difficulties. The parents had separated on a few occasions, and family conflict was reported by the interviewers at the 2-year, 10-year, and 18-year follow-ups. Her mother's mental health problems persisted into Shirley's teen years.

Shirley was the fifth of eight children. She was a "very active and cuddly" baby and "a friendly, independent, but restless" 2-year-old.

Both the 2- and 10-year psychological examinations indicated that she was of average ability. She had no problems at school at the time of the 10-year follow-up. The evaluation panel of pediatrician, psychologist, and public health nurse considered her adjustment to be satisfactory.

During adolescence her teachers noted "nervous tendencies" and "mood swings," but her grades continued to be B's and C's and she received superior ratings for industry, initiative, responsibility, and leadership. She was actively involved in the Big Sister Program, which appeared to be her major support during her teen years. Her SCAT and STEP scores in grades 8, 10, and 12 were in the 30–50th percentile range.

From the material obtained in her interview at 18, Shirley was rated as having a very favorable attitude toward school. "I loved it, just loved everything—I got to be part of it all and it took my mind off things at home . . . I could talk to my friends and liked my teachers." Achievement motivation was very high, and she participated extensively in school activities. Her future educational plans were realistic. She had been accepted at a junior college in Honolulu, where she planned to take a business course. She intended to postpone marriage and a family until she had established some career stability. She hoped to give her own children a good start. "I had a hard time and I don't want that to happen. As parents you can't get through to kids if you don't spend enough time with them."

Looking at her relationship with her parents and particularly at her mother's disturbance, she said, "To me my mother's emotionally sick, and the doctor has said it. Because she's sick, she can't help what she's doing."

Shirley had significant insight into her own moods and some of the factors that contributed to them. Her self-esteem had considerably improved since the beginning of adolescence.

Asked to describe herself, she said, "I'm somebody who's really involved with a lot of things—like I do a lot of thinking . . . Before, life was just pain. Now that I have something to look forward to, that feeling is getting away from me. It's changing now. I'm very emotional, very sensitive. I know I'm not a phony. I say and do as I feel and believe, really." She expressed strong feelings about the possibility of helping others deal with distress. "For others who have problems like I did, I'd want them to know how I did it and how, if I did it, they could do it, too. I'd say, 'Your problem is nothing compared to mine— if I could do it, you could, too!' I tell my girlfriends this, and it will help them help themselves.

Shirley's trust in her own control of her fate and her hope for the future differs markedly from the views expressed in the 18-year interview by some of her peers who were offspring of schizophrenic mothers.

Arthur: "I'd describe myself as different from most people. I don't worry about the problems of the world—not to the extent that I think the world will destroy itself. I think things will come pretty bad, but not to the extent of destroying itself. I don't worry about pollution problems as I think it will be solved, not by man, though." (He indicated that God would handle it all. He was a member of Jehovah's Witnesses.) "That way I don't have to worry about things. . . . I don't think I really have any weaknesses. My self-control is my strong point, but it's just about in-between, not that strong, not that good. But my goal is to get into a 'new order.' In the future a new order is going to come."

Sally: "I'm unhappy. I do a lot of thinking. I say and do what I think and feel. My weakness is giving in. I'm a lot of mouth. I should use more force, but I just talk and cry. I want to shut out what bothers me and just keep to myself now."

Ronald: "I'm quiet, I guess. I like being quiet, but sometimes people want me to talk more. My weakness is talking to other people. I worry a lot about what will happen in the future."

DISCUSSION

Our findings, though limited to a relatively small sample of children and their families, can be meaningfully linked to other longitudinal studies of high-risk children in the United States and Europe.

None have extended across the whole span of development from birth to young adulthood, but we can piece together related reports from segments of the life span of other children living in Europe or in urban centers of the United States (New York, Washington, D.C., Minneapolis, and St. Louis).

Only a few of these studies, notably those by Mednick and associates (1968, 1970) in Denmark and by Sameroff and Zax (1973) in New York, have included information on perinatal and birth complications. Mednick and Schulsinger's retrospective comparisons of reports of Danish midwives revealed a slightly higher rate of perinatal complications in 207 children born to schizophrenic mothers than among matched controls with normal parents. Research by Sameroff and Zax (1973) with four groups of 13 women each (schizophrenic, neurotic depressives, personality disordered, and normal, who were identified as such during their pregnancies) showed a tendency for the offspring of normal mothers to have fewer perinatal and birth complications than the offspring of schizophrenic and depressed mothers, but no differences were found between the two pathology groups.

We note a similar trend in our own small sample: Both the resilient and the "disturbed" offspring of parents with psychiatric problems had twice as high a rate of perinatal complications as the total 1955 birth cohort, but the resilient offspring of such parents had fewer congenital defects.

Fish (1979) has conducted a longitudinal prospective study of thirteen infants born to schizophrenic mothers in New York. They were examined in the first week of life, and at 1, 2, 3, 4, 7, 10, and 13 months. Subsequent follow-ups have been at yearly intervals, including a 10- and an 18-year follow-up. Her data, although based on a small sample, are comparable to the follow-up procedures used in the Kauai Longitudinal Study, and so are her findings.

In a comprehensive review of her research concerning the neurobiologic antecedents of schizophrenia in children, she concludes that a "pan-developmental" retardation is characteristic of preschizophrenic infants. Pan-developmental retardation involves gross-motor and visual-motor development, cognitive development, and proprioceptive and vestibular responses. She notes that children of schizophrenic mothers show more pan-developmental retardation in infancy, and have a higher rate of severe personality disorders at 10 years of age. In her study, pan-developmental retardation during the first 2 years of life was related to psychiatric morbidity and perceptual problems at 10 years.

Her results are strikingly similar to those we found among children from an entirely different ethnic background, some 6,000 miles apart. We noted consistent delays in adaptive, cognitive, and social self-help skills among the offspring of schizophrenic mothers at 20 months, and lower scores on measures of cognitive and perceptual-motor development at age 10, as well as a greater need for mental health care.

Corroborative findings come from Erlenmeyer-Kimling (1978), whose high-risk sample consisted of 80 white children, aged 7 to 12 years. Forty-four had a schizophrenic mother, 23 had a schizophrenic father, and 13 children were descended from two schizophrenic parents. Her two low-risk control groups included 25 children who had one parent with a psychiatric diagnosis other than schizophrenia, and 100 children of normal parents.

Erlenmeyer-Kimling, Cornblatt and Fleiss (1979) administered a number of neurological and perceptual-motor tests to these children when they were in grade school. The performance of the high-risk groups on the Bender-Gestalt test was significantly lower than that of the low-risk controls, suggesting a developmental lag. We found a similar lag at age 10, when we compared mean number-of-error scores on the Bender-Gestalt test for the resilient offspring of psychotic parents (mostly children of depressed mothers) and the offspring (mostly of schizophrenic mothers) who had developed serious learning or behavior problems by middle childhood.

Available data on measures of attention and cognitive functioning are fairly consistent in showing significant differences between children at high or low risk for psychopathology. Anthony (1974, 1978) in St. Louis, and Garmezy (1974) in Minneapolis, examined several groups of elementary school children. Among them were children of schizophrenic mothers, children of mothers hospitalized for depression or manic-depressive psychosis, and control children with normal parents, matched by age, sex, SES, ethnicity, and grade. Children of schizophrenic mothers showed marked attentional deficits and impairment in reality testing. Children of depressed mothers focused their attention better and their performance was accelerated when properly motivated.

We found similar differences between the offspring of schizophrenic and depressed mothers on Kauai. Children of the depressed mothers were able to concentrate better in the classroom than children of schizophrenic mothers. The latter displayed poorer problem-solving skills and had more difficulties in tests requiring perceptual acuity and adherence to a time limit than control children with normal parents.

In most of the research with offspring of psychotic parents, teachers' ratings of classroom behavior and peer relationships have discriminated significantly between groups at high and low risk for mental health problems. Mednick and Schulsinger (1968) noted in Denmark that high-risk children tend to become upset more easily in class. Among the "sick" group (i.e., offspring of schizophrenic mothers who themselves developed mental health problems), the majority was characterized by their teachers as being disturbing to the class, as discipline problems, and as aggressive, compared with a minority of the normal controls and of the "well" group (i.e., offspring of schizophrenic mothers who had not developed any problems by age 20).

In New York, Weintraub, Liebert, and Neale (1978) examined teachers' ratings of children of schizophrenic, depressed, and normal mothers. Children with either a schizophrenic or a depressed mother were perceived as more deviant than control children and exhibited higher levels of classroom disturbance, impatience, disrespect, defiance, and inattentiveness or withdrawal.

On Kauai, teachers' ratings also discriminated significantly among the offspring of the depressed mothers and the offspring of the schizophrenic mothers and their respective controls. Teachers also discriminated between the resilient offspring of psychotic mothers and offspring who developed serious coping problems by middle childhood. The resilient ones displayed fewer behavior disturbances in the classroom, bullied less, and were able to concentrate better.

Results from parental questionnaires (Beisser, Glasser & Grant, 1967) and from parental interviews (Grunebaum et al., 1978) are more inconsistent than the results of teachers' ratings. Beisser et al. found, as we did, that children of schizophrenic mothers were perceived as more maladjusted by their parents than children of normal parents. Grunebaum et al. report that the offspring of depressed mothers were perceived as more maladjusted by their parents than offspring of schizophrenic mothers, who, in turn, were judged by their parents to have more problems than the offspring of normal parents.

Anthony and his colleagues (1974, 1978) are among the few investigators who have included both black and white children in their samples, and who have examined the discriminating power of "standard" clinical evaluations and of psychological test batteries for children from different social class backgrounds. Clinical evaluations of the emotional status of children and adolescents differentiated between the offspring of psychotic and normal parents who were middle-class whites. They did *not* discriminate between normal children and the offspring of psychotic parents who were lower-class and black (Franklin et al., 1978). In fact, the characteristics of the lower-class black children who had normal parents approximated those of the white middle-class offspring with psychotic parents.

In short, more attention needs to be paid to the appropriateness of clinical measures of pathology and competence for lower-class children from different minority groups. In our own study, measures of adaptive and self-help skills in early childhood and nonverbal measures of problem-solving skills in middle childhood were better discriminators between the offspring of the psychotic parents, who came from non-white and predominantly poor families, and control children (matched by age, sex, SES, and ethnicity) than were behavior observations in the classroom. Problems recognized by the parents at home differentiated better between these groups than teachers' ratings.

While definitions and perceptions of abnormal behavior may vary from one ethnic and socioeconomic group to another, there seems to be more agreement on optimal functioning in children. Across ethnic and sociocultural barriers we noted a common set of characteristics that discriminated between the resilient offspring of psychotic parents and those who developed serious coping problems in the first two decades of life. These characteristics were found by Garmezy (1974, 1976) in white children; by Anthony (1974, 1978) with black and white children; and in our own study with Asian and Polynesian children and youth. They also appear to discriminate between monozygotic twins who are discordant for schizophrenia (Pollin & Stabenau, 1968). They include social responsiveness and an even temperament in infancy, independence and autonomy in toddlerhood, self-help and problem-solving skills that provide a sense of mastery in childhood, and a conviction of being in control of one's life in late adolescence.

The "invulnerable" offspring of psychotic parents also share another important asset: a predominantly positive interaction with their primary caregiver in the first year of life, the critical period for the development of attachment and trust. For, "without such a relationship . . . any child has less hope of surviving psychologically into adult life" (Anthony, 1974).

CHAPTER 12

SIGNIFICANT DISCRIMINATORS BETWEEN RESILIENT CHILDREN AND YOUTH, AND PEERS WITH COPING PROBLEMS

In this chapter we take a look at the relationships *across time* between child and caregiver variables that contributed to the "making of resiliency" among the children and youth in this birth cohort. We then introduce a model that shows the interrelationships between major risk factors at birth and stressful life events that increased *vulnerability*, and protective factors within the child and his caregiving environment that increased *stress resistance*. The *balance* between risk, stress, and protective factors appears to account for the range of adaptive and maladaptive outcomes observed in this study.

We first present a set of predictors that maximally differentiated between the high-risk resilient children and youth in the 1955 birth cohort on Kauai and their peers who developed serious coping problems at age 10 and age 18.

The predictors were entered in forward stepwise discriminant analyses that included a total of 37 variables (both characteristics of the child and of the caregiving environment) at age 10 and a total of 45 variables at age 18. One variable was either added to or removed from the equation until optimum discriminant functions were achieved. The variable added was the one, that when partialed on the previously entered variables, had the highest multiple correlations with the groups. The effectiveness of the discriminant functions was tested by reclassifying the original subjects into "resilient" and "problem" groups at age 10 and at age 18 and computing the rates of correct classifications.

Missing values were handled by substituting mean scores from the appropriate outcome groups for each sex at ages 10 and 18. The standardized discriminant function coefficients for females and males at ages 10 and 18 can be found in Appendix Tables A-10 and A-11.[1]

DISCRIMINANT FUNCTION ANALYSES: FEMALES

Resilient Females vs. Females with Problems at 10

Twenty of the 37 variables entered in the stepwise analysis separated the high-risk resilient girls from the high-risk girls with serious learning and/or behavior problems at age 10.

Eleven (55%) of the 20 discriminating variables were characteristics of the caregiving environment, nine (45%) of the variables were characteristics of the child. Fourteen variables (70%) were obtained between birth and age 2, the other six (30%) in the period between 2 and 10 years.

Among the variables making the *greatest* positive contribution to this discriminant function were: a relatively greater age of the father at the birth of his daughter; the amount of attention given to the infant during the first year of life; the physical status of the toddler as rated by the pediatrician at age 2; her information-processing and self-help skills at age 2; and the quality of the mother-daughter relationship observed during the developmental assessment by the psychologist.

Among the variables making the greatest *negative* contribution to this discriminant function were: late birth order; prolonged separation of the infant from the mother during year 1; parental discord between birth and year 2; serious or repeated childhood illnesses necessitating medical treatment; the girl's Bender-Gestalt error score; and a high number of stressful life events experienced between ages 2 and 10.

The 20-variable discriminant function analysis correctly classified 93.0% of the resilient girls, and 74.4% of the high-risk girls with serious learning and/or behavior problems at age 10. (The same proportion in each group had been correctly identified by the inclusion of *all* 37 pre-

---

[1]Each standardized discriminant function coefficient represents the relative contribution of its associated variable to the discriminant function. The sign denotes whether the variable is making a positive or a negative contribution.

dictors.) The separation between the two groups was highly significant (p<.0001). The canonical correlation for the 20-variable function was .93.

Resilient Females vs. Females with Problems at 18

Twenty-three out of 45 variables entered in the stepwise discriminant function analysis differentiated significantly between high-risk resilient girls and high-risk girls with a record of serious delinquencies and/or mental health problems at age 18.

Fifteen (65%) of these variables were characteristics of the caregiving environment; eight (35%) were characteristics of the child. Twelve (52%) of the variables were obtained between birth and age 2, six (26%) between ages 2 and 10 years, and five (22%) in adolescence.

Among the variables making the greatest *positive* contribution to this function were: a relatively greater age of the father at the birth of his daughter; the quality of the parent-child relationship observed during the 20-month developmental examination; the number of alternative caretakers in the household (besides the parent) in childhood; and the girl's self-concept at age 18.

Among the variables making the greatest *negative* contribution to this discriminant function were: late birth order; serious or repeated illnesses necessitating medical treatment during infancy; a high cumulative number of stressful life events experienced in the first two years of life; family discord during childhood; problems reported by the teenage girl in the relationship with her father during adolescence; and a high cumulative number of stressful life events reported by the girls for the period between ages 10 and 18.

The 23-variable discriminant function correctly classified 85.7% of the resilient girls and 93.0% of the high-risk girls with serious coping problems at age 18. (The inclusion of all 48 predictor variables raised the proportion of correctly classified resilient girls to 90.5%; the proportion of high-risk girls with coping problems who were correctly classified remained the same.[2]

The separation of the two groups on the 23 predictor variables was highly significant (p<.0001). The canonical correlation for the 23-variable function was .94.

---

[2]In the original 45-variable discriminant function, maternal mental illness was a significant discriminator between resilient girls and high-risk girls with coping problems at age 10 and age 18.

DISCRIMINANT ANALYSES: MALES

Resilient Males vs. Males with Problems at 10

Eighteen of the 37 predictors from infancy and childhood were retained in the set of variables that discriminated between the high-risk resilient males and high-risk males with serious learning and/or behavior problems at age 10. Half of the predictor variables were characteristics of the child, the other half were characteristics of his caregiving environment. Twelve of the eighteen variables (66%) were obtained in the period between birth and age 2, the other six (33%) in the period between ages 2 and 10.

Among the variables making the greatest *positive* contribution to this discriminant function were: the mother's perception of her infant son as "cuddly, affectionate" and "good-natured, even-tempered" at age 1; the positive interaction of the toddler with the examiner at age 2; and his autonomy and the quality of the mother-son interaction observed during the developmental assessment.

Among the variables making the greatest *negative* contribution to this function were: late birth order; prolonged separation of the infant from the mother during the first year of life; marital discord during the boy's infancy and childhood; the death of a sibling; the boy's Bender-Gestalt error score (a measure of CNS integrity) and a low parental IQ reported in the school records (see Appendix Table A-16 for correlations between the IQ of parents and their offspring).

The 18-variable discriminant function correctly classified 90.0% of the high-risk resilient boys and 80.4% of the high-risk boys with serious learning and/or behavior problems at age 10. (The original 37-variable function correctly identified 96.7% of the resilient boys and 82.4% of the boys with coping problems at age 10.) The separation between the two groups on the 18 predictors was highly significant (p<.0001). The canonical correlation for the 18-variable function was .85.

Resilient Males vs. Males with Problems at 18

Twenty-four of the 45 predictor variables (from infancy, childhood, and adolescence) were retained as significant discriminators between the high-risk resilient boys and high-risk boys with a record of serious delinquencies and/or mental health problems at age 18. Eight (33%) of these variables were characteristics of the youth; sixteen (66%) were characteristics of the caregiving environment. Thirteen

(54%) of the predictors were obtained in the period between birth and age 2, nine (38%) between ages 2 and 10 years, and two (8%) in adolescence.

Among the variables making the greatest *positive* contribution to this discriminant function were: the mother's perception of her infant son as "cuddly, affectionate" and the quality of the mother-son interaction observed at year 1 by home visitors; the autonomy of the toddler and the quality of the mother-son relationship observed during the developmental examination at 20 months; the psychologist's rating of the emotional support provided by the family for the child between the ages 2 and 10; and the boy's own rating of the quality of his family life during the period between 10 and 18.

Among the variables making the greatest *negative* contribution to this function were: late birth order; prolonged separation of the infant from the mother during the first year of life; serious and/or repeated illnesses of the child during the first two years of life; absence of the father during early and middle childhood; the death of a sibling (brother); and a high cumulative number of stressful life events reported by the youth for the period between ages 10 and 18.

This 24-variable discriminant function correctly classified 96.7% of the high-risk resilient males and 89.8% of the high-risk males with serious coping problems at age 18. (The proportion of correct classifications was identical to the one made when all 45 predictor variables were included in the analysis.) The separation between the two groups on the 24 predictor variables was highly significant ($p < .0001$). The canonical correlation for the 24-variable function was .88.

FACTORS CONTRIBUTING TO IMPROVEMENT IN ADOLESCENCE

Among the high-risk children who had developed serious learning and/or behavior problems by age 10, were 37 (21 boys and 16 girls) whose status was judged "improved" by the end of adolescence.[3]

None of these youth had been involved in any antisocial or delinquent acts between the ages of 10 and 18 years; none had developed any serious mental health problems in adolescence; all had graduated from high school with an adequate or better record of achievement.

[3]For a more detailed discussion, see Chapter 10 in *Kauai's Children Come of Age* (Werner & Smith, 1977).

During their 18-year interviews they appeared free of serious conflicts and anxieties, had realistic educational and vocational goals, and a satisfactory social and family life.

We examined the available longitudinal data on these children, as well as their test data in the records of Kauai's high schools (the SCAT, STEP) and all agency records that were available on them and their families (see Chapter 3). We compared these data with those available on the high-risk youth from the same birth cohort who had serious coping problems by age 18.

We found only a few, but apparently crucial variables that were related to improvement in the status of these high-risk children in late childhood and adolescence.

"Improved" high-risk youth grew up in families with a smaller number of children than peers of the same sex whose problem persisted from childhood through adolescence, and their fathers tended to be older at the birth of the child.

In infancy, more of the improved high-risk males were perceived as "good-natured" and "easy to deal with" by their mothers and more of the improved girls were judged to be well developed physically by the pediatrician at the 20-month examination.

Both improved boys and girls reported fewer problems in family relations during adolescence and a better relationship with their fathers than high-risk peers whose problems persisted. Improved girls reported better relations with their mothers as well and were less likely to be pregnant as teenagers.

Both the high-risk males and the high-risk females whose status improved between ages 10 and 18 reported a smaller number of stressful life events in adolescence than peers of the same age and sex whose status remained unchanged or deteriorated. Boys and girls whose status changed for the better also had significantly fewer contacts with community agencies during their teen years than high-risk youth whose problems persisted.

The improvement rate was higher (but not significantly so) among youth who had received some counseling or remedial help in late childhood, notably boys with learning disabilities and mental health problems at age 10. But more favorable parental (especially paternal) attitudes and support and a smaller load of stressful life experiences were the factors that appeared most consistently in the records and interviews of the "improved" high-risk youth in adolescence.

Similar findings have been noted in follow-up studies in late childhood and adolescence in Great Britain (Rutter, 1979; Shepherd et al.,

1971) and in the Growth and Guidance studies at the Institute of Human Development of the University of California at Berkeley (MacFarlane, 1964). A change for the better in family circumstances was associated with a marked reduction of psychiatric risk and mental health problems in adolescence in the British studies and with a reduction of learning difficulties in the Berkeley studies as well.

KEY DISCRIMINATORS

Table 23 presents a summary of the significant discriminators that separated the resilient children and youth from peers of the same age and sex who developed serious coping problems at age 10 and at age 18:

Characteristics of the child and of the caregiving environment were about equally represented among the discriminating variables. More than half of the significant predictors were from the first 2 years of life, another third from the period between age 2 and age 10. Less than 20% of the discriminating variables came from the adolescent period.

The relative contributions of child and caregiver variables changed from childhood to adolescence, as did the discriminating power of biological, ecological and interpersonal variables.

Among the significant predictors in infancy were age of the opposite-sex parent at the birth of the child, the mother's perception of her baby's temperamental characteristics and the health of the infant. The other early predictors were characteristics of the caregiving environment, critical for attachment and the establishment of a secure bond between infant and primary caretaker, i.e., the absence or prolonged separation of the infant from his primary caretaker; the amount of attention given to the infant by his mother during the first year of life and the quality of the early mother/child relationship.

Significant predictors in the second year of life were the toddler's social orientation, autonomy, and self-help skills observed during the 20-month developmental examination and the physical-status rating made independently by the pediatrician at that time. During childhood most of the significant discriminators dealt with the composition and coherence of the household: the number of children and adults in the household; the presence or absence of the father; the death or departure of siblings; the mother's long-term employment; and the presence or absence of chronic family discord and stressful life events. Among

Summary Table 23: Significant Discriminators Between High-Risk Resilient M and F and Children and Youth with Serious Coping Problems at 10 and 18 (low SES homes)

High-Risk M at 10	at 18		High-Risk F at 10	at 18
x	x	Birth order	x	x
x	x	Infant perceived as "cuddly," "affectionate" (year 1)		
x	x	Infant perceived as "good-natured," "even-tempered" (year 1)		
		Infant has (sleeping, feeding) habits distressing to mother (year 1)		x
	x	Mother's way of coping with infant (year 1) Ratio of positive/negative interactions		
		Attention given to infant (year 1)	x	x
x	x	Prolonged separation of infant from mother (year 1)	x	x
	x	Prolonged disruption of family life (year 1)		
		Father absent from household since birth	x	
	x	Serious or repeated illnesses of child (birth–year 2)	x	x
x	x	Physical status of child (20-month exam)	x	
x		Behavior patterns of child (during 20-month exam) Ratio of positive/negative interactions	x	
x		Social orientation of child (20 mos.)	x	x
x	x	Autonomy of child (20 mos.)		
		Information processing skills of child (20 mos.)		
x	x	Parent-child interaction (during 20-month exam) Ratio of positive negative interactions	x	x
x		Conflicts between parents (birth–2 years)	x	x
	x	Total cumulative life stresses (birth–2)	x	x

X		Serious or repeated illnesses of child (years 2–10)	X	X
	X	Emotional support in home (years 2–10)		
	X	Parents' illnesses (years 2–10)		
	X	Father died or permanently absent (years 2–10)	X	
		Father absent temporarily (years 2–10)	X	X
	X	Mother works long-term (> 1 year) outside of home (years 2–10)		
X	X	Death of sibling (years 2–10)		
X	X	Older sibling left home (years 2–10)		
X	X	Conflict between family members (years 2–10)	X	X
		Total cumulative life stresses (years 2–10)	X	
X	X	N of children in household (by year 10)		X
		N of additional adults in household (besides parents) (by year 10)		X
X	X	Bender-Gestalt error score (year 10)	X	X
	X	Problems in family relationships (years 10–18)		X
		Problems in relationship with mother (years 10–18)		X
		Problems in relationship with father (years 10–18)		X
		Self-concept (year 18)		X
	X	Total cumulative life stresses (years 10–18)		X
X	X	Age of opposite-sex parent	X	X
X		Low parental IQ (in school records)		X
		Parental mental health problems: infancy	X	
		Evidence of parental mental health problems during offspring's childhood		X
		Evidence of parental mental health problems during adolescence		X

characteristics of the child during that period that contributed to the making of resiliency were his or her health and central nervous system integrity.

Among significant discriminators in adolescence were the teenager's perception of the quality of his/her relationship with the family, especially with the father, and the cumulative number of stressful life events reported by him/her in adolescence. Additional significant discriminators for the girls were a positive self-concept and the absence of maternal mental health problems.

We are aware of the need to cross-validate the results of our study in settings that differ from the island of Kauai in ethnic make-up and "lifestyle," but we note a number of complementary findings in prospective studies of black and white children on the U.S. mainland and in Great Britain (Rutter, 1979).

Discriminant function analyses of infancy and childhood data from the largest of these investigations, the nationwide Collaborative Perinatal Project (CPP), by Broman et al. (1975) and Smith et al. (1972), have shown the relatively high predictive power of constitutional variables in infancy in samples of lower-class children from different regions of the country.

In a prospective study of a cohort of some one thousand children born in 1966 in St. Louis, Jordan & Spaner (1972) have examined, in multivariate analyses, a number of biological and ecological factors that influence the development of young children. Two aggregates of environmental data, one representing the micro-environment of the mother and child, the other, the macro-environment of the society (including SES and ethnicity), were found to have less of an effect on the early development of the children (at ages 24 and 36 months) than did constitutional variables.

Among developmental factors influencing exceptional status of the children at school entrance, six significant predictors were developmental factors in the child, four were social factors, and three (including age of mother) were characteristics of the primary caregiver. Life changes, i.e., changes in the number or intensity of stressful events, were primary sources of variance in these children (Jordan, 1976).

A similar set of factors—i.e., a combination of constitutional characteristics in the child, of characteristics of the caregiving environment, and cumulative life stresses—emerged as significant discriminators between resilient children and children with coping problems in our own study. The relative weight of the contribution of the biological, ecological, and social factors among these discriminators changed with age and differed for the sexes.

In our study both the age of the mother and of the father significantly discriminated between resilient children and peers who developed serious learning and/or behavior problems at age 10, or had a record of serious delinquencies and/or mental health problems at age 18. The *mother's* (greater) age consistently made a negative contribution to the discriminant functions for the boys, the *father's* (greater) age consistently made a *positive* contribution to the discriminant functions for the girls, even when the effect of birth order was controlled.

Among the high-risk children in this birth cohort, the age of a mother correlated significantly with her ratings of the temperamental characteristics of her son and the health status of the boys (see Appendix Table A-12 for correlations). Younger mothers perceived their sons more often as "high" in activity level and cuddliness, and, in turn, gave their sons more attention during the first year of life than older mothers. The sons of younger mothers had fewer and less serious childhood illnesses than the sons of older mothers. Daughters of younger mothers were less often and less seriously ill in childhood as well, had a lower incidence of central nervous system damage, and were more often rated "high" in social orientation by the psychologists during the 20-month examinations.

Daughters of older fathers were more often perceived to be "active, good-natured, and easy to deal with" than daughters of younger fathers, and were provided with more educational stimulation (i.e., verbal stimulation and encouragement of learning activities) in the home. There was a significant negative correlation between the father's age and the quality of the father-son relationship reported by the teenage boys in adolescence.

We are aware that a number of parent couples in this cohort had fairly large age differences (e.g., middle-aged Pilipino men married to younger Japanese or part-Hawaiian women). Our findings need replication in other settings and with larger numbers.

The importance of maternal age as a predictor of competence in the offspring has been recognized in a number of epidemiological studies in the U.S., such as the Collaborative Perinatal Project (Broman, et al., 1975) and in the study by Jordan and Spaner (1972), but the most comprehensive data available to date come from Europe. Associations of maternal age at birth and subsequent intelligence test scores in childhood and adolescence were reported for a series of 1500 young men (age 18) from the Netherlands (Zybert, Stein & Belmont, 1978).

Possible confounding by birth order, spacing interval, social class, and sex of sibling were examined. Significant (negative) correlations between a mother's age and her son's ability were found in three of the four possible birth order/social-class combinations among the Dutch youth.[4]

In spite of an extensive search of the literature, we found few references to the effect of parental, especially paternal age on the social development of offspring. This is a surprising gap in the child development literature, inasmuch as the age differences between spouses at first marriage is now decreasing (Tiger, 1979), but the number of divorces and second marriages—with additional children from spouses of unequal age—are increasing, and so are births to older mothers and adoptions of children by older parents.

Presser (1975), in an excellent review of secondery data on age differences between the spouses in the United States, has examined trends, patterns, and social implications that need to be more closely heeded by child development researchers. If we want to understand child development, we need to see it in the context of both the developmental needs and competencies of the child, and those of his primary caregivers. We consider the age of both parents important variables worthy of further investigation. They affect the relationship between the sexes and generations, the power structure within the family, sex-role expectations for sons and daughters, and, perhaps most importantly, the degree to which parents or peers (including older siblings) become role models for the next generation in times of rapid social change.

AMELIORATIVE FACTORS VS. ABSENCE OF RISK FACTORS

So far we have examined a set of predictors that maximally discriminated between high-risk resilient children and youth and peers of the same age and sex who had developed serious coping problems by ages 10 and 18. *Both* the index and the control groups lived in chronic poverty and experienced a series of stressful life events.

We now turn to additional data from our 1955 birth cohort to attempt a tentative answer to the question of whether there are protect-

---

[4]For a discussion of sex differences in parent-child correlates of ability, see Chapter 11 in *The Children of Kauai* (Werner, Bierman & French, 1971); App. A-16.

ive factors that are important in counterbalancing stress, deprivation, or disadvantage, but that are not important in the absence of such circumstances.

We sorted the children from the 1955 birth cohort into four groups, and each group by sex: Groups 1 and 2 consisted of middle-class and lower-class children, respectively, who had experienced one or several significant stressful life events, such as chronic family discord, absence of the father, parental mental illness, the death of a sibling, divorce or remarriage of parents, change of residence or schools, or who had a sibling with a chronic handicap or serious learning and/or behavior problems (for a list of stressful life events, see Chapter 5 and Figure I in this chapter). Groups 3 and 4 consisted of middle- and lower-class children, respectively, who had *not* experienced such serious or chronic life stresses. In each of the four groups we examined the variables that differentiated children who *did not* develop any problems in the first two decades of life from those who had difficulties in school by age 10 and/or a record of serious delinquencies and behavior disorders by age 18 (see Appendix Tables A-14 and A-15 for the results of the statistical tests of significance).

Among *middle-class* children *without* a record of serious or chronic life stresses, the following variables discriminated significantly between children who did and did not develop any serious coping problems in the first two decades of life: mother's level of education (for males and females); birth order and the number of children in the household (for males); the amount of attention given to the infant during the first year of life (for females); the mother's rating of the infant's activity level (for males) and social responsiveness (for females); the Cattell IQ at 20 months, and the PMA IQ and PMA Reasoning factor at age 10 (for both males and females); as well as verbal comprehension skills (for males) and perceptual-motor skills (for females).

Our analysis of the data in the three other comparison groups in the 1955 birth cohort identified additional protective factors that discriminated the children who *did not* develop any serious coping problems in the first two decades of life from those who did. These variables discriminated significantly between positive and negative developmental outcomes *only* when there was a series of stressful life events (in both middle- and lower-class families), or when children were exposed to deprivation or disadvantage (in the lower-class families). They *did not* discriminate between good and poor outcomes among middle-class children whose lives were relatively stress free.

Among such ameliorative factors in the child were: good health (for both sexes), autonomy and self-help skills (for males), and a positive social orientation and self-concept (for females). Among protective factors in the caregiving environment for both sexes were a positive parent-child relationship observed during the second year of life, and emotional support provided by other family members during early and middle childhood.

For boys, being a first-born son was an important protective factor, regardless of stress, disadvantage, or deprivation. For girls, the model of a mother who was steadily and gainfully employed was a significant protective factor, both among middle-class and lower-class families who experienced serious or chronic stress. For both sexes, the cumulative number of stressful life events discriminated significantly between positive and negative developmental outcomes in middle-class as well as lower-class homes.

In sum: Regardless of stress, deprivation, or disadvantage, the chances for a positive developmental outcome for children in this birth cohort were greater if they were reared by mothers with more education; if their temperamental characteristics elicited positive responses from the mother; if they received plenty of attention from their primary caregivers during the first year of life; and if they had age-appropriate perceptual-motor, communication, and reasoning skills at age 2 and 10 years.

The number of ameliorative factors that discriminated between positive and negative developmental outcomes in this cohort increased with stress (in both middle- and lower-class children) and deprivation (among lower-class children). The largest number of protective factors was found among the boys and girls who grew up in chronic poverty and were exposed to a number of stressful life events, but who managed to cope well in both childhood and adolescence.

As disadvantage and the cumulative number of stressful life events increased, more protective factors in the children and their caregiving environment were needed to counterbalance the negative aspects in their lives and to ensure a positive developmental outcome.

A TRANSACTIONAL MODEL OF DEVELOPMENT

The results of the Kauai Longitudinal Study appear to lend some empirical support to a transactional model of human development that takes into account the bidirectionality of child-caregiver effects.

In Figure I we show some of the interrelations between major risk factors at birth, and some of the most common stressful life events in childhood and adolescence that *increased vulnerability* in this birth cohort, and protective factors within the child and his/her caregiving environment that *increased stress resistance*.

It is the shifting balance between risk, stress, and protective factors in the child and his caregiving environment, the balance between "undergoing" and "doing" (Wertheim, 1978), that appears to account for the range of adaptive or maladaptive outcomes encountered in our study.

The majority of the children and youth in the 1955 cohort (some 422 out of 698) were exposed to low risk at birth, led lives that were not unusually stressful, grew up in a supportive caregiving environment, and coped successfully in childhood and adolescence.

Some 10% of the cohort, the 72 high-risk resilient children, were exposed to chronic poverty, higher-than-average rates of perinatal risk, and stressful life events, but they could draw on a number of ameliorative factors in themselves and in their caregiving environment that tilted the balance from "undergoing" to "doing" and led to successful developmental outcomes.

At the other end of the scale were the high-risk children—one out of five in this cohort (N:129)—who lived in persistently disordered family environments that provided little support and/or who had experienced biological insults that prevented adequate development. The overwhelming majority in this group tended to develop serious and persistent coping problems in childhood and adolescence. A smaller group (N:75) of low-risk children, born in better-off homes to educated mothers and exposed to little reproductive risk, also displayed maladaptive behavior in response to cumulative stressful life events that were not buffered by protective factors within the child and/or his caregiving environment.

In our study constitutional factors within the child (temperament, health) appeared to pull their greatest weight in infancy and early childhood; ecological factors (household structure and composition) gained in importance in childhood; and intrapersonal factors (self-esteem) in adolescence, judging from the weight assigned to these variables in the discriminant function analyses.

The relative contributions of risk factors, stressful life events, and protective factors within the child and his caregiving environment appear to change not only with the stages of the life cycle, but also with

Figure I: Model of Interrelations between Risk, Stress, Sources of Support, and Coping (based on data from the Kauai Longitudinal Study)

Major Risk Factors (at birth)
Chronic poverty
Mother with little education
Moderate-severe perinatal complications
Developmental delays or irregularities
Genetic abnormalities
Parental psychopathology

VULNERABILITY

Major Sources of Support

Caregiving Environment
Four or fewer children spaced more than two years apart
Much attention paid to infant during first year
Positive parent-child relationship in early childhood
Additional caretakers besides mother
Care by siblings and grandparents
Mother has some steady employment outside of household

Protective Factors Within the Child
Birth order (first)
CNS integrity
High activity level
Good-natured; affectionate disposition
Responsive to people
Free of distressing habits
Positive social orientation

Major Sources of Stress

In Childhood and Adolescence
Prolonged separation from primary caretaker during first year of life
Birth of younger sib within two years after child's
Serious or repeated childhood illnesses
Parental illness
Paternal mental illness
Sib with handicap or learning or behavior problem
Chronic family discord
Father absent

Loss of job or sporadic employment of parent(s)

Change of residence

Change of schools

Divorce of parents

Remarriage and entry of step-parent into household

Departure or death of older sib or close friend

Foster home placement (for F: teenage pregnancy)

Autonomy

Advanced self-help skills

Age-appropriate sensorimotor and perceptual skills

Adequate communication skills

Ability to focus attention and control impulses

Special interests and hobbies

Positive self-concept

Internal Locus of Control

Desire to improve self

Availability of kin and neighbors for emotional support

Structure and rules in household

Shared values—a sense of coherence

Close peer friends

Availability of counsel by teachers and/or ministers

Access to special services (health, education, social services)

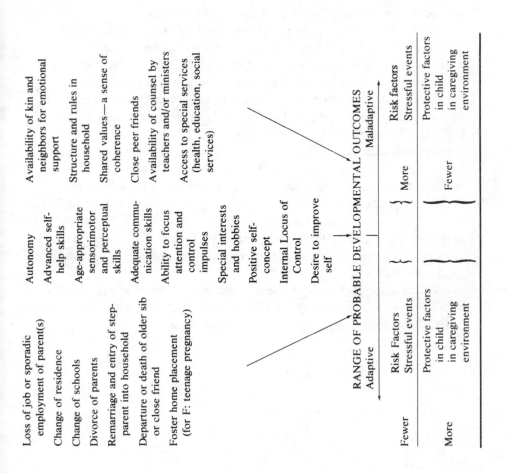

RANGE OF PROBABLE DEVELOPMENTAL OUTCOMES

Adaptive — Maladaptive

Fewer | Risk Factors Stressful events | More

More | Protective factors in child in caregiving environment | Fewer

the sex of the child and the cultural context in which s/he grows up. We have seen that in this culture boys appear to be more at risk than girls at birth and experience more stressful life events in the first decade of life, while the picture is reversed in the second decade.

To the extent that the men and women in this study were able to elicit predominantly positive responses from their environment, they were found to be stress-resistant at each stage of their life cycle, even under conditions of chronic poverty or in a home with a psychotic parent. To the extent that they elicited negative responses from their environment, they were found to be vulnerable, even in the absence of biological stress or financial constraints.

Optimal adaptive development thus appears to be characterized by a balance between the power of the person and the power of the social and physical environment. Intervention in behalf of children and youth may be conceived as an attempt to restore this balance, either by decreasing the young person's exposure to risk or stressful life events or by increasing the number of protective factors (competencies, sources of support) that one can draw on within oneself or one's caregiving environment.

The life stories of some of the resilient youth presented next illustrate some of the resources they called on to protect themselves and to counterbalance or conquer their vulnerabilities.

CHAPTER 13

SELECTED CASE STUDIES

In this chapter some of the resilient youth speak for themselves. Their stories, we trust, will illustrate some of the issues discussed in previous chapters, especially the interplay between inner resources and external support that helped buffer the impact of stressful events in the lives of these high-risk children and tipped the balance from vulnerability to invincibility.

We have drawn on our longitudinal records from infancy, childhood, and adolescence to highlight some of the significant biological, ecological, and social variables that contributed to the development of autonomy and competence in these children and youth. We hope thus to present an effective balance between the statistical findings of our study that depict group trends and individual life histories that capture some of the spirit of resiliency.

John and Mary, Michael and Kay are only a few of the resilient children who managed to cope successfully with chronic poverty, constitutional vulnerabilities, and family stress, but their sources of support—and above all their indomitable spirit—were shared by the others as well.

The contrast between John and Jim, high-risk twins who developed along divergent paths, provides a means for us to focus on some of these attributes.

John was the elder of a set of fraternal twins who were the sixth and seventh children of a Japanese mother and a part-Hawaiian father. The mother had some medical complications early in the pregnancy and her doctor suggested that it might be unwise to continue the pregnancy. She rejected this idea and the infants were born at term, weigh-

ing nearly 8 lb. each. During the pregnancy the mother had been described as calm and relaxed, not nervous or irritable, and one who had
a very happy married life—"no troubles"—a good understanding between her husband and herself, and pleasant relationships with other
family members, in spite of the poverty of the home.

The home atmosphere continued to be favorable, and at the time
of the 1-year interview the mother was described as "resourceful,
good-humored, energetic, affectionate, happy, sensibly permissive,
and patient." She was, on the whole, reasonably relaxed in a situation
demanding a great deal of energy.

John at year 1, was rated the "more active" of the twins by the
mother. He ate and slept well and seemed to be developing satisfacto-
rily. The visiting nurse felt he was "more alert" than his "placid,"
second-born twin brother. At 20 months the mother's attitude toward
her children was again described in positive terms—as "affectionate,
kind, temperate and easy-going." John appeared to have adequate self-
help skills (Vineland SQ: 100), but did not cooperate well enough on
the Cattell Infant Exam for his results to be scored. The psychologist
noted that he was very active, a child of apparently normal intelligence, who was described as determined, restless, and tense. His
"more placid" twin brother was also rated "normal" by both the pediatrician and psychologist, but the examiners noted that "these twins
are not alike in temperament," and the psychologist had made a rec-
ommendation that the mother treat them differently. Although socioeconomic status was low, overall family stability during these first 2
years of their lives was rated very high.

At the time of the 10-year follow-up, their socioeconomic status
seemed to have slightly improved, the educational stimulation provided in the home was rated "fair," and the emotional support adequate. The twins apparently had a good relationship with each other,
played well together, and were both making satisfactory progress in
school—until age 7, when the second-born twin, *Jim,* contracted asep-
tic meningitis. After his recovery, his teachers noted clumsiness, artic-
ulation difficulties, and a quick temper, and the mother indicated at age
10 that John was "easier to manage" than his brother.

At age 10 both boys received a PMA IQ score in the high average
range, but John was in much better condition physically. His twin
brother was already grossly overweight and by age 17 weighed more
than 200 lb.

During their adolescence, the twins' father was called on active
duty and served in the war in Vietnam. The older siblings grew up and

left home. The second-born twin became involved in a series of minor delinquencies, was often truant from school, received failing grades, and became a disciplinary problem. In high school he was retained one grade and his scores on the Locus of Control Scale at age 18 were in the external direction, expressing a lack of faith in his control of his fate.

John, however, took on a great deal of responsibility in the home during that time, and still managed to do well in school and to participate in extracurricular activities. Here are his views of himself during the interview at age 18:

"How would I describe myself? That's a tough one. I'm not too dumb—I'm smart enough to know things, to get around, to take care of myself. I've got average intelligence. If I were putting a want ad in the paper, I'd mention other things. Like I'm a firm believer in God. I'm not saying I follow the law." The youngster who was just beginning to "talk for himself" at 10 had become very articulate, insightful, and purposeful at 18—and very much impressed the interviewer with his qualities.

He had found school to be "very exciting and interesting," and wished that everyone could live the kind of life he had. He felt education was very important and planned to attend a 4-year college, majoring in music. Since finances continued to be a family problem, he planned initially to work while attending the local community college, then transfer to the University of Hawaii to concentrate on his music. In the meantime he planned to continue his music lessons locally. He had been very active in the field for a number of years and was considered to have a promising future. His school work had been C's and B's (A in music) and his STEP and SCAT scores ranged around the 50–60 percentiles. He scored in an internal direction on the Nowicki Locus of Control Scale.

John expressed positive feelings about his parents and identified with both of them. Of his mother he said, "She's very emotional, concerned about everything, a little hot-tempered, but not as much as my father. She's very loving and considerate." His father he felt was "about the same, but a little more prouder. I like him, I think everyone should admire his father. He should be someone to look up to, in authority." He felt close to both parents, got along with them well, although "everybody gets into skirmishes now and then, but nothing bad, nothing like leaving the house, not like my twin. I have my moods, but not that serious." He felt his parents had primarily influenced him in relation to right and wrong, respect and honor, but left the future up to him.

John indicated that he had a lot of friends. "I'm not saying I'm the most popular around, but I get along pretty well." He had several close male friends and a girlfriend, but "I don't plan on marriage yet, so count that out. It's going to take me about 7 or 8 years to get through my Masters in Music." When asked what he wanted to achieve most in life in addition to his specific career goals, John answered, "I want the satisfaction of planning something in the young stages and carrying it through, of making something out of myself. The field isn't that easy. I hope I can pull it through." He appeared to have a good chance of doing so. At 18 he was a youngster who expressed clear goals and values, high self-esteem, strong feelings of security as part of his family and an internal locus of control. In contrast to the majority of the youth his age (and his twin brother) he believed that his own behavior would determine the outcome and reinforcements he received from life.

A similar faith in her own assets and resources is echoed in *Mary's* responses to the same interview:

Mary at 18 Years: "If I say how I am, it sounds like bragging—I have a good personality and people like me. I'm not the greedy type—I'm jealous a lot of times, yes. And I don't like it when people think they can run my own life—I like to be my own judge. I know right and wrong, but I feel I have a lot more to learn and go through. Generally, I hope I can make it—I hope."

It looked as though Mary, a youngster of Caucasian-Pilipino ancestry, could make it. She had arrived at the threshold of adulthood displaying a resiliency that had served her well and would serve her in the future. Her immediate plans involved enrollment in a 2-year community college on Oahu, where she had applied for a general clerical/secretarial course. A tendency to test things out, noted earlier in her development and possibly a factor in her invulnerability, allowed her to say that she might change her plans at the end of 2 years and continue at the University of Hawaii. In that case she hoped to go into medical or legal secretarial work.

Mary's beginnings in life were not propitious. Her mother's pregnancy occurred after many unsuccessful attempts to conceive and a previous miscarriage. "We were so sure I couldn't have a baby, we even planned to adopt one, and the doctor calls this the miracle baby." The mother was very much overweight and had various minor medical problems during this pregnancy. She was hospitalized three times for severe false labor and eventually was in labor for more than 20 hours. She was described as a "temperamentally nervous person" and later was hospitalized for emotional disturbance.

However, the infancy years apparently provided a warm, supportive atmosphere for Mary. Her mother was very "thrilled—wanted a girl—feels she's wonderful," and her father, a plantation laborer with only 4 years of formal education, took his vacation after the infant's discharge from the hospital to help take care of her and early established a close relationship with his baby. The visiting nurse observed that the parents handled the baby well and that she was a plump, good-looking infant. The home, located in a plantation camp, was neat and clean.

At 1 year of age Mary's development seemed to be progressing well. She was described as "easy to deal with" and "very active," a "healthy, alert child who is apparently given much attention." The interviewer considered the mother "responsible, outgoing, self-confident, warm-hearted, affectionate, happy, and patient."

At age 22 months, Mary scored within the normal range on the Cattell Infant Intelligence Scale (MA: 20 months) and was advanced for her age in self-help skills (Vineland SA: 30 months). Both the examining pediatrician and the psychologist rated her physical and psychological development as normal (though allergies were noted). The psychologist saw her as an active, cheerful, energetic, and determined child who showed independence, perseverance, and feminine characteristics, but who also seemed somewhat excitable, distractible, and nervous. The mother-child relationship was described as an indulgent and easy-going one. The parents were experiencing financial difficulties, but the family stability was rated as high, as was the mother's intelligence.

The picture had changed by the time of the 10-year follow-up. The mother had found it necessary to work outside the home for a short period in the intervening years and had had several major illnesses, surgeries, and hospitalizations between Mary's fifth and tenth birthdays. She had also been hospitalized for emotional disturbance on two occasions during this period. Presenting symptoms included "unbearable tension," nervousness, annoyance with her children (a second girl had been born when Mary was 20 months old), and fears that she might harm them.

In the 10-year interview, the mother stated that she did not think her repeated hospitalizations had alarmed or upset Mary, but she did describe some crying spells and headaches, temper tantrums, and stubborn, contrary behavior in her daughter. Her mother considered Mary to have a mind and will of her own—"in some ways she is not easy."

Mary's performance in school throughout this period was adequate or better, and the teacher considered her behavior in class and her interaction with her peers to be satisfactory. At age 10, perceptual-motor development was age-appropriate, and she received a PMA IQ of 114. Over the years the family had attached importance to education, encouraged Mary, and provided opportunities for stimulation through outside reading and participation in many extracurricular activities—nature study, stamp collecting, scouting, hula lessons, Sunday School attendance. During the mother's many illnesses, there were other supportive relatives present in the household in addition to the father.

Looking at her relationship with her parents, Mary, at 18, described her mother as "very grumpy—well, she's going through change of life early—every little thing bothers her. She's lonely. My father leaves her a lot and we have our own life. When they're that age, they do get lonely." She said that she could talk to her mother when she wasn't grumpy, but added that she was much closer to her boyfriend's mother. Looking back to earlier years, she said, "I used to be blamed for every little thing that my sister did when my parents went out, and when my father went to work, my mother used to hit me and beat me. That's how come I'm not very close to my mother. In a way I used to hate her, but as I got older I understood her better, how she was going through that change of life—but we're not really close."

She described her father in glowing terms—"soft-hearted, very soft-hearted—he cares for our happiness and has always been like that. He's generous, not selfish. I feel very close to him." She indicated that her father had had the greatest influence on her, had guided her thinking and attitude toward life. Even in the midst of turmoil, his guidance, support, and values had apparently provided a framework in which to evaluate her own steps toward maturity.

When asked about some of the most important experiences that molded her, she referred again to her father's handling of particular incidents: "I used to sneak off before—you know, my father is Pilipino style, they're strict on their daughters. They don't really want them to get boyfriends until they're older. I was 16, and I figured I was going to have dates and my father wouldn't let me so I snuck out. And after he caught me one time, he started to be more lenient, you know, let me have a little fun. He told me then, 'if you want a boyfriend, you bring him over here and you can get to know him better because it's the natural way' . . . I guess if my father had kept being strict with me and I kept sneaking out, I guess I may have turned out more the rugged type."

Mary, at age 18, appeared to the interviewer as a young woman with a high degree of self-esteem and self-insight who had successfully worked through her conflict feelings.

School reports during her adolescent years continued to show average and above-average performance. She scored in the upper quartile of the population on scholastic aptitude and achievement tests (the SCAT and the STEP) in the tenth and twelfth grades. On the Nowicki Locus of Control Scale she reflected a strong internal orientation. More so than other girls in her age group, she believed that she had significant control over her own destiny.

On the California Psychological Inventory, she attained above-average scores on measures of sociability, dominance, self-acceptance, good impression, and achievement via conformance. She was outgoing, persistent, and concerned with others' responses to her; valued achievement; and was cooperative. She preferred avoiding tense situations, a fact she affirmed in talking about family disagreements. "Me, I don't start fights too much. My mother, she'll go around the house grumbling, until I finally get up to a point where I can't stand it. I can't stand to see a family fighting. Parents shouldn't fight, they should be able to talk things out."

Mary often expressed the need to test situations and felt comfortable only after being able to do so. This was a coping style noted at various points throughout her development. In looking back at high school, she said, "My freshman year I was scared, and the years went by and I got used to school, you know, it was like my second home in a way," and, looking ahead, "I'm kind of scared right now to go out without much experience" (she was referring to business college and jobs), "I'd like to wait until I have a little more experience." And again, testing relationships, "Well, I'm kind of shy before I get to know you, but once I get to know you, I don't want to brag, but I'm really outgoing and I like people."

Mary's opinions reflected a certain open-mindedness, but no lack of control, and a degree of maturity that held promise of an ability to cope with what the future might bring in spite of the difficulties encountered in the past.

Our interviews included questions on drug usage, racial prejudice, and premarital sex. Mary (on drugs): "I've never tried it, and I don't want to. I figure I'm happy enough and I don't have to get a high to feel better. I figure, what good is that stuff anyway? It's just to make you feel good, and then after that, you just go to sleep after that. I don't think it's right." On prejudice: "I don't like people that are prejudiced. I feel that everybody is the same, it's just their personalities are different. Just cuz their color is different, the race is different, that is nothing. You have to get to know the people before you judge them." In discussing premarital sex, she said, "I guess I'm broad-minded, and I guess the person has to get to know his mate; like my parents lived together for 6 months before they got married. I guess that's not influencing me in any way, but I feel the boy has to get to know the girl better so they know what they're going into before they get married. I think sex is OK if they're serious, but if it's not love, and he's just using her, I guess it's her tough luck. She should know the guy first, know if he's serious. I'm pretty well read up and broad-minded on the way things are now. Before I was the embarrassed type, but as I matured, I experienced things and learned."

The value Mary placed on experience, her recognition throughout of her need to learn more, and her willingness to open herself up to new possibilities after initial hesitancies and somewhat tentative steps forward, lead us to want to rephrase her opening quoted comments— "Generally, I hope I can make it—I *think* I can."

Michael at 18 Years: "I don't know how I'd describe myself. I think I'm pretty agreeable, but when it comes to things I have set ideas, and I can be just as stubborn as the next. I'm contented with what I did, and right now I'm just looking toward the future."

The future for Michael looked promising. He had already been accepted at a small college in the Pacific Northwest, had a scholarship from a local ethnic organization, had chosen his major (languages) and saw his goal in the teaching profession as realistic. He ranked in the top ten of his senior class, felt satisfied with his performance, but was somewhat critical of the educational standards in the school he attended: "They could have been higher. Four years in high school was a waste of time; the work accomplished in four years could have been done in three years."

Life had not always held such promise for him, however. First-born son of a 16-year-old Japanese mother and 19-year-old Pilipino father, whose marriage took place in the last trimester of her pregnancy, Michael was premature (weight, 4 lb. 10 oz.) and spent the first 3 weeks of life in an Army hospital. His hospital record was one of "steady improvement and weight gain." We may speculate that even at this early stage, Michael showed signs of a resiliency that carried him through life. Certainly the conditions surrounding the pregnancy had been less than ideal. His mother, who lived with her mother and grandmother, had not contacted a doctor until her seventh month, at which time her own mother, widowed and working on the plantations, discovered that her daughter was pregnant. At the time of her first medical contact she told the nurse, "I didn't tell my mother for a long time—she was very mad at me and scolded me. At first I was very unhappy and scared, but now I want my baby and I am happy to be pregnant. I'm going to be married and it's OK with him that I'm pregnant." Questioned about something good that might have happened recently, she said, "Getting married will be one happy thing," but her boyfriend's father was "very mad at the way his boys act and doesn't want us to be married." But "I want my baby and I will be fine." A hopeful but unfulfilled prediction. Following delivery and the infant's release from the hospital the mother and child returned to her home on Kauai. The father was sent with the Army to Korea, where he remained for nearly 2 years.

Infant examination at 21 months resulted in a rating of "normal" mental and physical development by the pediatrician. The psychologist found Michael to be an "agreeable, alert, and healthy" child, functioning at a slightly above-average level intellectually and socially. During this period Michael received a great deal of attention from the females in the household—mother, grandmother, and great-grandmother. These women were his constant caretakers. He was considered a cuddly infant, very active, good-natured, and easy to deal with. The visiting nurse viewed the mother, his primary caretaker, as "good-humored, affectionate, indulgent, and child-like." While we cannot help but feel that indeed she *was* a child, the presence of other adults to meet the infant's needs (as well as her own) doubtless helped the situation.

By the time Michael was 10 years old the picture had changed: The family now consisted of Michael, three younger siblings, and his father. His parents had divorced when Michael was 8 years old, and his mother had left the island. She eventually returned, but had no contact with the children. The family lived in the home of the paternal grandparents, but the children did not get along well with them, and their father felt they were too strict and tried to make up for this when with them. The interviewer noted considerable tension in the father, primarily in relation to any discussion of emotional problems. It appeared obvious that there were difficulties between him and his parents, and that the earlier conflicts in his marital situation had produced much stress.

The father felt Michael was lonesome for his mother and noted school problems when she initially left. He said that at 10 years old he seemed to be doing "OK" and seldom talked of her. The father stressed the importance of school work and reading, and supported Michael in these areas by both example and encouragement. Michael was described as "absent-minded, needs to be reminded," but basically his father saw him as a bright and helpful boy. Results of scholastic aptitude and achievement tests placed Michael in the upper quartile, and his reading was consistently above grade level. At age 10 years his PMA IQ was 122, and his perceptual-motor development was age-appropriate.

In reflecting on these years in his 18-year interview, Michael commented about his father, "I think I really respect him and think he's doing a good job. If it wasn't for him, I wouldn't be where I am today. He's pretty understanding and we learned to understand each other . . . I feel very close to him. He influenced me in my studies; my good grades came from him. We were taught we shouldn't do to others what we didn't want done to ourself." He recognized his mother as having been influential earlier. "When she was with us, she taught me a lot, and I had a lot of encouragement. Even before school she helped me with reading and numbers. I thought this was one of the main reasons why I did well in school." Dealing with the present he said, "I didn't see her since she left, and now I've made the decision that I don't want to see her any more. At first I thought this was silly, but now it's a silent thing, *over and done with*." By this time his mother had moved to the mainland U.S. and been twice remarried. Perhaps, like his father earlier, the boy needed to put an emotional as well as a physical distance between himself and his mother.

Michael had found support in his father and the community. Religion was important to him. The family was involved in a fundamentalist faith, and Michael believed he had been helped by his minister at times of stress, although he was not totally committed to the tenets of his church. He tried to live up to his own values, noting that "ever since freshman year I befriended the underdog. It got me into scraps. I felt it was right, so I have no regret about what I did." In relation to his own future, he commented that it was important to "be happy with oneself and what one was doing." Accomplishment was considered important, but not at the expense of satisfaction and happiness in the actual work. And, "I like to make friends with people for what they are, not just what they accomplished."

Michael's own accomplishments were considerable. Scholastic aptitute tests (SCAT) were at the 80th and 90th percentiles in grades 10 and 12, and educational achievement as measured by the STEP placed him in the 90th percentile. His grades were consistently A's and B's. He had been elected to offices in club and student government and held responsible positions on school projects.

On the Nowicki Locus of Control Scale, Michael received one of the most internal scores of his age group. Michael felt strongly that events in his life were largely contingent on his own efforts. On the CPI Michael scored well above the norm in measures of dominance, self-acceptance, communality, and femininity. His scores on measures of tolerance and a sense of well-being were equivalent to the mean for the resilient boys. On the basis of this profile he could be described as confident, persistent, self-assured, dependable, and realistic. He also possessed a strong core of those characteristics often labelled "feminine," aspects of human nature that contribute to the wholeness of the personality—patience, sincerity, helpfulness, and sympathy.

Thus, Michael, with considerable odds against him at birth, and subjected to a series of stressful life events in his early years, had reached the beginning of his adulthood as an individual of accomplishment and varied interests, high self-esteem and sound values, caring for others, and liked by his peers. His achievement motivation was high and his educational and vocational goals were realistic. He seemed invincible, indeed.

Kay was born of 17-year-old, part-Hawaiian, unmarried parents. They both had been asked to leave school because of the pregnancy, and the father was without a job. The young people had been going steady since their very early teens and wanted to get married in spite of her parents' opposition. Kay's mother was sent by the Family Court to a Salvation Army Home in Honolulu to have her baby; placing her for adoption was considered but rejected by the mother ("I'm really happy to be able to keep the baby"), and the parents were eventually married when Kay was 6 months old. She later had two siblings at 5 year intervals.

There were no perinatal complications, delivery was normal and spontaneous, and the infant weighed 7 lb. 13-½ oz. Her health was good during infancy with the exception of periodic bouts of atopic eczema associated with food allergies. She was described as an affectionate infant, easy to deal with, and very active. Interviewer's impressions were of a "healthy, robust, and alert" baby. The mother, who during her pregnancy had said that she did not want to finish school (in spite of teachers encouraging her to become a teacher)—"I'll stay home and care for my baby"—was doing just that. The interviewer rated her as an intelligent, resourceful, responsible, considerate, and self-controlled mother who "takes things in stride."

In her second year of life Kay's temperament and health continued to elicit positive evaluations. The pediatrician considered her physically and mentally normal, with the eczema the only health problem noted. The psychologist found Kay to be an agreeable, relaxed, and physically healthy child, cooperative about most of the tasks presented her and rated her emotional development as normal. At age 19 months, Kay received a mental age of 18 months on the Cattell Infant Intelligence Scale and an age equivalent of 25 months on the Vineland Social Maturity Scale. Her mother at this time was described as kind, temperate, and taking things in her stride.

At age 10 Kay's mother felt that her daughter lacked some self-confidence and was shy. Her teacher, however, observed no behavioral or emotional difficulties in the classroom, found her achievement satisfactory, and her grades average and above. Kay appeared to be achieving at capacity. Her PMA IQ was 96 and her perceptual-motor development (as measured by the Bender-Gestalt Test), appropriate to her age. Mild allergies continued, but her health was generally good.

The caretaking environment, in spite of a low socioeconomic status, was rated average in both educational stimulation and emotional support. The father had been working steadily, and the mother, with the exception of two brief periods of short employment, had carried out her decision to stay home and care for her child.

Mother and child seemed to have a good relationship—"She will sit and talk to me while I'm ironing and tell me what happened in school. She's very dependable and can be trusted with the baby . . . . I tell her that she did very good." The mother felt that the children preferred their father to her. "He plays with them and takes them places. He tells Kay, 'Gee, you've been too good today.' " The home environment was characterized by family cohesiveness and there were no serious conflicts between family members. Other evidence of the positive quality of the youngster's relationship with the parent of the opposite sex was seen.

The quality of this relationship was maintained throughout adolescence. At age 18 Kay was rated by the interviewer as "identifying" with her father, and "identifying strongly" with her mother. She herself said that she got along "fine" with both parents, felt "really close" to her mother and, "If I *had* to choose, the closest would be my mom, but we all get along fine and I'm close to my father, too." She reported similar feelings of closeness with her siblings.

Kay reported that her parents had separated and that she lived with her father. However, the mother often came and stayed with them, and the family participated in activities in various degrees of "togetherness." Kay commented on the separation—"I don't think they would really ever have a divorce. They like each other, but they do separate things and have separate lives."

Her description of both parents was positive and enthusiastic. In relation to her mother, she said, "For her age she's very attractive, a lot of people think she's my sister. She's pretty, tall, and understanding. I get along with her really well and we do a lot of things together. I'd like to be like my mother when I reach that age." And her father? "He's a very social type guy. I'm half like him and half like my mother. They've both influenced us . . . to be really neat, dress neat, eat right, have manners. They taught us good ones." They both stressed that "we work hard in school, and they especially wanted me to graduate since I'm the only daughter, and mother didn't have a chance to graduate. Dad, he always goes along with mother on this."

Apart from her parents' "separation" Kay experienced relatively few stressful life events in her preadolescent and adolescent years. Her health was stable and the earlier allergies were apparently under control. Although her STEP and SCAT scores were at a low average level, her school grades were A's and B's. She had a favorable attitude toward school, was satisfied with her achievement with the exception of one subject ("I'm worried about World History, it's too difficult to understand—lots of students feel the same way, too"), and felt it was "very important" to get good grades. She herself had no plans for education beyond high school as she had already chosen a career in the entertainment field. She had been dancing hula at one of the major hotels for some time and planned to go into this on a full-time basis. She enjoyed her work, wanted to make money, and get married, but then did not see herself working unless the additional income was necessary.

Kay was considered by the interviewer to be a fairly mature youngster whose self-esteem was high. She had a considerable amount of self-insight, clear values and goals, and expressed little in the way of conflict feelings. Her scores on the CPI confirmed the impressions received in the interview. She ranked high in socialization, self-control, good impression, communality, and femininity. She could be described as a serious, industrious, conscientious, and steady youngster, calm and patient, deliberate and thorough in her own work and her expectations of others. She had basic common sense and good judgment and, above all, was poised, sociable, self-assured, but respectful and accepting of others. She was not overly ambitious, but did make good use of the abilities she had. Her self-concept was quite in line with her strengths. As she entered adulthood, she could say, "I can get along well with people. I have enough talent to do things. I want to get married and live happily—and I really feel pretty good."

CHAPTER 14

SUMMING UP

It is man's role
in this evolving universe . . .
to teach the terrors of his nature
and his world to sing . . .

—*LILLIAN SMITH*
The Journey (1954)

Geologists estimate that the main islands at the northwest end of the Hawaiian chain are between 1 to 5 million years old. Molten lava, bubbling out of a rift in the floor of the Pacific, created the island on which our study took place. Its ancient name is "Kauai-a mono-ka-lani po"— "the fountainhead of many waters from on high and bubbling up from below."

While volcanic lava steadily pushed upward to the surface against the weight of the ocean and created the Hawaiian island chain, another event took place halfway around the world. In Ethiopia, East Africa, ten prehuman individuals, among them two young children, died together some 3 million years ago. Speculations about the possible catastrophe that overtook them range from a flash flood to a virulent disease.

Judging from the disposition of their bones, found by the French-American archaeological team of Don Johanson and Maurice Taieb, these individuals had lived together in close proximity to one another. From analysis of their dentition it is apparent that they were related. Lionel Tiger, in his book on *Optimism: The Biology of Hope* (1979), has called them the "first family."

This family, like most of humankind throughout our known existence as nomadic gatherer-hunters, must have had few material possessions. The shift to a more settled agricultural way of life, some 10,000 years ago, and the industrial revolution of the last century, has since brought a measure of affluence to some. Yet even today, more than three-fourths of all the children born on this planet grow up in chronic poverty, and in the rural areas of the developing world some 90% of the women can neither read nor write (Werner, 1979a).

Thus, most human beings throughout most of recorded history were poor and illiterate, exposed to an unending series of natural and manmade disasters. Families who lived after the "first one" survived diseases and droughts, floods and famines, earthquakes and hurricanes. They saw chiefs and landlords, shamans and priests, kings and emperors, presidents and dictators come and go. They escaped the Black Death, the Inquisition, the auction block of slave traders, indentured labor, and, in more recent times, global wars, saturation bombings, the Holocaust and concentration camps. Always some children survived to tell the tale.

The terrors of our nature and the world remind us forever how vulnerable we are. Hence biological and behavioral scientists have spent a great deal of time, energy, and resources exploring the roots of our aggression, alienation, disease, and unease. What is often overlooked, but seems more awesome and miraculous, is our resilience as a species.

Lately we have begun to look for the roots of this resiliency, for the self-righting tendencies within the human organism. This is a report of our journey to a Pacific island in search of the sources of human strength. The answers are tentative, but they invite other journeys to more distant shores.

A BRIEF RÉSUMÉ OF OUR FINDINGS

Our study group consisted of the children and grandchildren of immigrants who left the poverty of their Asian or European homelands to work for the sugar and pineapple plantations on the island of Kauai. Many intermarried with the local Hawaiians, who, oppressed by successive waves of newcomers, lost many lives and most of their land.

The children in our study had few material possessions, and most were raised by mothers who had not graduated from high school and by fathers who were semi- or unskilled laborers. They came of age during two and a half decades of unprecedented social change (1955–1979), which included statehood for Hawaii, the arrival of many newcomers from the U.S. mainland, and a prolonged and ill-fated war in Southeast Asia. During the first decade of their lives the children witnessed the assassination of one U.S. president, and during the second decade, the resignation, in disgrace, of another. In their teens they had access to contraceptive pills and mind-altering drugs, and they saw on television screens the space explorations that put man on the moon and his cameras within the range of other planets. Closer to home, they witnessed the undoing of the delicate balance of the island ecology that had evolved over millions of years by the rapid build-up of the tourist industry.

From an epidemiological point of view, these children were at high risk, since they were born and reared in chronic poverty, exposed to higher than average rates of prematurity and perinatal stress, and reared by mothers with little formal education. A combination of such social and biological variables correctly identified the majority of youth in this birth cohort who developed serious learning and behavior problems in childhood or adolescence.

Yet those in our index group (approximately one of ten in the cohort) managed to develop into competent and autonomous young adults who "worked well, played well, loved well, and expected well."

We contrasted their behavior characteristics and the features of their caregiving environment, from the perinatal period to the threshold of adulthood, with other high-risk children of the same age and sex who developed serious coping problems in the first and in the second decades of life.

SEX DIFFERENCES IN VULNERABILITY AND RESILIENCY

At birth, and throughout the first decade of life, more boys than girls were exposed to serious physical defects or illness requiring medical care, and more boys than girls had learning and behavior problems in the classroom and at home.

The physical immaturity of the boys, the more stringent expectations for male sex-role behavior in childhood, and the predominant feminine environment to which the boys were exposed, appeared to contribute both separately and in concert to a higher proportion of disordered behavior in childhood among the males than the females.

Trends were reversed in the second decade of life: The total number of boys with serious learning problems dropped, while the number of girls with serious behavior disorders rose. Boys seemed now more prepared for the demands of school and work, although they were still more often involved in antisocial and delinquent behavior. Girls were now confronted with social pressures and sex-role expectations that produced a higher rate of mental health problems in late adolescence and serious coping problems associated with teenage pregnancies and marriages.

While control of aggression appeared to be one of the major problems for the boys in childhood, dependency became a major problem for the girls in adolescence. For each sex, traditional sex-role expectations set limits to their behavior—limits on the expressive roles played by the boys, limits on the instrumental roles played by the girls.

Related to this trend was the cumulative number of stressful life events reported by each sex. Boys with serious coping problems experienced more adversities than girls in *childhood*; girls with serious coping problems reported more stressful life events in *adolescence*. In spite of the biological and social pressures, which in this culture appear to make each sex more vulnerable at different times, more high-risk girls than high-risk boys grew into resilient young adults.

COPING PATTERNS AND SOURCES OF SUPPORT AMONG RESILIENT CHILDREN AND YOUTH

The resilient high-risk boys and girls had few serious illnesses in the first two decades of life and tended to recuperate quickly. Their mothers perceived them to be "very active" and "socially responsive" when they were infants, and independent observers noted their pronounced autonomy and positive social orientation when they were toddlers. Developmental examinations in the second year of life showed advanced self-help skills and adequate sensorimotor and language development for most of these children. In middle childhood the resilient boys and girls possessed adequate problem-solving and communication skills, and their perceptual-motor development was age-appropriate. Throughout childhood and adolescence they displayed both "masculine" and "feminine" interests and skills.

In late adolescence the resilient youth had a more internal locus of control, a more positive self-concept, and a more nurturant, responsible, and achievement-oriented attitude toward life than peers who had developed serious coping problems. Their activities and interests were less sex-typed as well. At the threshold of adulthood, the resilient men and women had developed a sense of coherence in their lives and were able to draw on a number of informal sources of support. They also expressed a great desire to "improve themselves," i.e., toward continued psychological growth.

Among key factors in the caregiving environment that appeared to contribute to the resiliency and stress resistance of these high-risk children were: the age of the opposite-sex parent (younger mothers for resilient males, older fathers for resilient females); the number of children in the family (four or fewer); the spacing between the index child and the next-born sibling (more than 2 years); the number and type of alternate caretakers available to the mother within the household (father, grandparents, older siblings); the workload of the mother (including steady employment outside the household); the amount of attention given to the child by the primary caretaker(s) in infancy; the availability of a sibling as caretaker or confidant in childhood; structure and rules in the household in adolescence; the cohesiveness of the family; the presence of an informal multigenerational network of kin and friends in adolescence; and the cumulative number of chronic stressful life events experienced in childhood and adolescence.

THE NEED FOR A CROSS-CULTURAL PERSPECTIVE

As we pieced together the evidence from this longitudinal study of Asian and Polynesian children and compared it with findings of investigations of black and white youth in the U.S. and Europe, we recognized that the search for "resilience" requires a perspective that cuts across space and time. Singly, or in concert, similar factors seemed to be at work in longitudinal studies of children who came from different socioeconomic and ethnic backgrounds, who lived in urban, suburban, or rural areas in the U.S.A. and in Europe, and at different points in time.

The life stories of the "invulnerable" offspring of psychotic parents in our own and other studies and the biographies of the gifted told similar tales, and so have the poetry and prose of writers who surmounted grinding poverty, prejudice, and political persecution in their childhood and youth. All give us a glimpse of the universality of the enduring forces that allow the human species to overcome adversity.

The resilient children shared some enduring social bonds with our distant ancestors as well. These characteristics appear deeply rooted in man's "environment of evolutionary adaptedness" (Bowlby, 1968). They can be found among surviving societies of hunter-gatherers, such as the Kung San of the Kalahari Desert (Konner, 1977b), as well as among the families of the resilient boys and girls on Kauai.

These families were poor by material standards, but a characteristically strong bond was forged between the infant and the primary caretaker during the first year of life. The physical robustness of the resilient children, their high activity level, and their social responsiveness were recognized by the caregivers and elicited a great deal of attention. There was little prolonged separation of the infants from their mothers and no prolonged bond disruption during the first year of life. The strong attachment that resulted appears to have been a secure base for the development of the advanced self-help skills and autonomy noted among these children in their second year of life.

Though many of their mothers worked for extended periods and were major contributors to family subsistence, the children had support from alternate caretakers, such as grandmothers or older sisters, to whom they became attached.

Many resilient children grew up in multiage households that included members of the grandparent generation. As older siblings departed from the household, the resilient girls took responsibility for the care of younger siblings. The employment of their mothers and the need for sibling caretaking seems to have contributed to a greater autonomy and sense of responsibility in the resilient girls, especially in households where the father was dead or otherwise permanently absent. Their competence was enhanced by a strong bond between the daughter and the other females in the family—sometimes across three generations (mother, grandmother, older sisters, or aunts).

Resilient boys, in turn, were often first-born sons, lived in smaller families, and did not have to share their parents' attention with many additional children during the first decade of life. There were some males in their family who could serve as models for identification (fathers, older brothers, or uncles). There was structure and rules in the household, but space to explore in and less physical crowding. Last, but not least, there was an informal, multiage network of kin, peers, and elders who shared similar values and beliefs, and from whom the resilient youth sought counsel and support in times of crises and major role transitions.

These strong social bonds were absent among families whose children had difficulties coping under duress. The lack of this emotional support was most devastating to children with a constitutional tendency toward withdrawal and passivity, with low activity levels, irregular sleeping and feeding habits, and a genetic background (i.e., parental psychoses, especially maternal schizophrenia) that made them more vulnerable to the influences of an adverse environment.

Most of these infants were perceived as retiring, passive, placid, or inactive in infancy by their mothers, and some had feeding and sleeping habits or a temper distressing to their primary caretaker. They experienced more prolonged bond disruptions during the first year of life. Mothers in these families worked sporadically outside the household, but there were few alternative caregivers in the home, such as fathers, grandparents, or older siblings. This lack of dependable substitute care appears to have been especially hard on the boys.

During childhood and adolescence, these youngsters were sick more often, more seriously, and more repeatedly than the resilient children, and they moved and changed schools more often as well. During the same period, they were exposed to more family discord and paternal absence (which took a greater toll among the boys), and to episodes of maternal mental illness (which took a greater toll among the girls).

By age 18 most of these youth had an external locus-of-control orientation and a low estimate of themselves. They felt that events happened to them as a result of luck, fate, or other factors beyond their control. Professional assistance sought from community agencies was considered of "little help" to them.

Seligman (1975), an experimental psychologist speaking from the framework of learning theory, has attempted to diagnose what troubles these youngsters most. "Learned helplessness," he writes, "produces a cognitive set in which people believe that success and failure is independent of their own skilled actions" (p. 38). Crucial for these children was not failure *per se,* but a lack of control over reinforcement, an absence of synchrony between their actions and feedback from their environment. On the contrary, the experience of the resilient children in coping with and mastering stressful life events by their actions, appeared to build immunity against "learned helplessness," and an attitude of "hopefulness" instead—even in the midst of material poverty.

THE NEED FOR A TRANSACTIONAL MODEL OF HUMAN DEVELOPMENT

There is a great deal of concern today with the growing number of powerful and impersonal forces that affect our lives but that are beyond our control.

Bronfenbrenner (1979) has offered a provocative analysis of the interconnections between the microsystem of the immediate setting we live in and the meso-, exo-, and macro-systems that link us to the overarching patterns of organizations and to the ideologies of social institution so prevalent in the modern bureaucratic nation-state. The adult-centered assumption is that these wider socioeconomic, political, and ideological forces, in which the family is embedded, cause parents to act in certain ways toward their children (Tiger, 1979). The efficacy of children is often ignored in the study of such systems.

Bell and Harper (1977) have summarized a great deal of evidence that illustrates the powerful effect of the child on his or her caregivers and culture. Our longitudinal data indicate that constitutional and environmental influences not only interacted, but that their relative impact changed from infancy through childhood to late adolescence and young adulthood.

To the extent that children were able to elicit predominantly positive responses from their environment, they were found to be stress-resistant or "resilient," even when growing up in chronic poverty or in a family with a psychotic parent. To the extent that children elicited negative responses from their environment, they were found to be "vulnerable" even in the absence of biological stress or financial constraints.

The model of psychosocial development proposed by the Australian psychologist Eleanor Wertheim (1978) seems to be especially relevant. Wertheim's model attempts a synthesis of Piagetian concepts and principles of system analysis that takes into account not only a situational time scale, but an ontogenetic and phylogenetic time scale as well. This makes it especially useful for longitudinal and cross-cultural studies.

Wertheim's concern is the development of two parallel but interdependent qualities that we have seen at work in the resilient children in our study: autonomy and competence. The psychosocial development of an individual is perceived as an ongoing process of "doing" and "undergoing," beginning in the intrauterine experience and continuing throughout life. Optimal adaptive development is characterized by a balance between the power of the person and the power of the social and physical environment, a balance that may shift from one developmental stage to another, as we saw in the relative weight pulled by constitutional, ecological, and interpersonal variables in the lives of the resilient children in infancy, childhood, and adolescence.

Wertheim recognizes the need to broaden the study of the development of human "vulnerability" and "invulnerability." She is aware of the power of the early mother-infant bond, especially in the first year of life, but urges consideration of relationships with other members of the family and social systems in which the individual grows up.

We have glimpsed in our own data the impact of those relationships. They extend beyond the transactions between mother and child to relationships with the father, with older and younger siblings, with grandparents, friends and neighbors, and to other formal or informal "systems of support."

To prevent children from succumbing to their vulnerability, Wertheim argues, we must discover the biosocial laws that govern these processes of doing and undergoing. At the same time, we need to evaluate the outcome within the context of what is appropriate for a given age, sex, or culture.

In all cultures, however, there appear to be formal species-specific limits to child-caregiver transactions that are adaptive and whose transgression means trouble. The increasing time-lag between the phylogenetic and the modern ontogenetic time scales, and between the ontogenetic and situational time scales in Western societies, Wertheim warns, may contribute to greater developmental vulnerability.

Just as Western ecology, nutrition, and "way of life" have now stretched man's biological ability to cope and can be linked to specific diseases (e.g., cardiovascular disturbances and cancer), modern "engineering" of the human infant's birth and of his early transactions with his caregivers may have reached similar limits. Societies that undergo rapid social change, as does most of the developing world today, cannot afford to neglect these social bonds in a single-minded pursuit of technological or economic "progress" or environmental "control," without risking maladaptive anomalies of development in caregivers and children that are inimical to the survival of that society or culture.

IMPLICATIONS

What, then, are some of the implications of our still tentative findings? Repeatedly, we have been conscious that the life stories of these children could tempt us into an attitude of "return to nature" à la Rousseau or to a social policy of "benign neglect."

"Don't meddle too much in nature's design" may be a homespun and Taoist philosophy, but as we watched these children grow from babyhood to adulthood, we could not help but respect the self-righting tendencies *within them* that produced normal development under all but the most persistently adverse circumstances.

Maybe cooperation with nature's design, rather than wholesale intervention and control, would be the wisest policy in the face of our present ignorance about the long-term effects of many of our ambitio social policies and programs, and a humble recognition that some 3 million years of evolution have shaped our social behavior and set some constraints.

At present we need to know more about a wide array of what Antonovsky (1979) has called "generalized resistance resources," which seem to be as important as sources of strength for the survivors of concentration camps (whom he studied in Israel) as for the making of resiliency in children. Among them are: adaptability on the biological, psychological, social, and cultural levels; profound ties to concrete, immediate others; and formal or informal ties between the individual and the community.

We need to identify more systematically the positive effect of these variables in contributing to "resiliency" and "invulnerability"; provide some additional support to vulnerable individuals where these resources are lacking; and also recognize that sometimes social policies and programs create unintended consequences. In the name of "service," they separate fathers from their families in welfare programs and separate the old from the young in housing and neighbors from each other in "redevelopment" programs—breaking instead of strengthening social ties that enable us to hold up under duress.

We need to examine more systematically the consequences of sibling caretaking, which is prevalent around the world and even in our own country once we move beyond the study of small, nuclear, middle-class families. We know from cross-cultural studies (Weisner & Gallimore, 1977; Werner, 1979a) that child caretaking appears to be an important antecedent to nurturant and responsible behavior that leads to strong affective bonds. The Whitings (1975) argue that whether a child is told to take care of younger siblings or is sent to school instead, may have a more profound effect upon the profile of the child's social behavior than the manipulation of reinforcement schedules by his or her parents. Thus, major attention needs to be paid in future studies to the role of child caretakers as resilient models, as transmitters of new social values; and as links between the family and the rapidly changing outside world.

We need to take a look at the role of grandparents as "resistance resources," as sources of support for hundreds of thousands of children in our country who grow up in homes that are poor and "broken." We have some hints now from our own study and those of black children in urban ghettos that grandparents can provide continuity and support in an otherwise unstable situation and can buffer the effects of family strife and the dissolution of marital ties.

Some examples of the roles and influence of grandmothers as an-
cillary caretakers are available from cross-cultural studies (Werner,
1979a). A grandmother who is titular head of a household is likely to
function as a disciplinarian, whereas one with less status is more likely
to function in a nurturant, caretaking role. Cross-cultural studies indicate that grandparents tend to enjoy warm relationships with their
grandchildren, especially when they do not have the major responsibility for supervision and discipline.

We need to know more about the roles of other alternate caregivers in and outside the home, whether they be uncles, aunts, cousins,
"live-in" roommates, or members of communal living arrangements.
Cross-cultural studies and studies of child abuse have made us aware
that the effect of multiple caretakers on child behavior depends on the
ratio of adults to children. Regardless of culture and social class stand-
ing, a mother's emotional stability and warmth toward her children is
greater when there are more adults around to help and when she has
fewer of her own children to handle.

We need to examine more closely the implications of studies of
family size and birth order and what they can tell us about the contribution of these demographic variables to competence and resilience in
children. More than a decade ago the Coleman Report (1968) indicated
that the best predictor of success in the school system was not whether
one was white or black, rich or poor, but whether one was from a small
family. More recently, White et al. (1979) reported from the Harvard
Preschool Project that first-born children invariably developed more
competence than later-born offspring. We find in our own study of
Asian and Polynesian children that family size and birth order also appear related to the making of "resilience." Families with four children
or fewer were able to provide more attention to the growing boy or girl
during the first decade of their life than larger families. More first-born
sons in these families held up well under duress, as did more first- and
second-born daughters.

We need to examine more closely the effect of parental age, of
both the mother and the father, on their sons and daughters. In our
study, the age of the opposite-sex parent (younger mothers for males;
older fathers for females) consistently discriminated between resilient
children and peers with serious coping problems at 10 and 18, even
after the effects of birth order were partialled out. These findings need
replication or refutation. It made sense in the past that younger
mothers and older fathers might produce children who were biologi-
cally less vulnerable and who would grow up in a home where the

father was settled enough to provide a stable income. Does it "make sense" now, when the post–World War II "babies" are marrying spouses who are closer to them in age than any preceding generation in U.S. history and who are having their babies at later ages?

The women in this study are marrying younger men, who are psychologically and economically less prepared to deal with their adult lives, and they themselves reached sexual maturity (menarche) earlier than previous generations. Yet control of their reproductive processes is now more exclusively in their hands, thanks to contraceptive pills and liberalized abortion laws.

Do these trends relate to the greater dominance and autonomy noted among the females of this generation? How lasting will these trends be? How will they affect their sons and daughters? Will these women and their mates provide a different, perhaps more androgynous model of "competence" for their offspring that includes "being" as well as "doing," nurturance as well as risk-taking, for both sons and daughters?

We do not know, but we do find it surprising that so little attention has been paid in child-development research to such a basic demographic phenomenon as age differences between spouses and their social implications.

There is need to explore the impact of other role models outside the family circle. The three most frequently encountered in this study come to mind: the teacher, not just as a provider of skills essential for survival in a technological society, but as a confidant, counselor, and resilient role model; the minister or pastoral counselor; and the "good neighbor."

Support from an informal network of kin and neighbors and the advice of ministers and teachers were more often sought and more highly valued than the services of mental health professionals among the people of Kauai. The families of these children preferred personal rather than impersonal, bureaucratic relationships in times of stress, as do other minority cultures in the U.S. and the majority of people in the non-Western world.

In many situations, it may make better sense to strengthen available informal ties to kin and community than to introduce additional layers of bureaucracy into the delivery of social services, and it might be less costly as well.

During the early grades and especially during adolescence, there is need to explore the support that could be provided by peer counselors, by the growing reservoir of retired persons, by foster grandparents, by older children tutoring younger ones, or by teenagers assisting in running daycare centers and recreational facilities for children of working mothers.

There is also a need to tie the ministry and pastoral counseling to the work of other helping agencies. In many rural communities here and abroad, priests and ministers of all faiths are still among the most important links between the family and the community at large.

A strengthening of already existing informal support systems could focus especially on those children and families in a community who appear most vulnerable because they lack—temporarily or permanently—some of the essential social bonds that appear to buffer stress: working mothers of young children with no provisions for stable childcare; single, divorced, or teenage parents with no other adult in the household; hospitalized children and premature babies in need of special care who are separated from their families for extended periods of time; children of psychotic parents (and the "well" spouse in such a marriage); migrant and refugee children without access to regular schooling or roots in a permanent community; and, at the other end of the spectrum, old people living alone, separated from their children and grandchildren, especially in the large metropolitan areas of our country.

The central component of effective coping with the multiplicity of inevitable life stresses appears to be a sense of coherence (Antonovsky, 1979), a feeling of confidence that one's internal and external environment is predictable and that things will probably work out as well as can be reasonably expected. The real issue may well be whether the families and societies in which children grow up and live their daily lives facilitate or impede the development and maintenance of such a sense. Some unpredictable experiences that call forth unknown and unused resources may be essential for a strong sense of coherence.

A young child maintains a relatively small number of relationships that give feedback and shape a sense of coherence. We have seen that even under adverse circumstances, change is possible if the older child or adolescent encounters new experiences and people who give meaning to one's life, and a reason for commitment and caring.

The resilient children and youth in our study had such a sense of coherence, and some of their troubled peers may yet develop one. We cannot foretell how this generation will fare in the future, in the year

2000, when they enter a new millennium in middle age. But we are hopeful, having witnessed both their vulnerability and their invincibility when they were young. Hopeful that they will keep their roots in the island, with their families, within themselves.

> *"All living growth is pliant . . .*
> *and men who stay gentle are kin of life."*
> —*Lao Tzu (circa 604 B.C.)*
>   *Tao, The Way of Life*

APPENDIX

Data Base, Resiliency Study: 1955 birth cohort, Kauai (1955–1979)

Variables	Source
DEMOGRAPHIC CHARACTERISTICS	
Age of parents	Birth records
Educational level of parents	School records
Record of parental mental health problems	Study files and Mental Health Register, State of Hawaii
Socioeconomic status at birth, age 2, and age 10	Parental occupation, plantation pay scale
Number of persons in household by age 10	Home interviews by social and public health workers
Number of adults besides parents by age 10	
Number of children by age 10	
AT BIRTH	
Pre-perinatal stress score	Evaluation by pediatrician on basis of recorded events during prenatal, labor, delivery, and neonatal periods
1 YEAR	
Stressful life events	Social service records Postpartum interview
Mother's coping skills (adjective checklist)	1-year home interview by public health nurse
Mother's perception of infant's temperamental characteristics (activity level, responsiveness, nervous habits, temper, distressing habits)	Mother's assessment during 1-year home visit
20 MONTHS	
Cattell IQ	Developmental examinations by psychologists
Vineland SQ	Developmental examinations by psychologists

Data Base, Resiliency Study: 1955 birth cohort, Kauai (1955–1979) (*Continued*)

Variables	*Source*
Examiner's assessment of toddler's behavior patterns (adjective checklist)	Developmental examinations by psychologists
Examiner's assessment of quality of parent-child interaction (adjective checklist)	Developmental examinations by psychologists
Examiner's rating of toddler's psychological status	Developmental examinations by psychologists
Physical status of child	Pediatrician's rating
Stressful life events between birth and age 2	Interview with primary caretaker Social service records

2–10 YEARS

Medical problems and acquired physical handicaps	Public health, M.D.'s, and hospital records
Readiness and achievement test results Grades	School records (K–grade 5)
Behavior problems	School records (K–grade 5) Mental health service records Parent checklist
Stressful life events	Social service records 10-year home interview
Rating of educational stimulation provided by the home	Ratings made by clinical psychologist
Rating of emotional support in the home	Ratings made by clinical psychologist

10 YEARS

PMA IQ and factor scores (R,V,S,P,N)	Group tests
Bender-Gestalt error scores	Group tests
Classroom behavior	Teacher checklist

Variables	*Source*
Needs assessment: long-term remedial education, special class placement, long-term mental health care, and medical care	Panel consisting of pediatrician, psychologist and public health nurse (including diagnostic exams)

10–18 YEARS

Repeated or serious delinquency	Records of police and family court
Teenage pregnancy or abortion	Hospital records
Mental health problems	Mental health service records
SCAT (verbal, quantitative, total) scores	School records (grades 8–10, 12)
STEP (reading, writing, mathematics) scores	School records (grades 8–10, 12)
Stressful life events	Biographical questionnaire Social service records

18 YEARS

CPI dimensions	Group tests
Locus of Control (Nowicki)	Group tests
Interview ratings	Individual interview with youth

18–24 YEARS

Mental health problems	Mental Health Register, State of Hawaii (1972–1979)

Summary of Scoring System for Prenatal-Perinatal
Complications: Kauai Longitudinal Study

Mild (Score 1)	*Moderate* (Score 2)	*Severe* (Score 3)
mild: pre-eclampsia, essential hypertension, renal insufficiency or anemia; controlled diabetes or hypothyroidism; positive Wasserman and no treatment; acute genito-urinary infection 3rd trimester; untreated pelvic tumor producing dystocia; treated asthma	marked: pre-eclampsia, essential hypertension, renal insufficiency or anemia; diabetes under poor control; decompensated cardiovascular disease requiring treatment; untreated thyroid dysfunction; confirmed rubella 1st trimester; nonobstetrical surgery: general anesthesia, abdominal incision or hypotension	eclampsia; renal or diabetic coma; treated pelvic tumor
2nd or 3rd trimester vaginal bleeding; placental infarct; marginal placenta previa; premature rupture of membranes; amnionitis; abnormal fetal heart rate; meconium stained amniotic fluid (excl. breech); confirmed polyhydramnios	vaginal bleeding with cramping; central placenta previa; partial placenta abruptio; placental or cord anomalies	complete placenta abruptio; congenital syphilis of the newborn
rapid, forceful or prolonged unproductive labor; frank breech or persistent occiput posterior; twins; elective Cesarean section; low forceps	chin, face, brow, or footling presentation; emergency Cesarean section; manual or forceps rotation, mid forceps or high forceps or breech and oxygen	transverse lie; emergency Cesarean section; manual rotation, mid forceps or high forceps or breech extraction and oxygen administered 5 minutes or more

Mild (Score 1)	*Moderate* (Score 2)	*Severe* (Score 3)
with complications; cord prolapsed or twisted and oxygen administered to newborn	administered under 5 minutes	
breathing delayed 1–3 minutes; intermittent central cyanosis and oxygen administered less than 1 minute; cry weak or abnormal; bradycardia	breathing delayed 3–5 minutes; gasping; intermittent central cyanosis and oxygen administered more than 1 minute; cry delayed 5–15 minutes	breathing delayed 5 minutes or more; no respiratory effort; persistent cyanosis and oxygen administered continuously; cry delayed 15 minutes or more
birth injury excl. central nervous system; jaundice; hemorrhagic disease mild; pneumonia, rate of respiration less than 40 and oxygen administered intermittently; birthweight 1800–2500 gm and oxygen administered intermittently or incubator or other special care; oral antibiotic to newborn; abnormal tone or Moro reflex; irritability	major birth injury and temporary central nervous system involvement; spasms; pneumonia, rate of respiration more than 40 and oxygen administered intermittently; apnea and oxygen administered intermittently or resuscitation less than 5 minutes; birthweight 1800–2500 gm, fair suck and oxygen administered or incubator; antibiotics administered intravenously; cry absent	major birth injury and persistent central nervous system involvement; exchange transfusion; seizure; hyaline membrane disease; pneumonia, rate of respiration more than 60 and oxygen administered continuously, resuscitation more than 5 minutes; birthweight less than 1800 gm and oxygen administered or special feeding; meningitis; absent Moro reflex

Table A-1: Social class distribution of identified problems at age 10 and age 18 by sex (1955 birth cohort: Kauai Longitudinal Study)

Males

| | At Age 10 | | | | At Age 18 | |
	LR Ed. (N:54) %	LD (N:14) %	MR (N:13) %	LMH (N:14) %	Delinquent M (N:107) %	M with Mental Health problems (N:22) %
SES						
Upper (1,2)	1.8	8.3	—	—	7.4	4.5
Middle (3)	27.8	8.3	—	21.4	36.4	18.2
Lower (4,5)	70.4	83.4	100.0	78.6	56.2	77.3

Females

| | At Age 10 | | | | At Age 18 | | |
	LR Ed. (N:33) %	LD (N:9) %	MR (N:9) %	LMH (N:11) %	Delinquent F (N:57) %	F with Mental Health problems (N:47) %	F with teen-age pregnancy and other problems (N:25) %
SES							
Upper (1,2)	3.0	—	11.0	—	5.2	2.1	
Middle (3)	21.2	22.2	22.0	—	24.6	14.9	24.0
Lower (4,5)	75.8	77.8	67.0	100.0	70.2	83.0	76.0

LR Ed.: In need of long-term remedial education (>6 months)
LD : In need of placement in learning disability class
MR : In need of placement in special class for the mentally retarded (EMR)
LMH : In need of long-term mental health care (>6 months)

Table A-2: Multiple Correlation Coefficient and Best Single
Predictors or Problems (Kauai Longitudinal Study)

Predictors	Males (N=320)	Females (N=313)
CRITERIA AT AGE 2		
Cattell IQ below 80		
Multiple R	R =.55	R =.59
Congenital defects	r =.43	r =.45
Below normal physical development		
Multiple R	R =.47	R =.37
Congenital defects	r =.26	
Perinatal stress		r =.21
CRITERIA AT AGE 10		
Mental retardation		
Multiple R	R =.57	R =.66
Cattell IQ at 2	r =.46	r =.52
Learning disability		
Multiple R	R =.27	R =.49
Baby's activity level	r =.15	
Cattell IQ		r =.35
Need for long-term mental health care		
Multiple R	R =.36	R =.37
SES at 2	r =.18	
Standard of living at birth		r =.18
CRITERIA AT AGE 18		
Serious mental health problems in adolescence		
2-Year Predictors		
Multiple R	R =.35	R =.37
Standard of living at birth	r =.21	
SES at 2		r =.31
10-Year Predictors		
Multiple R	R =.88	R =.76
Need for long-term mental health care at 10	r =.65	
Learning disability at 10		r =.37
DELINQUENCY IN ADOLESCENCE		
2-Year Predictors		
Multiple R	R =.32	R =.44
Family instability at 2	r =.19	
Cattell IQ at 2		r =.38
10-Year Predictors		
Multiple R	R =.46	R =.74
Primary Abilities Test IQ	r =.24	
Need for long-term mental health care at 10		r =.30

Table A-3: Parental ages at birth of index child by sex (Resiliency Study: 1955 birth cohort, Kauai)

Variables	Females			Males		
	High Risk Resilient F (N:42) %	High Risk F Problems at 10 (N:39) %	High Risk F Problems at 18 (N:43) %	High Risk Resilient M (N:30) %	High Risk M Problems at 10 (N:51) %	High Risk M Problems at 18 (N:49) %
Mother's age at birth of child						
below 20	23.8	15.4	20.9	26.7	7.8	4.1
20–29	50.0	59.0	55.8	40.0	64.7	65.3
30–39	23.8	25.6	23.3	30.0	25.5	30.6
40 and above	2.4	0	0	3.3	2.0	0
Father's age at birth of child						
below 20	5.4	0	4.9	3.4	2.0	0
20–29	24.3	48.6	56.1	41.4	44.9	31.3
30–39	35.1	40.5	29.3	34.5	28.6	56.3
40 and above	35.1	10.0	9.8	20.7	24.5	12.5

Table A-4: Variables that differentiated between high risk
resilient children and peers with serious coping problems
at 10 during first decade of life

Variable	Females			Males		
	Chi square	df	p	Chi square	df	p
BIRTH–YEAR 1						
Age of mother				6.88	3	<.10
Age of father	9.91	3	<.01			
Congenital defect	8.69	1	<.01			
Birth order (first vs. later born)				6.30	1	<.01
Attention given to infant in year 1	2.89	1	<.10			
Mother's perspective of infant (year 1) as "cuddly, affectionate"	2.73	1	<.10			
" as "good-natured, easy to deal with"				3.12	1	<.10
" as "very active"				6.35	1	<.01
20 MONTHS	t		p	t		p
Mother-child interactions during developmental exam						
% positive	2.92		<.01			
% negative	−3.27		<.01			
Examiner's observations of child's behavior during exam						
% positive interactions				2.50		<.01
% negative interactions	−2.18		<.05	−2.59		<.01
Social Orientation						
% positive	3.18		<.01	2.18		<.05
% negative	−2.33		<.05			
Autonomy						
% positive				2.07		<.05
% negative	−2.19		<.01			
Cattell IQ	3.09		<.01	3.11		<.01
Vineland SQ	2.24		<.05	2.15		<.05
	Chi square	df	p			
Psychological Status Rating	5.05	1	<.05			
10 YEARS						
Rating of emotional support provided by family	8.24	1	<.01			
	t		p	t		p
PMA IQ	8.23		<.001	6.82		<.001
PMA Verbal Comprehension Factor	6.61		<.001	5.72		<.001

Table A-4 (*Continued*)

Variable	Females		Males	
	t	*p*	*t*	*p*
PMA Reasoning Factor	6.79	<.001	5.19	<.001
Bender-Gestalt Error Score	−3.16	< 001	−3.52	<.001
N of children in household			−1.66	<.10
N of persons in household			−2.04	<.05

STRESSFUL LIFE EVENTS IN FIRST DECADE	*Chi square*	*df*	*p*
Father absent since before birth of child	6.02	1	<.01
Prolonged separation from mother during year 1	4.21	1	<.05
Parental mental health problems during first two years of child's life	3.36	1	<.10
Conflict between parents during first two years of child's life	3.21	1	<.10
Repeated or serious illnesses or accidents during first two years of child's life	4.07	1	<.05
Father permanently absent during early and middle childhood	3.62	1	<.05
Older sib died while child was between 2 and 10 years old	4.53	1	<.05
Older sib left home when child was between 2 and 10 years old	4.74	1	<.05

Table A-5: Variables that differentiated between high risk resilient children and peers with serious coping problems in childhood during first decade of life

Variable	Females			Males		
BIRTH–YEAR 1	*Chi square*	*df*	*p*	*Chi square*	*df*	*p*
Age of mother				11.27	3	<.01
Age of father	10.75	3	<.01			
Congenital defect	12.34	1	<.001			
Birth order (first vs. later born)				8.71	1	<.01
20 MONTHS	*t*		*p*			
Mother-child interactions during developmental exam						
% positive	2.72		<.01			
% negative	−2.89		<.01			
Examiner's observations of child's behavior during exam						
% negative	−2.12		<.05	−2.56		<.01
Social Orientation						
% positive	2.20		<.05			
% negative				−1.91		<.05
Autonomy						
% negative	−2.39		<.05	−1.92		<.05
10 YEARS	*Chi square*	*df*	*p*			
Rating of emotional support provided by family	8.74	1	<.01			
	t		*p*	*t*		*p*
PMA IQ	5.96		<.001	4.16		<.001
PMA Verbal Comprehensive Factor	4.96		<.001	3.98		<.001
PMA Reasoning Factor	5.16		<.001	3.01		<.005
Bender-Gestalt Error Score	−2.19		<.05	−2.53		<.01
N of children in household				−2.71		<.01
N of persons in household				−3.22		<.01
STRESSFUL LIFE EVENTS IN FIRST DECADE	*Chi square*	*df*	*p*	*Chi square*	*df*	*p*
Repeated or serious illnesses of child in infancy (birth–2)	3.50	1	<.10			
Maternal mental health problems necessitating prolonged absence of mother (birth–2)	3.11	1	<.10			

Table A-5 (*Continued*)

Variable	Females			Males		
	Chi square	*df*	*p*	*Chi square*	*df*	*p*
Permanent father absence (since birth of child)	3.90	1	<.05			
Temporary father absence (between 2–10)				3.98	1	<.05
Chronic family discord (between 2–10)				4.05	1	<.05
				t		*p*
Cumulative number of stressful life events (birth–10)				−2.16		<.05

Table A-6: Variables that differentiated between high risk resilient youth and peers with serious coping problems at 18 during second decade of life

Variable	*Females*		*Males*	
GRADES 8 – 10	*t*	*p*	*t*	*p*
SCAT Total Score	6.39	<.001	3.68	<.001
STEP Reading	5.26	<.001	2.58	<.01
Writing	3.92	<.001	2.62	<.01
GRADE 12				
SCAT Total Score	4.98	<.001	3.00	<.005
STEP Reading	4.23	<.001	3.85	<.001
Writing	5.01	<.001	3.98	<.001
CPI SUBSCALES				
Responsibility	3.61	<.001	2.52	<.01
Socialization	5.11	<.001	2.76	<.01
Communality	4.68	<.001	3.83	<.001
Achievement via Conformance	3.95	<.001	2.40	<.02
Femininity	1.97	<.05	2.31	<.05
Dominance	2.32	<.05		
Capacity for Status	2.29	<.05		
Sociability	2.68	<.01		
Sense of well-being	2.72	<.01		
Achievement via independence	2.93	<.01		
Intellectual efficiency	3.95	<.001		
NOWICKI LOCUS OF CONTROL SCALE	−2.84	<.01		

	Chi square	*df*	*p*	*Chi square*	*df*	*p*
18-YEAR INTERVIEW						
Structure and rules in family	3.52	1	<.10	5.41	1	<.05
Self-esteem	8.36	2	<.01	8.33	2	<.01
Attitude toward school	9.32	1	<.01			
Achievement motivation	6.00	1	<.01			
Participation in school activities	7.84	2	<.01			
Realism of plans beyond high school	8.38	1	<.01			
Social life	13.69	2	<.001			
Family as a whole talks together about problems	6.57	2	<.05			
Mother's understanding	4.76	1	<.05			
Father's support	2.60	1	<.10			
Identification with father				4.09	1	<.05
Sources of support				9.78	2	<.01

Table A-6 (*Continued*)

Variable	Females			Males		
STRESSFUL LIFE EVENTS DURING SECOND DECADE						
Maternal mental health problems during S's adolescence	4.32	1	<.05	3.80	1	<.05
Problems in relationship with father	14.09	1	<.001	3.89	1	<.05
Family discord	22.76	1	<.001			
Teenage pregnancy	12.64	1	<.001			
Financial problems	10.67	1	<.001			
Problems in relationship with mother	9.00	1	<.01			
Serious or repeated illnesses or accidents	7.75	1	<.01			
Permanent absence of mother	4.81	1	<.05			
Temporary absence of father	4.30	1	<.05			
	t		p	t		p
Cumulative N of stressful life events between 10–18	−7.06		<.001	−4.55		<.001

Table A-7: Variables that differentiated between high-risk youth whose status improved between 10 and 18 and peers with serious coping problems at 18

Variable	Females			Males		
	Chi square	df	p	Chi square	df	p
Father's age at birth of child	15.20	6	<.02	15.48	6	<.02
Mother's perspective of infant as "good-natured, easy to deal with"				4.16	1	<.05
	t		p	t		p
N of children in household by age 10	−2.32		<.05	−2.32		<.05
	Chi square	df	p	Chi square	df	p
Family discord between 10–18	12.74	1	<.001	4.35	1	<.05
Problems in relationship with father between 10–18	4.26	1	<.05	5.59	1	<.05
Problems in relationship with mother between 10–18	4.26	1	<.05			
Teenage pregnancy	4.84	1	<.05			
	t		p	t		p
Cumulative N of stressful life events between 10–18	−3.55		<.001	−3.89		<.001
N of contacts with community agencies between 10–18	−2.91		<.005	−4.12		<.001

Table A-8: Behavior characteristics that differentiated the
resilient offspring of psychotic parents from offspring who
developed serious coping problems in the first two decades of
life

Variables	Age	Source	p
Maternal mental health problems	Birth	Study files & Mental Health Register	<.05
Congenital defects	Birth	Pediatrician	<.10
Baby perceived as "good-natured"; "easy to deal with"	1 year	Mother	<.05
Mother's way of coping with infant	1 year	Home observations by social worker	<.10
Quality of toddler's interaction with examiner and caretaker during developmental screening	20 months	Psychologist's behavior observations	<.05
Autonomy/Independence	20 months	Behavior observations	<.05
Information Processing Skills	20 months	Behavior observations	<.05
Social Orientation	20 months	Behavior observations	<.05
IQ (measure of adaptive and language skills)	20 months	Cattell Infant Intelligence Scale	<.001
SQ (measure of self-help skills)	20 months	Vineland Social Maturity Scale	<.05
Psychological status rating	20 months	Tests and behavior observations	<.05
PMA factor R (nonverbal measure of problem-solving skills)	10 years	Primary Mental Abilities Test (PMA)	<.001
PMA factor V (verbal comprehension skills)	10 years	PMA Test	<.001
Perceptual-motor coordination	10 years	Bender-Gestalt Test (errors)	<.01

Variables	Age	Source	p
Ability to concentrate	10 years	Teacher's observations in classroom	<.001
Not bullying			<.05
Total N of behavior problems observed in classroom	10 years	Teacher's checklist	<.10
Emotional control	10 years	Parent checklist	<.05
No chronic nervous habits	10 years	Parent checklist	<.10
Locus of Control: Internal-External	17–18 years	Nowicki Locus of Control Scale (self-description)	<.01

Table A-9: Behavior characteristics that differentiated the offspring of schizophrenic mothers (N:8) from offspring of depressed mothers and from normal controls matched by age, sex, SES and parental ethnicity

Variables	Differences from Offspring of Depressed Mothers (N:10) p	Differences from Offspring of Matched Normal Controls (N:8) p
Cattell IQ at 20 months	<.05	<.01
Vineland SQ at 20 months	<.05	<.01
Psychological status rating at 20 months	<.10	<.05
PMA IQ at 10 years		<.01
PMA factor R at 10 (non-verbal problem-solving skills)		<.05
PMA factor P at 10 (perceptual acuity and speed)		<.10
Total N of behavior problems checked by teacher at age 10	<.01	
Nervous habits in classroom (age 10)	<.02	
Inability to concentrate (age 10)	<.02	
Total N of behavior problems checked by parents at age 10	<.02	<.05
Emotional control (at home)	<.10	<.05
Need for mental health care by age 10	<.10	.001
Anti-social behavior or mental health problems by 18	<.02	
Need for mental health care by age 24	<.10	

Table A-10: Significant discriminators between high-risk
resilient children and peers with serious coping problems at 10
(low SES homes)

Variables entered in stepwise discriminant function analysis	Standardized Discriminant Function Coefficients	
	For Females	For Males
Age of opposite sex parent at birth of child	+1.01	− .33
Birth order	− .92	− .84
Attention given to infant during year 1	+ .82	
Prolonged separation of infant from mother (year 1)	− .67	− .61
Infant perceived as "cuddly, affectionate" (year 1)		+ .42
Infant perceived as "good-natured, easy to deal with" (year 1)		+ .47
Physical status of child (20 months)	1.34	+ .29
Behavior patterns (ratio ±) (20 months)	+ .91	+1.08
Social orientation (20 months)	+ .68	+ .42
Autonomy (20 months)		+ .85
Information processing skills (20 months)	+ .85	
Self-help skills (ratio ±) (20 months)	+ .72	
Parent-child interactions (20 months)	+1.50	+1.22
Conflict between parents (birth–2 years)	− .66	− .73
Father absent since birth	+ .59	
Serious or repeated illnesses of child (birth–2 years)	− .26	− .42
Cumulative N of stressful life events (birth–2 years	− .41	
Serious or repeated illness of child (2–10)	− .83	
Father dead or permanently absent (2–10)	+ .50	

Table A-10 (*Continued*)

Variables entered in stepwise discriminant function analysis	Standardized Discriminant For Females	Function Coefficients For Males
Father temporarily absent (2–10)	– .98	
Chronic family discord (2–10)	– .47	– .54
Death of sibling (2–10)		–1.00
Departure of sibling from household (2–10)		+ .45
N of children in household by age 10		– .29
Cumulative N of stressful life events (2–10)	– .67	
Bender-Gestalt error score at age 10	–1.88	– .59
Evidence of low mental functioning in parents		– .60

Table A-11: Significant discriminators between high-risk
resilient youth and peers with serious coping problems at 18
(low SES homes)

Variables entered in stepwise discriminant function analysis	Standardized Discriminant For Females	Function Coefficients For Males
Age of opposite sex parent at birth of child	+ .94	− .70
Birth order	−1.32	− .80
Attention given to infant (year 1)	+ .28	
Prolonged separation of infant from mother (year 1)	− .35	−1.36
Distressing habits of infant (year 1)	− .58	
Infant perceived as "cuddly, affectionate" (year 1)		+ .68
Infant perceived as "good-natured, easy to deal with" (year 1)		+ .26
Mother's way of coping with infant (ratio ±) (year 1)		+ .66
Physical status of child (20 months)		+ .41
Social orientation (20 months)	+ .41	
Autonomy (20 months)		+ .48
Self-help skills (20 months)	+ .43	+ .38
Parent/child interaction (ratio ±) (20 months)	+1.45	+ .36
Serious or repeated illnesses of child (birth–2)	−1.61	−1.26
Prolonged disruption of family life (year 1)		− .32
Conflict between parents (birth–2)	− .29	
Cumulative N of stressful life events (birth–2)	−1.54	− .66
Serious or repeated illnesses of child (2–10)	− .45	
Repeated or chronic parental illnesses (2–10)		− .64
Father absent temporarily (2–10)	− .65	
Father absent permanently (2–10)		− .73
Chronic family discord (2–10)	− .71	− .31
Mother worked long-term (2–10)		.78
Death of a sibling (2–10)		− .64

Table A-11 (*Continued*)

Variables entered in stepwise discriminant function analysis	Standardized Discriminant For Females	Function Coefficients For Males
Departure of sibling from household (2–10)		+ .58
N of children in household by age 10	– .33	– .40
N of additional adults in household (besides parents) (by year 10)	+ .87	
Emotional support in home (2–10)		+ .80
Bender-Gestalt error score (10)	– .95	– .65
Quality of family relationships (10–18)	+ .45	+1.30
Quality of relationship with mother (10–18)	+ .64	
Quality of relationship with father (10–18)	+ .88	
Cumulative N of stressful life events (10–18)	–2.43	–2.64
Self-concept (18)	+1.29	
Evidence of low mental functioning in parents	–1.27	

Table A-12: Significant correlations across time (birth to age 18) between selected child and caregiver variables for high-risk F: Kauai Longitudinal Study

Variable	Birth–Year 1	20 Months	Year 10	Year 18	Cumulative N of Stressful Life Events Reported up to Age 18
Mother's educational level	Birth order -.31 Mother's age at birth of F -.31	Physical status of child .30 Quality of caretaker/child relationship during developmental exam .21	Educational stimulation provided by home .27	Quality of mother/daughter relationship .21	
Mother's age at birth of F	Birth order .55	Child's social orientation -.30	N of serious childhood illnesses -.25 Bender-Gestalt error score -.25		
Father's age at birth of F	Birth order .36 Baby's activity level .22 Baby perceived as "good-natured, easy to deal with" .25		Educational stimulation provided by home .27 Physical handicap .21	N of serious illnesses of F in adolescence .23	

Table A-12 (Continued)

Variable	Birth–Year 1	20 Months	Year 10	Year 18	Cumulative N of Stressful Life Events Reported up to Age 18
Birth order of F	Low birthweight, remained in hospital for special care .41	Autonomy −.30	N of children in household .47 Bender-Gestalt error score .34 Educational stimulation provided by home −.32 PMA IQ −.22 Mother has long-term employment .24	Problems in F's relationship with family −.26 Teenage pregnancy −.28	
Congenital defect.		Cattell IQ −.45 Social orientation −.34 Autonomy −.33 Quality of caretaker/child relationship −.28		Quality of father/daughter relationship −.26	
Baby's activity level (mother's perception) Year 1	Mother's way of coping with baby .53 Habits distressing to mother −.28	Physical status of child .22	Emotional support provided by family .24		

Variable	Birth–Year 1	20 Months	Year 10	Year 18	Cumulative N of Stressful Life Events Reported up to Age 18
Baby perceived as "cuddly, affectionate" by mother–Year 1	N of additional adult caretakers in household besides mother .26	Social orientation of child during developmental exam .38 Quality of caretaker/child relationship .27 Vineland SQ .26	Emotional support by family .30 PMA factor verbal comprehension .31 PMA IQ .26 Physical handicap –.21	Self-esteem .26	
Baby perceived as "good-natured, easy to deal with" by mother–Year 1	Attention given to baby –.30				
Baby has habits (eating, sleeping) distressing to mother–Year 1	Mother's way of coping with baby –.28		Emotional support provided by family –.36 Bender-Gestalt error score .21		.25
Attention given to baby–Year 1	Baby perceived as "cuddly, affectionate" by mother .30 N of additional adult caretakers in household besides mother .24	Physical status of child .23	Educational stimulation provided by family .22		

Table A-12 (Continued)

Variable	Birth–Year 1	20 Months	Year 10	Year 18	Cumulative N of Stressful Life Events Reported up to Age 18
Mother's way of coping with F (home observations) Year 1	Baby's activity level .53 N of baby's illnesses -.26 Baby has habits distressing to mother -.21	Psychologist's rating of child's emotional status .29			
F's social orientation during 20 mos. developmental exam	Baby perceived by mother as "cuddly, affectionate", .38 Congenital defect -.34 Mother's age -.30	Cattell IQ .55 Quality of caretaker/child relationship .42 Vineland SQ .29	Presence of physical handicap in F -.28	Quality of father/daughter relationship .24	
F's autonomy at 20 mos. developmental exam	Birth order -.30	Vineland SQ .22	Mother has long-term (>12 mos.) employment outside of household .22	Self-esteem .22	.22

Variable	Birth–Year 1	20 Months	Year 10	Year 18	Cumulative N of Stressful Life Events Reported up to Age 18
Cattell IQ at 20 mos.	Congenital defect −.45	Vineland SQ .55 Quality of caretaker/child relationship .52	PMA IQ .39	Quality of father/daughter relationship .28	
Vineland SQ at 20 mos.	Congenital defect −.27 Baby perceived as "cuddly, affectionate" .26 as "good-natured, easy to deal with" .24	Quality of caretaker/child relationship .38	N of children in household −.31		
Quality of caretaker/child relationship observed during developmental exam at 20 mos.	Congenital defect −.28 Baby perceived as "cuddly, affectionate" .27 Mother's educational level .21	Cattell IQ .52 Child's social orientation .42 Vineland SQ .36 Physical status of child .23	N of children in household −.35 PMA reasoning factor .29 Mother has long-term (>12 mos.) employment .28	Quality of mother/daughter relationship .38 Problems in family relationship −.26	−.49
Physical status of child at 20 mos. (pediatric exam)	Low birthweight required special care −.30	Vineland SQ .31 Child's social orientation .26	N of children in household −.35 Educational stimulation provided by home .21	Self-esteem .33 Quality of mother/daughter relationship .31	−.27

Table A-12 (Continued)

Variable	Birth–Year 1	20 Months	Year 10	Year 18	Cumulative N of Stressful Life Events Reported up to Age 18
Physical status of child at 20 mos. (pediatric exam)	Mother's educational level .30 Attention given to baby–Year 1 .23 Baby's activity level .22	Quality of caretaker/child relationship .23		Problems in family relationship –.30	
PMA IQ at 10	Baby perceived as "cuddly, affectionate" .26 LBW, remained in hospital for special care .26	Cattell IQ .30	Cumulative N of stressful life events up to age 10 –.33 Emotional support in family .28		–.25
Bender-Gestalt error in score (at 10)	Birth order –.34 Mother's age at birth of F –.25 Perinatal stress .23 Distressing habits of baby .21		PMA reasoning factor –.49	Self-esteem –.37 Problems in family relationship .43	.36

Variable	Birth–Year 1	20 Months	Year 10	Year 18	Cumulative N of Stressful Life Events Reported up to Age 18
Self-esteem at 18 years	Baby perceived as "cuddly, affectionate" .26	Physical status of child .33 Autonomy .22	Bender-Gestalt error score −.37 Chronic family discord −.29	Teenage pregnancy −.53 Quality of father/daughter relationship .52 Quality of mother/daughter relationship .48	−.44
Evidence of low mental functioning in family members	Congenital defect .36 Activity level of baby −.25	Physical status of child −.39 Cattell IQ −.37 Vineland SQ −.33 Autonomy −.22 Quality of caretaker/child relationship −.44	Bender-Gestalt error score .29 PMA IQ −.27 N of children in household .26 Permanent father absence .24 Chronic family discord .24	Problems in family relationship .42 Quality of mother/daughter relationship −.32 F's self-esteem −.32	.47
Maternal mental health problems	Mother's way of coping with baby −.29	Quality of caretaker/child relationship −.38 Child's autonomy .22	N of additional caretakers in household .49	Quality of mother/daughter relationship −.24	.29

195

Table A-12 (*Continued*)

Variable	Birth–Year 1	20 Months	Year 10	Year 18	Cumulative N of Stressful Life Events Reported up to Age 18
Chronic family discord	Distressing habits of baby .52		Bender-Gestalt error score .44 PMA reasoning factor −.32 N of children in household .26	Teenage pregnancy .34 Self-esteem −.29	.46
Father absence	Mother's educational level −.29		Chronic family discord .39 PMA reasoning factor −.26 Physical handicap in F .24		.32
Teenage pregnancy	Birth order −.28	Psychologist's rating of emotional status −.30 Physical status of child −.27	Chronic family discord .34 Father absence .30	Self-esteem −.53 Quality of father/daughter relationship −.51	.37
Mother's long-term employment	Birth order .24	Autonomy of child .22 Quality of caretaker/child relationship .22	Bender-Gestalt error score −.23	Teenage pregnancy −.33 Problems in family relationship −.24	−.12

Table A-13: Significant correlations across time (Birth to Age 18) between selected child and caregiver variables for High-Risk M: Kauai Longitudinal Study

Variable	Birth–Year 1	20 Months	Year 10	Year 18	Cumulative N of Stressful Life Events Reported up to Age 18
Mother's educational level	Mother's way of coping with baby .36 Mother's age at birth of M −.31 Birth order −.31 Attention given to baby .24		Bender-Gestalt error score −.29 PMA factor verbal comprehension .26 Physical handicap −.24 Emotional support provided by family .21		
Mother's age at birth of M	Birth order .49 Mother's level of education −.31 Baby's activity level −.28 Baby perceived as "cuddly, affectionate" −.25		N of serious childhood illnesses −.24		−.22
Father's age at birth of M	Birth order .42			N of children in household −.28 Quality of father/son relationship −.26	

Table A-13 (Continued)

Variable	Birth–Year 1	20 Months	Year 10	Year 18	Cumulative N of Stressful Life Events Reported up to Age 18
Birth order of M	Baby's activity level −.39 Attention given to baby −.29 Baby perceived as "good-natured" "easy to deal with" .26	Autonomy .30	N of children in household .47 N of additional adults in household besides parents −.23 Mother's employment .26		−.21
Congenital defect		Social orientation −.39	Bender-Gestalt error score .34 Physical handicap .32 PMA IQ −.28		
Baby's activity level—Mother's perception—Year 1	Birth order −.39 Mother's age at birth of M −.28 Mother's way of coping with baby .28	Social orientation .24 Vineland SQ .24 Quality of caretaker/child interaction during developmental exam .23	PMA IQ .30 Bender-Gestalt error score −.23 Mother's employment .24 Emotional support provided by family .22	Problems in family relationship −.48 Quality of father/son relationship .39 Self-esteem .21	

Variable	Birth–Year 1	20 Months	Year 10	Year 18	Cumulative N of Stressful Life Events Reported up to Age 18
Baby perceived as "cuddly, affectionate" by mother–Year 1	Attention given to baby .36 Mother's age at birth of M –.25	Psychologist's rating of M's emotional status .39 Cattell IQ .30 Vineland SQ .24		Quality of mother/son relationship .29 Problems in family relationship –.24	–.26
Baby perceived as "good-natured," "easy to deal with" by mother–Year 1	Birth order .26 Attention given to baby –.23		PMA IQ .24 Mother's employment .23	Problems in family relationship –.35	–.35
Attention given to baby–Year 1	Baby perceived as cuddly, affectionate .36 N of baby's illnesses .35 Birth order of M –.29 LBW, remained in hospital for special care .28 Mother's educational level .24	Quality of caretaker/child interaction during developmental exam .32 Cattell IQ .25			

Table A-13 (Continued)

Variable	Birth–Year 1	20 Months	Year 10	Year 18	Cumulative N of Stressful Life Events Reported up to Age 18
Mother's way of coping with M (home observations) Year 1	Mother's educational level .36 Baby's activity level .28	Quality of caretaker/child interaction during developmental exam .29 Child's physical status .25 Vineland SQ .22		Problems in family relationship –.32 Quality of father/son relationship .31 Quality of mother/son relationship .29	
M's social orientation during 20 mos. developmental exam	Congenital defect –.30 Baby's activity level .24	Psychologist's rating of M's emotional status .30 Cattell IQ .28 Vineland SQ .23	PMA factor verbal comprehension .26 Emotional support provided by family .26		
M's autonomy at 20 mos. developmental exam	Birth order .30	Cattell IQ .45 Vineland SQ .45 Quality of caretaker/child interaction .37 Child's physical status .34		Self-esteem .27	

Variable	Birth–Year 1	20 Months	Year 10	Year 18	Cumulative N of Stressful Life Events Reported up to Age 18
Cattell IQ at 20 mos.	Baby perceived as "cuddly, affectionate" – 1 year .30 Attention given to baby by primary caretaker .25	Vineland SQ .65 Quality of caretaker/child interaction .40 Physical status .28 Social orientation .28	PMA factor verbal comprehension .44 PMA IQ .33		
Vineland SQ at 20 mos.	Baby's activity level .24 Baby perceived as "cuddly, affectionate" .24 Mother's way of coping with baby .22	Cattell IQ .65 Autonomy .45 Quality of caretaker/child interaction .36 Social orientation .23	PMA factor verbal comprehension .31 PMA IQ .23		
Quality of caretaker/child interaction during 20 mos. developmental exam	Attention given to baby .32 Mother's way of coping with M .29 Baby's activity level .23	Cattell IQ .40 Vineland SQ .36 Physical status .22	N of childhood illnesses .33 Mother's employment .23	Quality of mother/son relationship .27 Quality of father/son relationship .27	

Table A-13 (*Continued*)

Variable	Birth–Year 1	20 Months	Year 10	Year 18	Cumulative N of Stressful Life Events Reported up to Age 18
Physical status of M at 20 mos. (pediatric exam)	Perinatal stress −.24 Mother's way of coping with M .25	Autonomy .34 Cattell IQ .28 Quality of caretaker/child relationship .22	N of childhood illnesses −.38 Educational stimulation provided by home .28 PMA IQ .28 Bender-Gestalt error score −.22		
PMA IQ at Year 10	LBW remained in hospital for special care .35 Baby's activity level .30 Congenital defect −.28 Mother's educational level .26 Baby perceived as "good-natured," "easy to deal with" .23	Cattell IQ .33 Physical status .28 Vineland SQ .23 Social orientation .23	Bender-Gestalt error score −.56 Educational stimulation provided in home .34 N of persons in household −.26		−.26

Variable	Birth–Year 1	20 Months	Year 10	Year 18	Cumulative N of Stressful Life Events Reported up to Age 18
Bender-Gestalt error score at Year 10	Congenital defect .34 Perinatal stress .25 Baby's activity level -.22	Physical status -.22	PMA IQ -.56 N of persons in household .25		
Self-esteem at Year 18	Baby's activity level .21	Autonomy .27	Chronic family discord -.41 Emotional support provided by family .27	Problems in family relationship -.43 Quality of father/son relationship .36	
Evidence of low mental functioning in family members	Attention given to baby -.40 Mother's age at birth of F .32 Baby has habits distressing to mother .25	Vineland SQ -.28 Cattell IQ -.26	PMA factor verbal comprehension -.26 Physical defect .24		
Maternal mental health problems	N of serious illnesses of baby .31 Activity level of baby -.27			Quality of mother/son relationship -.36 Problems in family relationship .23	.33

Table A-13 (Continued)

Variable	Birth–Year 1	20 Months	Year 10	Year 18	Cumulative N of Stressful Life Events Reported up to Age 18
Chronic family discord	Baby perceived as "cuddly, affectionate" −.40 Mother's way of coping with M −.28		Permanent father absence .29 Parental mental health problems .27	Self-esteem −.41 Problems in family relationship .40 Quality of father/son relationship .36	.38
Father absence	Baby perceived as "cuddly, affectionate" −.31 Baby perceived as "good-natured, easy to deal with" −.25		Parental mental health problems .42 N of additional children in hospital −.29 PMA reasoning factor −.29 Bender-Gestalt error score .27	Quality of mother/son relationship −.41 Problems in family relationship	.59
Mother's long-term (>12 mos.) employment outside of household	Mother's educational level .24 Birth order of M .26 Baby's activity level .24 Baby perceived as "good-natured, easy to deal with" .23		N of additional children in household .26 Family discord −.21	Quality of mother/son relationship .21	−.21

Table A-14: Variable that differentiated between F with and without serious coping problems in childhood and adolescence (1955 birth cohort, Kauai)

Middle-Class F with Significant Stressful Life Events	*(N:30)*	*Middle-Class F without Significant Stressful Life Events*	*(N:104)*
	p		*p*
Mother's education	<.05	Mother's education	<.05
Toddler's social orientation (20 months)	<.05	Perinatal stress	<.01
Cattell IQ (20 months)	<.05	Baby perceived as "cuddly, affectionate" (year 1)	<.05
N of childhood illnesses (2–10)	<.05	Attention given to baby (year 1)	<.05
PMA IQ (age 10)	<.01	Cattell IQ (20 months)	<.05
PMA Verbal Comprehension (age 10)	<.01	PMA IQ (age 10)	<.05
Mother's long-term (>12 mos.) employment (2–10)	<.05	PMA Reasoning factor (age 10)	<.01
Emotional support provided by family (2–10)	<.05	Bender-Gestalt score (age 10)	<.01
Cumulative N of stressful life events	<.05		

Lower Class F with Significant Stressful Life Events	*(N:84)*	*Lower Class F without Significant Stressful Life Events*	*(N:103)*
	p		*p*
Quality of parent-child relationship (20 mos.)	<.05	Social orientation (20 mos.)	<.05
Social orientation (20 mos).	<.05	Cattell IQ (20 mos.)	<.05
N of childhood illnesses (2–10)	<.05	Presence/absence of physical handicap	<.05
PMA IQ (age 10)	<.001	PMA IQ (age 10)	<.001
PMA Verbal factor (age 10)	<.001	PMA Verbal factor (age 10)	<.001
PMA Reasoning factor (age 10)	<.001	PMA Reasoning factor (age 10)	<.05
Bender-Gestalt score (age 10)	<.01	Self-concept (age 18)	<.01
Mother's long-term (>12 mos.) employment (2–10)	<.05		
Emotional support provided by family (2–10)	<.01		
Educational stimulation provided by family (2–10)	<.05		
Self-concept (age 18)	<.01		
Cumulative N of stressful life events	<.01		

Table A-15: Variables that differentiate between M with and without serious coping problems in childhood and adolescence (1955 birth cohort, Kauai)

Middle-Class M with Significant Stressful Life Events	(N:37)	Middle-Class M without Significant Stressful Life Events	(N:110)
	p		p
Mother's education	<.05	Mother's education	<.05
Birth order	<.05	Birth order	<.05
Social orientation (20 mos.)	<.01	N of children in household	<.05
Cattell IQ (20 mos.)	<.01	Baby's activity level (year 1)	<.05
Vineland SQ (20 mos.)	<.05	Cattell IQ (20 mos.)	<.05
Presence/absence of physical handicap	<.05	PMA IQ (year 10)	<.001
PMA IQ (age 10)	<.01	PMA Verbal factor (year 10)	<.001
PMA Verbal factor (age 10)	<.01	PMA Reasoning factor (year 10)	<.001
PMA Reasoning factor (age 10)	<.01		
Bender-Gestalt score (age 10)	<.001		
Emotional support provided by family (2–10)	<.05		
Educational stimulation provided by family (2–10)	<.01		
Cumulative N of stressful life events	<.05		

Lower Class M with Significant	
Stressful Life Events	*(N:97)*
	p
Mother's education	<.05
Birth order	<.05
Baby perceived as "cuddly, affectionate"	<.05
Mother's way of coping (year 1)	<.01
Quality of parent-child relationship (20 mos.)	<.01
Toddler's autonomy (20 mos.)	<.01
Cattell IQ (20 mos.)	<.001
Vineland SQ (20 mos.)	<.05
PMA IQ (age 10)	<.001
PMA Verbal factor (age 10)	<.001
PMA Reasoning factor (age 10)	<.001
Bender-Gestalt score	<.01
Educational stimulation provided by family (2–10)	<.05
Cumulative N of stressful life events	<.01

Lower Class M without Significant	
Stressful Life Events	*(N:65)*
	p
Birth order	<.05
Presence/absence of distressing habits (year 1)	<.05
Vineland SQ (20 mos.)	<.05
N of childhood illnesses (2–10)	<.01
PMA IQ (age 10)	<.001
PMA Verbal factor (age 10)	<.001
PMA Reasoning factor (age 10)	<.001
Bender-Gestalt score (age 10)	<.001
Educational stimulation provided by family (2–10)	<.05

Table A-16: Correlations between children's IQs at 20 months and 10 years and measures of parental ability and socioeconomic status (1955 birth cohort, Kauai Longitudinal Study)

Variables	Cattell IQ at 20 Months		PMA IQ	
	F	M	F	M
Father's IQ				
Total	.29**	.13	.32**	.21*
Verbal	.33*	.19*	.40**	.31**
Nonverbal	.33**	.14	.24**	.13
Mother's IQ				
Total	.19*	.05	.28**	.30**
Verbal	.03	.06	.20**	.29**
Nonverbal	.26**	.09	.38**	.32**
Father's Education	.26**	.15	.31**	.31**
Mother's Education	.21**	.19*	.28**	.33**
Socioeconomic Status	.09	.23**	.34**	.24**

* $p < .05$
** $p < .01$

REFERENCES

Ainsworth, M. D. S. *Infancy in Uganda: Infant care and the growth of love.* Baltimore: The Johns Hopkins Press, 1967.

Ainsworth, M. D. S. Attachment theory and its utility in cross-cultural research. In P. H. Leiderman, S. R. Tulkin & A. Rosenfeld (Eds.), *Culture and infancy: Variations in the human experience.* New York: Academic Press, 1977, 49–68.

Angelou, M. *I know why the caged bird sings.* New York: Random House, 1970.

Anthony, E. J. A risk vulnerability intervention model (a); and The syndrome of the psychologically invulnerable child (b). In E. J. Anthony, & C. Koupernik (Eds.), *The child in his family: Children at psychiatric risk,* Vol. III. New York: Wiley, 1974, 100–109; 529–544.

Anthony, E. J. From birth to breakdown: A prospective study of vulnerability. In E. J. Anthony, C. Koupernik & C. Chiland (Eds.), *The child in his family: Vulnerable children,* Vol. IV. New York: Wiley, 1978, 273–285.

Antonovsky, A. *Health, stress and coping: New perspectives on mental and physical well-being.* San Francisco: Jossey-Bass, 1979.

Arend, R., Gore, F. L. & Sroufe, L. A. Continuity of individual adaptation from infancy to kindergarten: A predictive study of ego resiliency and curiosity in preschoolers. *Child Development,* 1979, *50,* 950–959.

Bacon, M., Child, I. L. & Barry, H. A cross-cultural study of correlates of crime. *Journal of Abnormal Psychology,* 1963, *66,* 291–300.

Bell, R. & Harper, L. V. *Child effects on adults.* Hillsdale, N.J.: Erlbaum, 1977.

Belmont, L. Birth order, intellectual competence and psychiatric status. *Journal of Individual Psychology,* 1977, *33,* 97–103.

Beisser, A. R., Glasser, N. & Grant, M. Psychosocial adjustment in children of schizophrenic mothers. *Journal of Nervous and Mental Disease,* 1967, *145*(6), 429–440.

Bem, D. L. Sex role adaptability: One consequence of psychological androgyny. *Journal of Personality and Social Psychology,* 1975, *31,* 634–643.

Benjamin, J. A. A study of the social psychological factors related to the academic success of Negro high school students. Dissertation Abstracts International, 1970, 30(8-A). 343 (abstract).

Bertalanffy, L. Von *General systems theory.* New York: Braziller, 1968.

Bleuler, M. *Die schizophrenischen Geistesstoerungen im Lichte langjahriger Kranken und Familien Geschichten.* Stuttgart: Georg Thieme Verlag, 1972.

Bleuler, M. The offspring of schizophrenics. *Schizophrenia Bulletin,* 1974, *8,* 93–107.

Block, J. *Lives through time.* Berkeley: Bancroft Books, 1971.

Block, J. & Block, J. H. The developmental continuity of ego control and ego resiliency.

Paper delivered at the Symposium on the Organization of Development and the Problem of Continuity in Adaptation. Biannual Meeting of the Society for Research in Child Development, New Orleans, 1977.

Block, J. H. & Block, J. The role of ego-control and ego-resiliency in the organization of behavior. Paper presented at the Conference on Research Directions for Understanding Stress Reactivity and Stress Resistance in Adolescence, National Institute of Mental Health, Bethesda, Md., September 17, 1980.

Bowlby, J. *Attachment*. New York: Basic Books, 1969, 58–64.

Brislin, R. W., Lonner, W. J. & Thorndike, R. M. *Cross-cultural research methods*. New York: Wiley, 1973.

Broman, S. H., Nichols, P. L. & Kennedy, A. *Preschool IQ: Prenatal and early developmental correlates*. Hillsdale, N.J.: Erlbaum, 1975.

Bronfenbrenner, U. *The ecology of human development*. Cambridge, Mass.: Harvard University Press, 1979.

Bryant, B. & Trockel, J. Personal history of psychological stress related to locus of control orientation. *Journal of Consulting and Clinical Psychology*, 1976, *44*, 266–271.

Cattell, P. *The measurement of intelligence of infants*. New York: Psychological Corporation, 1940.

Chavez, A., Martinez, C. & Yashine, T. The importance of nutrition and stimuli on child mental and social development. In J. Cravito, L. Hombreaux & B. Vallquist (Eds.), *Early nutrition and mental development*. Uppsala, Sweden: Almquist and Wiksell, 1974.

Cherry, F. & Eaton, E. L. Physical and cognitive development in children from low income mothers working in the child's early years. *Child Development*, 1977, *48*, 158–166.

Clarke-Stewart, K. A. Interaction between mothers and their young children: Characteristics and consequences. *Monograph of the Society for Research in Child Development*, 1973, *38*, 153.

Clausen, J. A. Family structure, socialization and personality. In L. W. Hoffman & M. L. Hoffman (Eds.), *Review of Child Development Research*, 1966, *2*, 1–55.

Cohen, S. L. & Beckwith, L. Caregiving behavior and early cognitive development as related to ordinal position in pre-term infants. *Child Development*, 1977, *48*, 152–157.

Cohler, E. J., Galland, D. H., Grunebaum, H. U., Weiss, J. L. & Gamer, E. Pregnancy and birth complications among mentally ill and well mothers and their children. *Social Biology*, 1975, *22*, 269–278.

Coleman, J. S. *Equality of educational opportunity*. Washington: U.S. Office of Education, 1966.

Coles, R. *Children of Crisis, Vol. I: A study of courage and fear*. Boston: Little, Brown and Co., 1967.

Coles, R. *Children of Crisis, Vol. II: Migrants, sharecroppers, mountaineers*. Boston: Little, Brown and Co., 1972.

Coles, R. *Children of Crisis, Vol. III: The South goes North*. Boston: Little, Brown and Co., 1973.

Coles, R. *Children of Crisis, Vol. IV: Eskimo, Chicanos, Indians*. Boston: Little, Brown and Co., 1978.

Cowen, E. Social and community intervention. *Annual Review of Psychology*, 1973, *24*, 423–460.

Crandall, V. J. Differences in parental antecedents of internal-external control in children and in young adulthood. Paper presented at the American Psychological Association Convention, Montreal, 1975.

Crockenberg, S. Infant irritability, mother responsiveness and social support influences on the security of infant-mother attachment. *Child Development*, 1981 (in press).

Darrel, S. *A sparrow in the snow*. New York: Penguin Books, 1973.

Diamond, R. E. & Hellkamp, D. T. Race, sex, ordinal position of birth and self-disclosure in high school students. *Psychological Reports*, 1969, *25*, 235–238.

Doll, E. A. *Measurement of social competence*. Minneapolis: Educational Testing Bureau, 1953.

Douvan, E. Employment and the adolescent. In F. J. Nye & L. W. Hoffman (Eds.), *The employed mother in America*. Chicago: Rand McNally, 1963.

Duke, M. P. and Nowicki, S. Personality correlates of the Nowicki-Strickland locus of control scale for adults. *Psychological Reports*, 1973, *33*, 267–270.

Elder, G. H., Jr. *Children of the Great Depression: Social Change in Life Experience*. Chicago: University of Chicago Press, 1974.

Erikson, E. H. Identity and the life cycle. *Psychological Issues*, *1*, Monograph I, 1959.

Erlenmeyer-Kimling, L. A program of studies on children at risk for schizophrenia. In E. J. Anthony, C. Koupernik & C. Chiland (Eds.), *The child in his family: Vulnerable children*, Vol. IV. New York: Wiley, 1978, 268–272.

Erlenmeyer-Kimling, L., Cornblatt, B. & Fleiss, J. High risk research in schizophrenia. *Psychiatric Annals*, 1979, *9*.

Escalona, S. K. *The roots of individuality*. Chicago: Aldine, 1968.

Fish, B. Neurobiologic antecedents of schizophrenia in children. In S. Chess & A. Thomas (Eds.), *Annual Progress in Child Psychiatry and Child Development, 1978*. New York: Bruner/Mazel, 1979.

Franklin, L., Worland, J., Cass, L., Bass, L. & Anthony, E. J. Studies of children at risk: Use of psychological test batteries. In E. J. Anthony, C. Koupernik & C. Chiland (Eds.), *The child in his family: Vulnerable children*, Vol. IV. New York: Wiley, 1978, 313–324.

Freedman, D. G. *Human Sociobiology: A holistic approach*. New York: The Free Press, 1979.

Gal, R. & Lazarus, R. S. The role of activity in anticipating and confronting stressful situations. *Journal of Human Stress*, 1975, *1*, 4–20.

Gallimore, R., Boggs, J. W. & Jordan, C. E. *Culture, behavior and education: A study of Hawaiian-Americans*. Beverly Hills: Sage Publications, 1974.

Garmezy, N. Children at risk: The search for the antecedents of schizophrenia. Part I: conceptual models and research methods. *Schizophrenia Bulletin*, 1974a, *8*, 14–90.

Garmezy, N. Children at risk: The search for the antecedents of schizophrenia. Part II: Ongoing research programs, issues and intervention. *Schizophrenia Bulletin*, 1974b, *9*, 55–125.

Garmezy, N. The study of competence in children at risk for severe psychopathology. In E. J. Anthony & C. Koupernik (Eds.), *The child in his family: Children at psychiatric risk*, Vol. III. New York: Wiley, 1974c, 77–98.

Garmezy, N. Vulnerable and invulnerable children: Theory, research and intervention. Master lecture on developmental psychology. Washington, D.C.: American Psychological Association, 1976 (No. 1337).

Garmezy, N. & Nuechterlein, K. H. Invulnerable children: The fact and fiction of competence and disadvantage. *American Journal of Orthopsychiatry*, 1972, *77*, 328–329 (abstract).

Gersten, J. C., Lagner, T. S., Eisenberg, J. G. & Orzeck, L. Child behavior and life events: Undesirable change or change per se? In B. S. Dohrenwend & B. P. Dohrenwend (Eds.), *Stressful life events: Their nature and effects.* New York: Wiley, 1974, 159–170.

Gill, L. J. & Spilke, B. Some non-intellectual correlates of academic achievement among Mexican-American secondary school students. *Journal of Educational Psychology*, 1962, *53*, 144–149.

Giovannini, J. & Billingsley, A. Child neglect among the poor: A study of parental adequacy in families of three ethnic groups. *Child Welfare*, 1970, 196–204.

Goertzel, M. G., Goertzel, V. & Goertzel, T. G. *Three hundred eminent personalities: A psychosocial analysis of the famous.* San Francisco: Jossey-Bass, 1978.

Goldberg, S. Social competence in infancy: A model of parent-infant interaction. *Merrill-Palmer Quarterly*, 1977, *23*, 163–177.

Gough, H. *California Psychological Inventory Manual.* (Rev. Ed.) Palo Alto: Consulting Psychologists Press, 1969.

Gove, W. R. Sex differences in the epidemiology of mental disorders: Evidence and explanations. In E. S. Gomberg & V. Franks (Eds.), *Gender and disordered behavior.* New York: Bruner/Mazel, 1979, 23–70.

Graves, P. L. Infant behavior and maternal attitudes: Early sex differences in West Bengal. *Journal of Cross-Cultural Psychology*, 1978, *9*, 45–80.

Grunebaum, H., Cohler, B. J., Kauffman, C. & Gallant, G. Children of depressed and schizophrenic mothers. *Child Psychiatry and Human Development*, 1978, *8*, 219–228.

Haan, N. Proposed model of ego functioning: Coping and defense mechanisms in relationship to IQ changes. *Psychological Monographs: General and Applied*, 1963, *77*, 1–23.

Haan, N. Coping and defense mechanisms related to personality inventories. *Journal of Consulting Psychology*, 1965, *29*, 373–378.

Haan, N. Personality development from adolescence to adulthood in the Oakland Growth and Guidance Studies. *Seminars in Psychiatry*, 1972, *4*, 399–414.

Haan, N. The implications of family ego patterns for adolescent members. Unpublished doctoral dissertation, California School of Professional Psychology, San Francisco, 1974.

Haan, N. *Coping and defending: Processes of self-environment organization.* New York: Academic Press, 1977.

Halverson, C. F. & Waldrup, M. P. Relations between preschool barrier behaviors and early school-age measures of coping, imagination and verbal development. *Developmental Psychology*, 1974, *10*, 716–720.

Hamburg, D. A. & Adams, J. E. A perspective on coping behavior: Seeking and utilizing information in major transitions. *Archives of General Psychiatry*, 1967, *17*, 277–284.

Hamburg, D. A., Coelho, G. V. & Adams, J. E. Coping and adaptation: Steps toward a synthesis of biological and social perspectives. In G. V. Coelho, D. A. Hamburg & J. E. Adams (Eds.), *Coping and adaptation*. New York: Basic Books, 1974, 403–440.

Heider, G. M. Vulnerability in infants and young children: A pilot study. *Genetic Psychological Monographs*, 1966, *73*, 1–216.

Heston, L. L. & Denney, P. Interaction between early life experience and biological factors in schizophrenia. In D. Rosenthal & D. Katz (Eds.), *The transmission of schizophrenia*. Oxford: Pergamon Press, 1968.

Hoffman, L. W. The effects of maternal employment on the child: A review of the research. *Developmental Psychology*, 1974, *10*, 204–228.

Johnston, K. Children of parents treated for mental health problems: A longitudinal assessment. M.S. thesis in Child Development, University of California at Davis, 1981.

Jordan, T. E. & Spaner, S. D. Biological and ecological influences on development at 24 and 36 months of age. *Psychological Reports*, 1972, *31*, 319–332.

Jordan, T. E. Developmental factors influencing exceptional status at age 6 years. *Contemporary Educational Psychology*, 1976, *1*, 4–19.

Kellam, S. G., Baruch, J. D., Agrawal, K. C., et al. *Mental health and going to school*. Chicago: University of Chicago Press, 1975.

Kellam, S. G., Ensminger, M. E. & Turner, R. J. Family structure and the mental health of children. *Archives of General Psychiatry*, 1977, *34*, 1012–1022.

King, S. H. Coping and growth in adolescence. *Seminars in Psychiatry*, 1972, *4*, 355–366.

Konner, M. Evolution of human behavior development (a); and Infancy among the Kalahari Desert Sari (b). In P. H. Leiderman, S. R. Tulkin & A. Rosenfeld (Eds.), *Culture and Infancy: Variations in the Human Experience*. New York: Academic Press, 1977, 69–118; 287–338.

Koppitz, E. *The Bender-Gestalt test for young children*. New York: Grune and Stratton, 1964.

Lamb, M. E. Proximity seeking attachment behavior: A critical review of the literature. *Genetic Psychology Monographs*, 1976, *93*, 63–89.

Lander, H. S., Anthony, E. J., Cass, L., Franklin, L. & Bass, L. A measure of vulnerability to risk of parental psychosis. In E. J. Anthony, C. Koupernik & C. Chiland (Eds.), *The child in his family: Vulnerable children*, Vol. IV. New York: Wiley, 1978, 325–334.

Lefcourt, H. M. *Locus of control: Current trends in theory and research*. Hillsdale, N.J.: Lawrence Earlbaum Associates, 1976.

Lefcourt, H. M. The experience of stress and its moderation by perceptions of control. Paper presented at the Stress Conference at the University of Sasketchewan, Saskatoon, February 1976.

Lefcourt, H. M. & Hogg, E. Coping with challenges: An antecedent of an internal locus of control (unpublished manuscript), 1978.

Leon, G. R., Butcher, J. N., Kleinman, M., Goldberg, A. & Almagor, M. Survivors of the Holocaust and their children: Current status and adjustment. University of Minnesota, Minneapolis (unpublished manuscript), 1980.

Lewis, M. Parents and children: Sex role development, *School Review*, 1972, *80*, 229–240.

Lynn, D. B. *The father: His role in child development.* Monterey, Calif.: Brooks/Cole, 1974.

Lynn, D. B. *Daughters and parents: Past, present and future.* Monterey, Calif.: Brooks/ Cole, 1979.

Maccoby, E. E. & Jacklin, C. E. *The psychology of sex differences.* Stanford, Calif.: Stanford University Press, 1974.

MacFarlane, J. W. Perspectives on personality consistency and change from the guidance study. *Vita Humana,* 1964, *7,* 115–128.

Mason, E. P. Comparison of personality characteristics of junior high school students from American Indian, Mexican and Caucasian ethnic backgrounds. *Journal of Social Psychology,* 1967, *73,* 145–155.

Masterson, J. F., Jr. *The psychiatric dilemma of adolescence.* Boston: Little, Brown and Co., 1967.

McCord, J., McCord, W. & Thurber, E. Effect of maternal employment on lower class boys. *Journal of Abnormal and Social Psychology,* 1963, *67,* 177–182.

Mednick, S. A. & Schulsinger, F. Some premorbid characteristics related to breakdown in children with schizophrenic mothers. *Journal of Psychiatric Research,* 1968, *6,* 267–291.

Mednick, S. A., Mura, E., Schulsinger, F. & Mednick, B. Perinatal conditions and infant development in children with schizophrenic parents. *Social Biology,* 1971, *18,* 103–113 (supplement).

Megargee, E. I. *The California Psychological Inventory Handbook.* San Francisco: Jossey-Bass, 1972.

Miller, S. M. Effects of maternal employment on sex role perception, interests and self-esteem in kindergarten children. *Developmental Psychology,* 1975, *11,* 405–406.

Minturn, L. A. & Lambert, W. W. *Mothers of six cultures: Antecedents of child-rearing.* New York: Wiley, 1964.

Minturn, L. A. A survey of cultural differences in sex role training and identification. In N. Kretschmer & D. Walcher (Eds.), *Environmental influences on genetic expression.* Washington, D.C.: U.S. Government Printing Office, 1969.

Monat, A. & Lazarus, R. S. Stress and coping: Some current issues and controversies. In A. Monat & R. S. Lazarus (Eds.), *Stress and coping: An anthology.* New York: Columbia University Press, 1977, 1–11.

Moriarty, A. & Toussieng, P. *Adolescent coping.* New York: Grune and Stratton, 1976.

Murphy, L. & Moriarty, A. *Vulnerability, coping and growth from infancy to adolescence.* New Haven, Conn.: Yale University Press, 1976.

Nowicki, S. Correlates of locus of control in secondary school populations. *Developmental Psychology,* 1971, *4,* 477–478.

Nowicki, S. and Strickland, B. A locus of control scale for children. *Journal of Consulting and Clinical Psychology,* 1973, *40,* 148–154.

Nuechterlein, K. H. Competent disadvantaged children: A review of research. Unpublished summa cum laude thesis. University of Minnesota, 1970.

Offer, D. *The psychological world of the teenager.* New York: Basic Books, 1969.

Osofsky, E. (Ed.). *Handbook for research on infant development.* New York: Wiley, 1979.

Piaget, J. *Biology and knowledge.* Chicago: University of Chicago Press, 1971.

Pines, M. Superkids. *Psychology Today,* 1979 (January), 53–63.

Pollin, W. and Stabenau, J. R. Biological, psychological and historical differences in a series of monozygotic twins discordant for schizophrenia. In D. Rosenthal and S. S. Kety (Eds.) *Transmission of schizophrenia.* Oxford: Pergamon Press, 1968, 317–332.

Presser, H. Age differences between spouses: Trends, patterns and social implications. *American Behavioral Scientist,* 1975, *19,* 190–205.

Rees, A. N. & Palmer, F. H. Factors related to change in mental test performance. *Developmental Psychology Monographs,* 1970, *3* (2, Part 2).

Rivenbark, W. H. Self-disclosure patterns among adolescents. *Psychological Reports,* 1971, *26,* 35–42.

Robins, L. *Deviant children grown up.* Baltimore: Williams and Wilkins, 1966.

Robinson, A. Sex differences in development. *Developmental Medicine and Child Neurology,* 1969, *11,* 245–246.

Rogoff, B., Sellers, M. J., Pioratta, S., Fox, N. & White, S. Age of assignment of roles and responsibilities in children: A cross-cultural survey. *Human Development,* 1975, *18,* 352–369.

Rohner, R. *They love me, they love me not: A world-wide study of the effect of parental acceptance and rejection.* New Haven, Conn.: HRAF Press, 1975.

Rowland, T. S. Mother-son interaction and the coping behavior of young boys. *Dissertation Abstracts International,* 1969, *30*(1-B), 389–390.

Rutter, M. Sex differences in children's response to family stress. In E. J. Anthony & C. Koupernik (Eds.), *The child in his family,* Vol. I. New York: Wiley, 1970, 165–196.

Rutter, M. Epidemiological strategies and psychiatric concepts in research on the vulnerable child. In E. J. Anthony & C. Koupernik (Eds.), *The child in his family: Children at psychiatric risk,* Vol. III. New York: Wiley, 1974, 167–179.

Rutter, M. Parent-child separation: Psychological effects on the children. In A. M. Clarke & A. B. D. Clarke (Eds.), *Early experience: Myth and evidence.* New York: Free Press, 1977, 153–186.

Rutter, M. Early sources of security and competence. In J. Bruner & A. Garton (Eds.), *Human growth and development.* Oxford: Clarendon Press, 1978, 33–61.

Rutter, M. Maternal deprivation, 1972–1978: New findings, new concepts, new approaches. *Child Development,* 1979, *50,* 283–305.

Sameroff, A. and Chandler, M. J. Reproductive risk and the continuum of caretaking casualty. In F. D. Horowitz (Ed.) *Review of Child Development Research,* Vol. IV. Chicago: University of Chicago Press, 1975, 87–244.

Sameroff, A. & Zax, M. Perinatal characteristics of the offspring of schizophrenic women. *Journal of Nervous and Mental Disease,* 1973, *157,* 191–199.

SCAT (Cooperative School and College Ability Tests), Grades 10–12. Princeton, N.J.: Cooperative Tests and Services, Educational Testing Service, 1966.

Seligman, M. E. P. *Helplessness.* San Francisco: W. H. Freeman, 1975.

Shepherd, M., Oppenheim, B. & Mitchell, S. M. *Childhood behavior and mental health.* New York: Grune and Stratton, 1971.

Shipman, V. C. Notable early characteristics of high and low achieving Black low SES children. Princeton, N.J.: Educational Testing Service, 1976.

Singer, J. E., Westphal, M. & Niswander, K. Sex differences in the incidence of neonatal abnormalities and abnormal performance in early childhood. *Child Development,* 1968, *39,* 103–112.

Smith, A. C., Glick, G. L., Ferris, G. & Sellmann, A. Prediction of developmental outcome at seven years from prenatal, perinatal and postnatal events. *Child Development,* 1972, *43,* 495–507.

Smith, L. *The Journey.* New York: Norton, 1954.

Smith, R. S. High risk families in rural communities. In S. Haurel (Ed.), *The at risk infant.* Amsterdam: Excerpta Medica, 1980.

STEP (Sequential Tests of Educational Progress) Grades 10–12. Princeton, N.J.: Cooperative Tests and Services, Educational Testing Services, 1966.

Stewart, C. W. *Adolescent religion.* Nashville: Abingdon, 1967.

Super, C. M. Differences in the care of male and female infants: Data from non-American samples. Worcester, Mass.: Clark University, October 1977 (mimeograph).

Tatsuoka, M. M. Discriminant analysis: The study of group differences. In *Selected topics in advanced statistics: An elementary approach,* No. 6. Institute for Personality Assessment and Testing, University of Illinois, 1970.

Thomas, A. & Chess, S. *Temperament and Development.* New York: Bruner/Mazel, 1977.

Thurstone, L. & Thurstone, T. G. SRA Primary Mental Abilities: Examiner's Manual. Chicago: Science Research Associates, 1954.

Tiger, L. *Optimism: The biology of hope.* New York: Simon and Schuster, 1979.

Vogel, S. R., Broverman, I. K., Broverman, D. M., Clarkson, F. E. & Rosenkrantz, P. S. Maternal employment and perception of sex roles among college students. *Developmental Psychology,* 1970, *3,* 384–391.

Waddington, C. H. *Principles of development and differentiation.* New York: MacMillan, 1966.

Weibe, B. & Williams, J. D. Self-disclosure to parents by high school seniors. *Psychological Reports,* 1979, *31,* 690.

Weinstock, A. R. Longitudinal study of social class and defense preferences. *Journal of Consulting Psychology,* 1967a, *31,* 539–541.

Weinstock, A. R. Family environment and the development of defense and coping mechanisms. *Journal of Personality and Social Psychology,* 1967b, *5,* 67–75.

Weintraub, S., Liebert, D. E. & Neale, J. M. Teacher rating of children vulnerable to psychopathology. In E. J. Anthony, C. Koupernik & C. Chiland (Eds.), *The child in his family: Vulnerable children,* Vol. IV. New York: Wiley, 1978, 335–346.

Weisner, T. S. & Gallimore, R. My brother's keeper: Child and sibling caretaking. *Current Anthropology,* 1977, *18,* 169–190.

Werner, E. E. Personality characteristics of men and women who successfully assimilated stress during their formative years. Paper presented at the Biannual Meeting of the Society for Research in Child Development. State College, Penn., 1961.

Werner, E. E. *Cross-cultural child development: A view from the Planet Earth.* Monterey, Calif.: Brooks/Cole, 1979a.

Werner, E. E. The transactional model: Application to the longitudinal study of the high risk child on the island of Kauai, Hawaii. Paper presented at the Biannual Meeting of the Society for Research on Child Development. San Francisco, 1979b.

Werner, E. E. Sources of Support for High Risk Children. In N. Anastasiow, W. K. Frankenburg, & A. Fandall (Eds.), *Identification of high risk children.* Baltimore, Md.: University Park Press, 1981.

Werner, E. E., Bierman, J. M. & French, F. E. *The Children of Kauai: A longitudinal study from the prenatal period to age ten.* Honolulu: University of Hawaii Press, 1971.

Werner, E. E. & Smith, R. S. *Kauai's children come of age.* Honolulu: University Press of Hawaii, 1977.

Wertheim, E. S. Person-environment interaction: The epigenesis of autonomy and competence: I. Theoretical considerations (normal development). *British Journal of Medical Psychology,* 1975a, *48,* 1–8.

Wertheim, E. S. Person-environment interaction: The epigenesis of autonomy and competence: II. Review of the developmental literature (normal development). *British Journal of Medical Psychology,* 1975b, *48,* 95–111.

Wertheim, E. S. Person-environment interaction: The epigenesis of autonomy and competence: III. *British Journal of Medical Psychology,* 1975c, *48,* 237–256.

Wertheim, E. S. Person-environment interaction: The epigenesis of autonomy and competence: IV. *British Journal of Medical Psychology, 1975d, 48,* 391–402.

Wertheim, E. S. Developmental genesis of human vulnerability: Conceptual re-evaluation. In E. J. Anthony, C. Koupernik & C. Chiland (Eds.), *The child in his family: Vulnerable children,* Vol. IV. New York: Wiley, 1978, 17–36.

White, B. L. & Watts, J. *Experience and environment: Major influences on the development of the young child,* Vol. I. Englewood Cliffs, N.J.: Prentice-Hall, 1973.

White, B., Kaban, B. T. & Attanucci, J. S. *The origins of human competence: The final report of the Harvard Preschool Project.* Lexington, Mass.: Lexington Books (D.C. Heath and Co.), 1979.

White, R. Strategies of adaptation: An attempt at systematic description. In G. V. Coelho, D. A. Hamburg & J. E. Adams (Eds.), *Coping and adaptation.* New York: Basic Books, 1974, 47–67.

Whiting, B. B. & Whiting, J. W. M. *Children of six cultures: A psychocultural analysis.* Cambridge, Mass.: Harvard University Press, 1975.

Wiesel, E. *Night.* New York: Avon Books, 1969.

Wilson, E. O. *On human nature.* Cambridge, Mass.: Harvard University Press, 1978.

Wolff, S. *Children under stress.* London: Penguin Press, 1969.

Woods, M. B. The unsupervised child of the working mother. *Developmental Psychology,* 1972, *6,* 14–25.

Zelkowitz, P. Children's support networks: An exploratory analysis. Special Qualifying Paper accepted by the Harvard Graduate School of Education, 1978. Cited by C. Longfellow, P. Zelkowitz, E. Saunders, & D. Belle. The role of support in moderating the effects of stress and depression. Paper presented at the Biannual Meeting of the Society for Research in Child Development, San Francisco, March 15–18, 1979.

Zybert, P., Stein, Z. & Belmont, L. Maternal age and children's ability. *Perceptual-Motor Skills,* 1978, *47,* 815–818.

NAME INDEX

SUBJECT INDEX

Ability and achievement tests, 20–22
Aggressiveness, sex differences in
  vulnerability and, 44
Alternate caregivers, 76–77, 160–61
Anglo-Caucasians *(haoles)*, 9
  absence from resiliency study of, 49*n*.
  in Kauai population, 1
  in longitudinal study population, 12
Attrition rates of longitudinal studies, 23
Autonomy and independence of resilient
  toddlers, 63

Bayley Scales of Infant Development,
  42
Behavior characteristics of resilient
  offspring of mentally ill parents *(see*
  Resiliency, of offspring of parents
  with psychiatric problems)
Behavior problems:
  at age 18, 26–27
  in first decade of life, 25, 26
    stressful life events associated with,
    38–39
  (See also Delinquency; Teenage
    pregnancy)
Bender-Gestalt, (B-G) test, 18, 32, 74
Berkeley (University of California)
  longitudinal studies, 3, 102
Bidirectionality of child-caregiver effects,
  31–35
Big Brothers and Big Sisters Association
  of Kauai, 11, 113
Biographical questionnaire, 22
Birth-order studies, 58
Boy Scouts, 11

California, University of, at Berkeley:
  Ego Resiliency Study at, 3
  Growth and Guidance Study at, 3
  longitudinal studies at, 3, 102
  personality development study at, 91
California Psychological Inventory (CPI),
  20, 22, 83–88

Caregivers:
  alternate, 76–77, 160–161
  bidirectionality of effects of relationhips
    with children of, 31–35
  resilient infants and characteristics of,
    54–58
  sibling, 78, 160
  variables for, correlated across time: for
    high-risk females, 189–196
    for high-risk males, 197–204
Caregiving environment, 6, 7
  methodology of assessment of: for birth
    through second year, 16–17
    for second decade of life, 22–23
    for years 2 through 10, 18–20
  and outcomes of perinatal stress, 29–31
  in prediction of developmental
    outcomes, 4–5
  of resilient children: infants, 53–56
    toddlers, 61–65
    years 2 through 10, 76–81
Casualties:
  of first decade of life, 24–26
  in pregnancy, 24, 26
  of second decade of life, 26–27
Catholic Youth Organization, 11
Cattell Infant Intelligence Scale (Cattell
  IQ), 16, 25, 29–30, 64, 110
  in prediction of coping problems, 46,
    47, 131
Caucasians *(see* Anglo-Caucasians)
Census, household, 14
Central nervous system (CNS) impairment:
  perinatal stress and, 28
  (See also Physical health problems)
  Children of Kauai, The (Werner,
    Bierman & French), 2, 14, 130*n*.
Chinese:
  in Kauai population, 1, 9
  social mobility of, 9
Civil Air Patrol, 11
Class *(see* Social class; Socioeconomic
  status)
CNS *(see* Central nervous system
  impairment)